Doves into Hawks

Doves into Hawks

*Talking about Saving Strangers
to Build Public Support for War*

SARAH MAXEY

OXFORD
UNIVERSITY PRESS

OXFORD
UNIVERSITY PRESS

Oxford University Press is a department of the University of Oxford.
It furthers the University's objective of excellence in research, scholarship,
and education by publishing worldwide. Oxford is a registered trade mark of
Oxford University Press in the UK and in certain other countries.

Published in the United States of America by Oxford University Press
198 Madison Avenue, New York, NY 10016, United States of America.

Library of Congress Cataloging-in-Publication Data
Names: Maxey, Sarah author
Title: Doves into hawks : talking about saving strangers
to build public support for war / Sarah Maxey.
Description: New York, NY : Oxford University Press, [2026] |
Includes bibliographical references. |
Identifiers: LCCN 2025041498 (print) | LCCN 2025041499 (ebook) |
ISBN 9780197832691 hardback | ISBN 9780197832707 paperback |
ISBN 9780197832714 epub | ISBN 9780197832738
Subjects: LCSH: Politics and war—United States | War—Public opinion |
Humanitarian intervention—United States—Public opinion |
Executive power—United States | Presidents—United States |
Rhetoric—Political aspects—United States | United States—Foreign relations
Classification: LCC JZ6385 .M39 2026 (print) | LCC JZ6385 (ebook)
LC record available at https://lccn.loc.gov/2025041498
LC ebook record available at https://lccn.loc.gov/2025041499

DOI: 10.1093/9780197832738.001.0001

Paperback printed by Integrated Books International, United States of America

The manufacturer's authorized representative in the EU for product safety is
Oxford University Press España S.A. of Parque Empresarial San Fernando de Henares,
Avenida de Castilla, 2 – 28830 Madrid (www.oup.es/en or product.safety@oup.com).
OUP España S.A. also acts as importer into Spain of products made by the manufacturer.

Contents

Acknowledgments

A generous and broad coalition of people made this book possible. The project began at Cornell University where I am particularly indebted to advisers who saw the potential in its earliest, wildest versions. Matthew Evangelista provided key feedback and constant encouragement well beyond my time in Ithaca. His guidance, questions, and patience strengthened the project in countless ways and I am tremendously grateful. Sarah Kreps opened the doors to the discipline, challenging and championing me at every step. Her belief that I should and could write a book that mattered was the project's lodestar. Chris Way's support and engagement shaped my approach to research design and kept the project on the tracks at critical junctures. Peter Enns was an unwavering source of public opinion wisdom and encouragement.

The broader Cornell community also provided invaluable support. I am grateful for the guidance and thoughts of Richard Bensel and Jessica Chen-Weiss in dissertation colloquia. Steven Ward served as the external reader, offering a fresh perspective and exceptional comments. Tina Slater, Dinnie Sloman, and Laurie Dorsey made the logistics of this research possible. Countless graduate student colleagues and friends also served as sounding boards and sources of moral support. Elizabeth Acorn, Caitlin Ambrozik, Manfred Elfstrom, Triveni Gandhi, Matthew Hill, Natalie Letsa, Wendy Leutert, Josh Meyer-Gutbrod, Martijn Mos, Elizabeth Plantan, Abigail Post, Kathleen Powers, Catherine Reyes-Housholder, and Mariano Sanchez merit particular thanks. Delphia Shanks and Mallory SoRelle have been constant writing partners and exemplars of friendship for over a decade. For reading all the drafts, protecting my sanity, and lending your brilliance to this work, I owe you. Steffen Blings has been there from day one of this project. It is not an understatement to say this book would not exist without his unwavering belief that it was worthwhile and generosity with his intellect and humor.

The early stages of this project received financial support from a Doctoral Dissertation Research Improvement Grant from the National Science

Foundation (No. 1559741) and the Reppy Institute for Peace and Conflict Studies' Bluestone Peace Fellowship. This funding facilitated archival travel and I owe tremendous thanks to the librarians and staff at the George H. W. Bush Presidential Library and the William J. Clinton Presidential Library.

The book developed during my time at the University of Pennsylvania's Perry World House and Loyola University Chicago, both of which provided professional and financial support for completing the project. At Penn, Ryan Brutger, Michael Kenwick, Michael Horowitz, Rebecca Lissner, and Diana Mutz provided helpful feedback and advice on navigating the publication process. Loyola University Chicago provided a supportive and intellectually engaging environment for bringing this project to fruition. I am particularly appreciative of feedback and advice from Meghan Condon, Jennifer Forrestal, Alexandru Grigorescu, and Molly Melin.

Throughout the writing process, I was also fortunate to receive valuable comments from audiences and discussants at Stockholm University, the Emerging Scholars in Grand Strategy Conference at the University of Notre Dame, the Harvard International Security Conference, and the International Studies Association's Junior Scholars Symposium. I owe particular thanks to Allison Carnegie, Michael Desch, and Joshua Kertzer, whose engagement with the project at these forums provided transformative feedback at critical junctures. Bridging the Gap's International Policy Summer Institute was key to polishing the project's main ideas and—hopefully— clarifying why they matter for the real world. I am grateful to the entire BTG team and cohort, with extra thanks to Jordan Tama.

At Oxford University Press, I thank David McBride for his support of the project throughout the publication process. Two anonymous reviewers deserve my sincerest thanks for suggestions that were a rare combination of thoughtful, concrete, and actionable, all of which dramatically improved the manuscript.

Finally, none of this would be possible without family. I am grateful to my parents, Neil and Susan, and grandparents who encouraged and made opportunities for my intellectual curiosity at every stage of life. Thank you.

1

Humanitarian justifications
in security crises

Two months before the US launched Operation Iraqi Freedom, George W. Bush used his State of the Union address to send a message to "the brave and oppressed people of Iraq: Your enemy is not surrounding your country; your enemy is ruling your country. And the day he and his regime are removed from power will be the day of your liberation" (G. W. Bush 2003a). This direct message was only one of the many instances in which Bush talked about the welfare of the Iraqi people while making the case for an intervention primarily framed as part of "The war on terror [that] also requires us to confront the danger of catastrophic violence posed by Iraq and its weapons of mass destruction" (G. W. Bush 2002c). As US military action became imminent, Bush linked Security Council resolutions that focused on the security threats posed by Iraq's purported weapons of mass destruction to a chemical weapons attack on the village of Halabja where, "the regime killed thousands of Iraq's Kurdish citizens. Whole families died while trying to flee clouds of nerve and mustard agents descending from the sky" (G. W. Bush 2003c). He continued, "We know from human rights groups that dissidents in Iraq are tortured, imprisoned, and sometimes just disappear; their hands, feet, and tongues are cut off; their eyes are gouged out; and female relatives are raped in their presence" (G. W. Bush 2003c).

While the 2003 US invasion of Iraq was distinct and controversial in many ways, the Bush administration's use of humanitarian justifications— statements that focus on the protection or welfare of foreign civilians—in a security crisis was not an anomaly. Bush (2002b) himself used similar statements to explain military action in Afghanistan, where links to US security were more direct and credible, asserting that US troops were "freeing women and children from incredible oppression." A closer look at official justifications for military action reveals that every US president since at least the end of the Cold War chose to include humanitarian rationales in their speeches about security crises. The pattern extends across party lines,

Doves into Hawks. Sarah Maxey, Oxford University Press. © Oxford University Press (2026).
DOI: 10.1093/9780197832738.003.0001

including George H.W. Bush's (1990g) assertion at the beginning of the Gulf War that "Iraq's brutality against innocent civilians will not be permitted to stand" and Barack Obama's (2014) statement about the US fight against the Islamic State that "the brutality of ISIL is not a match for the yearning of millions who want to live in security and dignity." Donald Trump (2017c) later echoed this same brutality against civilians, noting that "ISIS is on a campaign of genocide, committing atrocities across the world." More recently, Joseph Biden (2022c) pledged US aid to Ukraine after outlining how, "Putin is inflicting appalling—appalling—devastation and horror on Ukraine: bombing apartment buildings, maternity wards, hospitals. I mean, it's God awful. [...] These are atrocities. They're an outrage to the world. And the world is united in our support for Ukraine and our determination to make Putin pay a very heavy price."

Again, humanitarian justifications stand out in these security crises because they were not the main reason for US action. Instead, the interventions focused on eliminating threats to US security and national interests, with implications for the wellbeing of American citizens. The Gulf War responded to Iraq's invasion of Kuwait, while the battle against the Islamic State aimed to prevent terrorist attacks on the US and its allies. Similarly, while US involvement in Ukraine is so far limited to military aid, Russia's actions are a direct threat to North Atlantic Treaty Organization (NATO) allies and territorial integrity, in addition to carrying the risk of nuclear escalation.

Why do leaders so consistently use humanitarian justifications when US security is at stake? The answer, this book argues, lies in whom humanitarian appeals persuade and the role these individuals play in domestic coalitions of support for military action. Combining humanitarian justifications with security rationales appeals to doves while maintaining the support of hawks.[1] Doves are skeptical of the use of force, but I show that they can be reliably persuaded to support military interventions under the right circumstances. Leaders create the right circumstances for doves to become hawks by offering other-regarding goals for military action such as the protection of foreign civilians and human rights.

---

[1] In Chapter 3, I define doves as individuals who prioritize using cooperative methods like diplomacy to achieve other-regarding goals. This definition expands on the standard account of doves as individuals who are "not hawks," defined by their lack of militant internationalism. To understand whether and when individuals can be persuaded to support military action, I argue, it is important to define these groups based on their policy priorities, not just their opposition. Following a similar logic, I define hawks as individuals who prioritize military strength and competition.

These dynamics were evident in the build-up to the US invasion of Iraq in 2003, where references to Saddam Hussein's record of human rights abuses evoked concern and support for intervention from prominent human rights activists. Vocal activists included Nobel laureate and Holocaust survivor Elie Wiesel, who Bush quoted as saying, "We have a moral obligation to intervene where evil is in control. Today, that place is Iraq" (G. W. Bush 2003c). High-profile doves were such significant supporters of the war that Bill Keller (2003) labeled them "The I-Can't-Believe-I'm-A-Hawk-Club." The self-described "wary warmongers" in this club were individuals who had "an aversion to the deployment of American power [that] was formed by Vietnam but had a kind of epiphany along the way—for most of us, in the vicinity of Bosnia" where the humanitarian costs of inaction were too grave to ignore (Keller 2003).[2] By expanding statements about weapons of mass destruction and terrorism to include humanitarian rationales, Bush's communication strategy was able to turn these traditional doves into temporary hawks.

Despite the red flags raised by the Iraq case, I show that humanitarian justifications do not undermine the public's ability to influence or constrain military action. In fact, broad domestic coalitions that include hawks and doves are good for democracy. When leaders raise the prospect of helping people in other countries, they activate the support of doves, who are particularly attentive to the wellbeing of foreign civilians. By broadening the domestic coalition of support to include doves, humanitarian justifications also increase opportunities for the public to hold leaders accountable for what they say. If the leader makes insincere humanitarian promises, doves notice and care, creating an additional risk of political backlash. The same doves who incentivize humanitarian appeals therefore also limit their use. In the Iraq case, the eventual accountability imposed by doves is visible in the defection of early supporters to the antiwar movement (Heaney and Rojas 2015) and in public statements from human rights advocates like Michael Ignatieff (2007), who called his support of the intervention a mistake, crediting it to emotional memories of how Saddam Hussein treated Kurdish populations at the end of the Gulf War.

By accounting for the presence of humanitarian justifications, this book presents a new and more comprehensive picture of the relationship between

---

[2] For other examples of doves who cite human rights concerns as the reason they supported intervention, see Malone's (2021) overview of liberals who supported invading Iraq.

leaders, the public, and war. The argument offers a middle ground between two strands of existing wisdom about public attitudes towards military action, asserting that the public can be moral and prudent at the same time. As a result, humanitarian appeals are both more powerful and better for democracy than they are conventionally assumed. Identifying both the power and limits of humanitarian justifications in security crises clarifies what it takes to win the public's consent for war. Gaining public support for military action is critical for democratically elected leaders (Tomz, Weeks, and Yarhi-Milo 2020). When the public is convinced that intervention is necessary, its support loosens constraints on the use of force and leaders are empowered to act. Without public consent, presidents who move forward with military action risk paying high political costs, from stalled domestic agendas to losing their bids for reelection (Gelpi and Grieco 2015; Kriner 2010; Tomz and Weeks 2013). Public statements are the central tool presidents have to shape public perceptions of international crises and build support for military action (Baum and Groeling 2010; Druckman and Jacobs 2015). How leaders choose to justify military interventions and how the public responds to these justifications are directly connected to whether military action is sustainable and to whether presidents will be held accountable for their foreign policy decisions.

While I focus primarily on how humanitarian justifications persuade doves—because the power of humanitarian appeals is important but overlooked and doves are not conventionally expected to support military action—the book also adds nuance to our understanding of security justifications. The domestic coalition argument outlined in Chapter 3 identifies the foreign policy constituencies who prioritize security rationales. It also highlights how hawks, because of their focus on national security interests, hold leaders accountable for the misuse of security justifications. It is when official justification strategies mobilize a diverse coalition of doves and hawks that leaders' pursuit of intervention is most constrained by the domestic audience.

To support this domestic coalition argument, the book provides evidence at the speech, individual, and intervention levels. An original dataset of US presidents' justifications for post-Cold War interventions reveals patterns of perceived demand and restraint in leaders' use of humanitarian appeals (Maxey 2020). On the one hand, presidents from both parties frequently justify security interventions in humanitarian terms. On the other hand, they are careful not to overstate humanitarian rationales.

Survey experiments then identify the micro-foundations behind demand and restraint, focusing on the preferences of different foreign policy constituencies. Doves are a distinct, politically relevant constituency that responds most strongly to humanitarian rationales and evaluates the use of force differently when these justifications are present—they create the demand for humanitarian claims in security cases. Critically, doves are also a source of political backlash when humanitarian justifications appear insincere, while hawks constrain the misuse of security justifications. Together, these groups explain why leaders demonstrate restraint—both doves and hawks would punish leaders who stretch claims too far. Finally, archival evidence from US interventions in the Gulf War and Bosnia demonstrates that the White House's use of humanitarian claims is intentional and designed to achieve the domestic political benefits that stem from appealing to distinct foreign policy constituencies.

The remainder of this chapter considers how the prevalence of humanitarian appeals challenges existing wisdom about effective justifications for the use of force, explaining why it is important to take humanitarian claims seriously. It then presents an overview of the domestic coalition argument, which resolves the puzzling prevalence of humanitarian claims by explaining how democratically elected leaders benefit from building broad coalitions of public support and how humanitarian justifications make these coalitions possible. The argument carries new implications for how political science approaches both the use of force by democracies and humanitarian norms. The chapter concludes by offering definitions that separate the justifications for an intervention from the type of underlying crisis, establishing the scope of the argument, and outlining the plan of the book.

Challenging what we know about public support for military action

Explaining the influence of humanitarian claims in speeches about security crises corrects two common misunderstandings about public opinion: (1) that security threats alone can sufficiently mobilize public support, and (2) that a public concerned with humanitarian outcomes is a problem for foreign policy because it incentivizes overreach. These assumptions map onto two strands of existing wisdom about effective justifications: the rational public and the emotional public. The domestic coalition argument, outlined in a later section, resolves both misunderstandings and offers a new middle ground between these two perspectives.

First, scholars who view the public as rational and prudent expect support for military action to be the highest when interventions respond to security threats (Drezner 2008; Gadarian 2010; Gelpi, Feaver, and Reifler 2009; Herrmann, Tetlock, and Visser 1999; Hildebrandt et al. 2013). With high-profile cases like the 9/11 attacks and threats of nuclear war in mind, these accounts of public opinion assume that all individuals prioritize their own interests and security. A public made up of such individuals will rally in the face of security threats (Baum and Groeling 2010; Gadarian 2010), put national interests before human rights goals (Drezner 2008; Zvobgo 2019), and weigh the prospects for success against the potential human and financial costs of action (Gelpi, Feaver, and Reifler 2009). From this perspective, presidents' humanitarian claims in cases like Ukraine, Afghanistan, and Iraq are not false, but they do appear superfluous and likely to distract attention from security interests without bolstering public support. Instead of spending time on humanitarian explanations, leaders would seem to do a better job of persuading the public if they talked about nuclear security, counterterrorism, or regional stability and oil prices, respectively. The consistent presence of humanitarian justifications in security crises from Iraq to Afghanistan to Ukraine reveals a critical piece missing from this conventional picture of what it takes to sell war to the public: It is not enough to protect national security; the action must also appear to help foreign civilians. The reason, I argue below, is that humanitarian claims have unique power over an important political constituency—doves—that focuses as much on protecting foreign civilians as national security.

Second, earlier studies of public opinion recognized that domestic constituencies might prefer humanitarian appeals but saw their existence as a problem. These scholars warned that the emotional public's humanitarian tendencies could create pressure for a volatile and overly ambitious foreign policy (Kennan 1984; 1985; Lippmann 1922; Morgenthau 1951). Such concerns resurfaced with the arrival of 24/7 news coverage, which broadcast images of humanitarian crises directly into the country's living rooms (Kennan 1993; Mandelbaum 1996; Robinson 1999). A public that responds to humanitarian appeals would represent an "unduly legalistic and moralistic" force in foreign policy that misdirects policymakers and causes the US "to lose effectiveness in the international arena" (Kennan 1985, 205).

These critiques mistakenly assume that reactions to humanitarian concerns are impulsive. Instead, I show that the persuasive power of humanitarian claims is rooted in predictable foreign policy priorities. Because doves reliably prioritize other-regarding policy goals, they are also well-equipped to vet presidents' humanitarian rationales and impose punishment for insincere humanitarian claims. Hawks offer similar forms of accountability for the misuse of security justifications. By engaging a broader segment of the domestic audience, the presence of humanitarian justifications in security crises bolsters the constraints expected to stop democratically elected leaders from making bad foreign policy decisions.

The importance of taking humanitarian justifications seriously

By identifying and explaining the domestic power of humanitarian appeals, this book's findings change how we think about mobilizing public support for the use of military force. It is not enough for an intervention to protect US national security interests. To broaden public support, the intervention must also appear to benefit foreign civilians. Focusing only on security justifications has overlooked an important foreign policy constituency that can be convinced to support military action but does not always assign top priority to national security concerns. White House communications teams recognize both the importance of turning persuadable doves into temporary hawks and that humanitarian justifications are the best way to accomplish this goal. Presidents' consistent use of humanitarian justifications in security crises reflects an attempt to mobilize a broad domestic coalition of support while acting within the boundaries set by public accountability.

Additionally, humanitarian claims have counterintuitive, positive implications for public engagement and accountability. On the one hand, the pattern of humanitarian justifications in recent interventions shows that White House communications teams have a sophisticated understanding of what it takes to sell intervention to the public. Presidential speeches consistently combine humanitarian and security appeals to mobilize a broad coalition of domestic support, regardless of the main impetus for military action. If the right combination of words increases presidents' leeway in pursuing military interventions, the strategic use of humanitarian claims would warrant concern about undermined democratic accountability. Instead, the same individuals who respond to humanitarian appeals also limit their misuse. By engaging both hawks and doves in decisions about the use of force and drawing attention to other-regarding concerns, the broad coalitions built with humanitarian justifications increase the likelihood that leaders will be held accountable for what they say. Human rights groups can also use this increased public attention and reference official statements to create domestic pressure for humanitarian outcomes.

Finally, the power of humanitarian narratives is not limited to humanitarian interventions, where they are most often studied (Bellamy 2006; Booth Walling 2013; Crawford 2002; Finnemore 2003; Kreps and Maxey 2018). Instead, these justifications are especially important in the context of security crises. Because the domestic benefits of humanitarian claims stem from the public's foreign policy predispositions, which are difficult to change, the political importance of this rhetoric can be decoupled from the practice of humanitarian intervention. Doing so helps make sense of the presence of humanitarian claims in security contexts that long precede the rise of humanitarian intervention norms. It also has implications for the future. Even if humanitarian interventions lose their international legitimacy, leaders will continue to benefit from offering humanitarian rationales for the use of force.

Why presidents use humanitarian claims: Overview of the argument

To explain the use of humanitarian claims in security crises, I establish the pattern of humanitarian justifications across conflicts and address three related questions: (1) Who responds to humanitarian appeals? (2) Do humanitarian justifications help leaders avoid accountability for military action? (3) Are humanitarian claims an intentional part of leaders' justification strategies? These questions cover multiple levels of analysis. To capture the pattern of humanitarian justifications in need of explanation, I examine the use and emphasis of different claims at the speech level. The first and second questions then focus on individual-level attitudes to establish the public incentives that presidents face, accounting for patterns of perceived demand and restraint in official speeches. The third question considers White House communication strategies in actual cases of intervention to show that leaders recognize and act on the domestic political incentives for humanitarian appeals. Together, the answers explain the domestic power of humanitarian justifications and provide a comprehensive picture of when and at what costs the White House is able to sell intervention to the public.

By answering these questions, the book shows that humanitarian justifications are a critical part of strategies designed to mobilize the domestic audience, even when US security is at stake. I demonstrate that humanitarian justifications hold this power because they are uniquely capable of maximizing support among doves—a key domestic constituency that is otherwise skeptical of the use of force—facilitating a broader and more durable coalition of support for military action. Leaders benefit from mobilizing a broad domestic coalition of support because wide-ranging popularity increases their ability to sustain support for the duration of the operation while also minimizing the risk of dissent from Congress and other political elites (Gelpi and Grieco 2015; Kriner 2010).

Expanding the domestic coalition requires leaders to mobilize support across constituencies with different views of when and how the United States should engage with the world. These views form three distinct foreign policy constituencies: doves, hawks, and isolationists. When it comes to supporting the use of military force, isolationists are unlikely coalition members. These individuals represent a relatively small segment of the American public and are characterized by their belief that it is better for the US to mind its own business and let other countries deal with their own problems (Chaudoin, Milner, and Tingley 2010; Kertzer 2013; Smeltz, Daalder, and Kafura 2014). As a result, isolationists are skeptical of engagement in general, especially high cost and risky actions like military intervention. They will be difficult to persuade, and leaders are unlikely to view isolationists as a target audience for their communication strategies. These individuals do not explain why leaders rely on humanitarian justifications in security crises.

Instead, the strength of the domestic coalition of support for military action depends on a leader's ability to mobilize internationalists, including doves who can be persuaded to support military action under the right circumstances and hawks whose support can be sustained in the long-term. Internationalist doves and hawks share the belief that the US should play an active role in the world, but have different preferences for the form that US engagement should take (Kertzer et al. 2014; Kreps, Saunders, and Schultz 2018; Mattes and Weeks 2019; Rathbun et al. 2016). Individuals who view the world through a hawkish lens will be primarily concerned with military strength and national security goals. While not opposed to humanitarian rationales, these individuals already offer their strongest support in response to security justifications alone. Their preferences do not incentivize leaders to include humanitarian justifications when US security is at stake—consistent with the conventional wisdom, adding a humanitarian justification does not further increase support among hawks when security justifications are available.

The incentives for and power of humanitarian justifications lie with the remaining group: internationalist doves. Doves have cooperative priorities, which means they "embrace the world with open arms" (Rathbun et al. 2016, 125). They are primarily concerned with promoting common, global goods and prefer for US engagement to take the form of diplomatic actions. This preference for cooperative solutions also reflects a skepticism with the effectiveness of military force and the primacy of national security goals. Humanitarian justifications—especially in the context of security crises—give doves an other-regarding goal to focus on besides national security threats. The presence of an other-regarding logic changes how doves evaluate interventions and helps override their skepticism about the use of force. The support of doves is maximized by humanitarian justifications instead of security claims and it is this group that incentivizes leaders to talk about foreign civilians even when US security is on the line.

Contrary to the concern that other-regarding impulses in foreign policy promote overreach and create ethical dilemmas in the long term (Desch 2003; Mandelbaum 1996), doves also place important constraints on the usefulness of humanitarian appeals. Because these individuals value common global interests, they are attentive to the humanitarian consequences of US actions. If leaders stretch humanitarian justifications too far and appear insincere—or rely on humanitarian appeals and then fail to protect civilians—they can expect backlash from otherwise persuadable doves that undermines the domestic coalition. Hawks create a similar risk of backlash against the misuse of security justifications. By reaping the benefits of a broad coalition of doves and hawks, leaders also broaden opportunities for accountability.

After establishing the pattern of justifications and the public incentives for humanitarian claims, the book shows that the White House recognizes and responses to these incentives, designing communication strategies with the goal of persuading doves and hawks. Through polling and experience, administrations understand the need to appeal to foreign policy constituencies with diverse preferences. The opportunity to choose justifications and frame military action gives the White House significant power over public opinion, but communications teams also acknowledge the limits of justifications. When stretched so far as to appear insincere, justifications carry the risk of backlash and political costs. The lowest risk strategy for presidents is to reference credible humanitarian aspects of security crises, without casting military action primarily as a humanitarian intervention. This limit assuages the most severe concerns that humanitarian rhetoric can provide a pretext for otherwise illegitimate military actions (Bellamy 2004).

In short, humanitarian justifications are necessary to sell military action to the domestic audience, even when US security is at stake. Presidents have incentives to build broad domestic coalitions of support for intervention, and humanitarian claims are critical to achieving this goal. Humanitarian appeals have domestic power because they persuade doves—who are usually skeptical of military force—to temporarily set aside their hesitation and support intervention. White House communications teams recognize and respond to these incentives, but also exercise restraint to avoid appearing insincere. Taken as a whole, this domestic coalition argument expects the public to respond to White House narratives, but this responsiveness does not mean leaders have a blank check or can easily avoid accountability for their actions.

Separating justifications and interventions

The domestic coalition is not a theory of the decision to initiate a military intervention, but of the strategies leaders use to manage the domestic politics of intervention once this decision has been made—and their consequences for democracy. In this regard, the argument is distinct from the insights provided by studies of foreign policy decision-making that focus on when and why democratically elected leaders decide to engage in or escalate conflicts towards military action.[3] Anticipated public opposition constrains the range of politically feasible policy options and can make leaders think twice about pursuing military action. The launch of coordinated communication strategies designed to mobilize broad domestic coalitions of support, however, follows the initial decision to escalate a conflict towards intervention. The domestic coalition theory's expectations thus begin after the decision to pursue intervention is made.

[3] See, for example, Friedman (2023), Payne (2023), and Saunders (2011).

Additionally, a key claim of this book is that humanitarian justifications are important outside of humanitarian interventions. Humanitarian rationales can and do play an essential role in military operations that respond to humanitarian crises. They are equally vital, however, for building domestic coalitions of support for interventions that respond to national security threats. Evaluating this claim requires separating the justifications presidents use to legitimate interventions from the primary and proximate impetus for the intervention.

Types of justifications

Justifications are the overt and public rationales presidents use to convince the domestic audience that military action is legitimate and worth the potential costs. Justifications assert the need for intervention, often by introducing the risk of bad outcomes if the US fails to act or the prospect of good outcomes that US action could bring about. In the post-Cold War period, there are two types of justifications that offer a solely sufficient, legally accepted rationale for the use of force: security justifications and humanitarian justifications (Finnemore 2003). Security justifications explain the need for action in terms of the protection and promotion of US interests. They encourage individuals to evaluate an intervention in terms of its consequences for their own safety and for the safety of the nation as a whole. For example, George W. Bush offered a security justification for the US intervention in Afghanistan in 2001 when he said, "Our Nation faces a threat to our freedoms, and the stakes could not be higher. We are the target of enemies who boast they want to kill" (G. W. Bush 2001b). In this case, US military action is presented as necessary because without it, American lives would be at risk.

Humanitarian justifications, on the other hand, explain the need for military action in terms of the protection and promotion of the human rights and welfare of foreign civilians. These justifications encourage individuals to evaluate the intervention in terms of its implications for the wellbeing of others and for the common good. In the same address to the nation on Afghanistan, George W. Bush also offered an example of humanitarian justifications when he noted, "We care for the innocent people of Afghanistan, so we continue to provide humanitarian aid, even while their Government tries to steal the food we send. When the terrorists and their supporters are gone, the people of Afghanistan will say with the rest of the world: Good riddance" (G. W. Bush 2001b). This statement captures the defining features of humanitarian appeals because it focuses attention on the benefits that US military forces would provide for civilians in the short term—food and aid—as well as the greater good of freeing people from an oppressive government.

Types of interventions

Bush's statements about Afghanistan reiterate that humanitarian justifications are not limited to cases where the US has no security interests at stake. Interventions rarely have a single objective, but to evaluate the power of humanitarian justifications, it is necessary to draw some distinctions between the types of crises in which these claims could be important. To this end, I sort crises into security and humanitarian categories based on the proximate and primary impetus for military action.[4] I define military interventions as the deployment of combat troops across international borders with the purpose of coercion that lasts at least one week.[5]

Security interventions respond primarily and proximately to an increasing threat to US national interests or to the safety of individuals within the US. These interventions can achieve humanitarian outcomes, but their initiation is not a reaction to intensifying human rights abuses. The 2001 US invasion of Afghanistan continues to provide a helpful illustration. Prior to the US intervention, the Taliban government was responsible for grave human rights abuses. Additionally, US operations included efforts to improve the welfare of the country's civilians. Despite this record of oppression and the provision of aid, the US military intervention took place when it did because of the 9/11 terrorist attacks, not because of escalating human rights abuses. For this reason, I classify this case as a security intervention.

Alternatively, humanitarian interventions are cases that primarily and proximately respond to escalating harm or threats posed to foreign civilians. The US may be more likely to react to humanitarian crises in areas where it has strategic interests, but military action is not preceded by a direct attack on US troops, citizens, or interests. The 2011 US intervention in Libya offers a helpful example of the boundaries of humanitarian interventions. The US had clear strategic interests in the region and the Gaddafi regime

---

[4] I rely on news reports—from before the first official presidential speech on the crisis whenever possible—to determine the impetus for intervention. Classifying interventions based on precipitating events rather than leaders' statements is key for separating the type of justification from the type of intervention. This process is described in more detail in Chapter 2.

[5] This definition is standard in recent scholarship, including Finnemore (2003), Kreps (2011), and Saunders (2011). I add the one-week criteria because short and limited operations may carry a different burden of justification.

had directly threatened US security in the past. The timing and primary objective of the 2011 intervention, however, was driven by evidence that the regime intended to launch indiscriminate attacks on civilians in Benghazi. I thus classify this case as a humanitarian intervention.

This distinction between security and humanitarian interventions is consistent with Jentleson and Britton's (1998) discussion of principle policy objectives. By these definitions, from 1990 to 2013, the United States engaged in eight military interventions, four primarily security-focused and four that were humanitarian. Security interventions include the 1991 Gulf War, operations in Haiti in 1994,[6] the war in Afghanistan beginning in 2001, and the 2003 invasion of Iraq.[7] Cases of humanitarian intervention include US operations in Somalia from 1992 to 1993, action in Bosnia beginning in 1994, Kosovo 1999, and Libya 2011.

Humanitarian justifications across interventions

Across all of the eight cases of military intervention—both security and humanitarian—US presidents used humanitarian justifications to explain the need for action to the domestic public. Unsurprisingly, humanitarian claims abound in speeches about the four cases of humanitarian intervention. George H. W. Bush introduced the need for action in Somalia by telling the public that, "The people of Somalia, especially the children of Somalia, need our help. We're able to ease their suffering. We must help them live. We must give them hope. America must act" (G. H. W. Bush 1992). Under the Clinton administration, military action in Bosnia was also linked to increasing attacks on civilians, with justifications noting, "Two weeks ago, in a murderous attack, a single shell killed 68 people in the city's market. And last week with our NATO allies, we said that those who would continue terrorizing Sarajevo must pay a price" (Clinton 1994b). When launching airstrikes against Serbian forces in Kosovo almost five years later, Clinton's

---

[6] The 1994 intervention in Haiti is particularly difficult to classify. The intervention's objective was to reinstall the democratically elected leader and stop the flow of civilians fleeing to the United States. Because the precipitating crisis was directly a threat to US interests, it is coded as a security intervention. However, the crisis also had clear humanitarian components from the beginning. All of the analyses that follow code Haiti both ways as a robustness check and the findings consistently hold.

[7] As Chapter 5 discusses in more detail, the security concerns raised in the Iraq case were ultimately found to be misleading. However, for the purposes of classification, it remains the case that Iraq's variable track record of allowing UN inspectors into the country and potential interest in weapons of mass destruction, in the context of the broader war on terror narrative, provided the initial impetus for action.

justifications carried a similar focus on the wellbeing of civilians, claiming, "I think the most important thing now is for us to save lives, return people to their homes, get them the humanitarian aid they need, and to remove completely and irrevocably the threat of aggression by the Serb military and other forces in Kosovo" (Clinton 1998). More than a decade later when Obama explained why he ordered an intervention in Libya in 2011, concern about attacks on civilians remained a central theme: "...as president, I refused to wait for the images of slaughter and mass graves before taking action" (Obama 2011).

Contrary to conventional expectations, examples of humanitarian justifications are also common in presidential speeches about security interventions. In the build-up to the Gulf War—the first major US military intervention after the end of the Cold War—George H. W. Bush asserted that, "We have no argument with the people of Iraq; indeed, we have only friendship for the people there" (G. H. W. Bush 1990f). He also emphasized the protection of Kuwaiti civilians, noting, "The tales of rape and assassination, of cold-blooded murder and rampant looting are almost beyond belief. The whole civilized world must unite and say: This kind of treatment of people must end. And those who violate the Kuwait people must be brought to justice" (G. H. W. Bush 1990f). When the US returned to Iraq years later, George W. Bush maintained that, "We care about those who suffer under the hands of a dictator in Iraq. We care deeply about those who dissent and then are tortured, about those who express an opinion other than what the dictator thinks and are raped and mutilated" (G. W. Bush 2003b). This statement echoed his claim in the immediate aftermath of 9/11 that "Afghanistan's people have been brutalized. Many are starving, and many have fled. Women are not allowed to attend school. You can be jailed for owning a television" (G. W. Bush 2001a). While operations in Haiti in 1994 remain difficult to classify, there is no doubt that humanitarian rationales were part of the communication strategy, with Clinton asserting, "Our reasons are clear: to stop the horrific atrocities that threaten thousands of men, women, and children in Haiti" (Clinton 1994a).

The scope of the argument

The domestic coalition theory has implications for the use of humanitarian justifications across time and countries, but I first establish the validity of this argument by focusing on the pattern of justifications used in US military interventions from 1990 to 2013. This pattern includes the eight cases of military intervention mentioned above, but also extends to security and humanitarian crises that did not ultimately end in the use of US military force. All elected leaders stand to benefit from gaining public support for military action; however, I limit the analysis to justifications offered by US presidents because, for the time period in question, the US was unique in its ability to project military power around the world (Pickering and Kisangani 2009). Additionally, the United States was the country most often involved in post-Cold War interventions. Understanding how the US mobilizes domestic support for interventions thus has wide-ranging consequences for international security and helps explain a significant number of contemporary uses of military force.

Humanitarian justifications in potential interventions

The eight cases in which the US pursued military interventions in the post-Cold War period confirm that humanitarian justifications are not limited to instances of humanitarian intervention. Turning to the broader set of cases in which the US considered military action during this period demonstrates that the pattern of justifications also applies to potential interventions. Figure 1.1 illustrates how many times each year from 1990 to 2013 presidents used humanitarian and security statements in their speeches about ongoing conflicts—including cases that did not ultimately escalate to the use of military force.[8] This broader set of crises captures multiple Republican and Democratic administrations, as well as conflicts before and after the beginning of the US war on terror. Across administrations, crises, and time, humanitarian claims are consistently present and were occasionally the most used justification for action. In fact, presidents used at least one humanitarian claim in 59 percent of their national addresses about potential interventions, regardless of the nature of the underlying crisis.

Across cases of actual and potential military interventions, humanitarian justifications thus play a pivotal role in US foreign policy. Understanding the power of these claims, especially in security interventions, offers new insight

---

[8] The following chapter outlines how I constructed this dataset and analyzes the pattern of speeches in more detail.

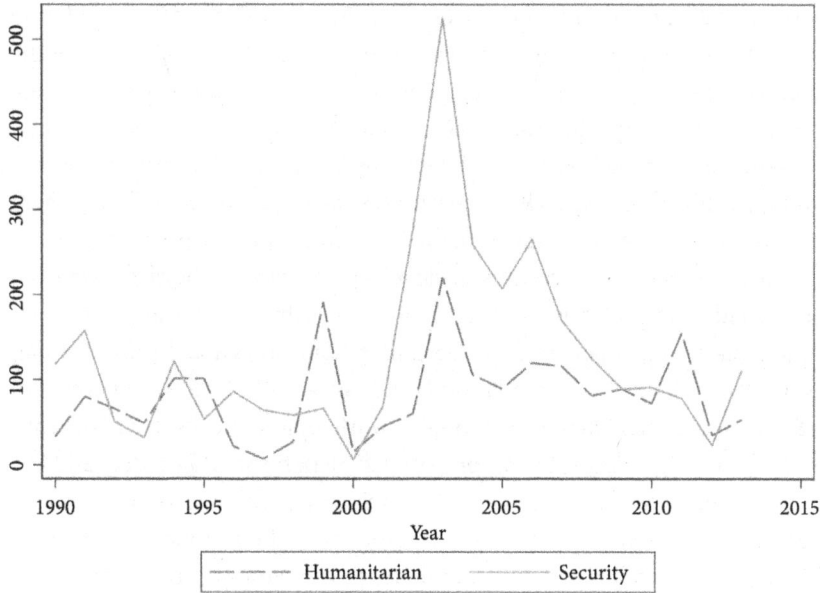

Figure 1.1 Number of justifications for potential interventions by year

into the process of domestic mobilization and corrects misperceptions about what it takes to build and sustain support for the use of force.

Humanitarian justifications beyond the US context

Although the book is limited to the US context for the reasons outlined above, I expect the logic of the domestic coalition argument to extend to any democracy that engages in military action. Whether humanitarian justifications will be equally important in mobilizing public support in other countries depends on the prevalence of doves and how their political power is divided or concentrated across electoral blocs. Where dovish preferences make up a non-negligible and politically relevant portion of the population,[9] elected leaders have a strong incentive to explain how military action will benefit foreign civilians, even when the intervention protects national interests. Relative to other advanced industrialized democracies, the US is a hard case for observing the domestic benefits of humanitarian claims for

---

[9] Criteria I define in more detail in Chapter 3.

two reasons: (1) doves likely make up a smaller proportion of the population compared to European countries, and (2) the two-party system dampens the effect of minority policy preferences compared to multi-party systems where appeasing smaller parties can be key to maintaining governing coalitions.

Public opinion on both sides of the Atlantic supports this distinction. For example, during key security interventions in Afghanistan and Iraq, there were three times as many hawks in the US as in Europe (Asmus 2004). Consistent cross-national measures of doves and hawks are hard to come by, but variation in preferences for engaging with China offers suggestive evidence that this gap between the US and its allies remains. In the German Marshall Fund's 2023 Transatlantic Trends survey (2023, 56), 40 percent of US respondents said that the US should "work diplomatically to end the conflict" if China invaded Taiwan, compared to 50 percent of Canadian and UK respondents, as well as 52 percent of French and German respondents. Support for humanitarianism also appears higher in the European context. In 2023, 91 percent of European respondents viewed funding humanitarian aid activities as "very" or "fairly" important (Eurobarometer 2024), compared to 71 percent of US respondents who viewed foreign humanitarian aid as "very" or "somewhat important" (CNBC 2023).

Given that doves are at least as prevalent in the domestic audiences of US allies, it is no surprise that humanitarian justifications appeared prominently in European leaders' speeches about contemporary security crises. For example, in his address to Parliament about British involvement in Afghanistan, Prime Minister Tony Blair (2001) gave significant attention to humanitarian issues, explaining that "I believe the humanitarian coalition to help the people of Afghanistan to be as vital as any military action itself." He went on to promise that "We will do what we can to minimize the suffering of the Afghan people as a result of the conflict; and we commit ourselves to work with them afterwards inside and outside Afghanistan to ensure a better, more peaceful future, free from the repression and dictatorship that is their present existence" (Blair 2001).

Humanitarian justifications were also central in Chancellor Gerhard Schröder's efforts to gain support for deploying German troops in Afghanistan (Connolly 2001). Facing opposition from the Green Party—members of the governing coalition at the time—Schröder (2001) outlined the potential humanitarian risks and benefits of action directly, noting, "War impacts innocent people. This is not a question. But the example of Afghanistan shows: only with the help of military force could the endless suffering of innocent people be prevented in the future."[10] In addition to establishing the cross-national use of humanitarian claims, the German case also highlights the importance of building broad support that includes persuadable doves, even when other majorities are feasible. While the vote to deploy troops had sufficient support from the opposition to pass, Schröder tied the vote to confidence in his government and used humanitarian appeals to directly counter the concerns raised by Green Party members (Finn 2024).

As these examples show, humanitarian justifications are not an exclusively US phenomenon. Instead, they are a persistent part of the rhetoric used by global leaders across multiple countries. If anything, their presence in the US case is the most surprising, given the public's relatively high tolerance for the use of force and the comparably narrower channels that two-party systems provide for dissenting opinions.

The post-Cold War period and beyond

I also focus the initial analysis on the period following the end of the Cold War, beginning in 1990, to hold constant the global balance of power and the feasibility of humanitarian justifications as a primary rationale for action. Before the end of the Cold War, humanitarian crises were viewed as the internal affairs of states whose sovereignty could not be violated without also violating the UN Charter (Finnemore 1996). As a result, humanitarian appeals alone could not legitimate intervention (Finnemore 1996; Wheeler 2000). Prior to the end of the Cold War, it is thus not possible to determine whether presidents' emphasis of humanitarian justifications in security interventions was limited by the risk of backlash from the domestic audience or because primarily humanitarian interventions were not considered legitimate uses of force.

After the empirical chapters establish that leaders have domestic political incentives to link military action to the wellbeing of foreign civilians, the conclusion applies the domestic coalition logic to earlier historical cases. Drawing on examples from Vietnam and the World Wars, it shows that leaders' use of humanitarian claims in security crises is not an exclusively

---

[10] Translated from the original: "Krieg trifft Unschuldige. Das ist keine Frage. Aber das Beispiel Afghanistan zeigt: Nur mithilfe militärischer Gewalt konnte verhindert werden, dass auch in Zukunft Unschuldige unendlich leiden müssen."

post-Cold War phenomenon. Instead, the domestic coalition logic helps explain the long-standing and widespread appeal of humanitarian claims and more appropriately captures their breadth and power.

Plan of the book

This book reveals and explains the necessity of humanitarian claims for military intervention. It does so by showing that leaders intentionally offer humanitarian appeals to reap domestic benefits, highlighting which constituencies respond to humanitarian rationales, and demonstrating that broad domestic coalitions increase opportunities for democratic accountability. I first establish the pattern of humanitarian justifications in contemporary interventions, highlighting evidence of perceived demand and restraint that is out of sync with existing explanations. I then investigate the domestic incentives leaders have to offer humanitarian justifications, comparing how presidents actually talk about interventions with what they *should* say to broaden public support. Finally, I examine the intent behind the White House's rhetorical choices, demonstrating officials' concern with broad domestic coalitions and political backlash. The result is evidence that humanitarian appeals are important for mobilizing domestic support in both theory and practice.

Chapter 2 describes the overall pattern of humanitarian justifications based on the analysis of an original dataset of presidents' justifications for every potential US military intervention from 1990 to 2013. This speech-level data shows that humanitarian claims play a common and central role in security crises, reinforcing the puzzling prominence of these justifications. Across administrations and political parties, leaders consistently include humanitarian justifications in their speeches about intervention, even when US security is at stake. Presidents also, however, limit the emphasis they place on humanitarian explanations in security crises. The main takeaway from this pattern of humanitarian justifications is that it reveals both perceived demand and restraint.

Chapter 3 presents the domestic coalition explanation for this pattern of justifications, accounting for both the demand and restraint that appear in the speech data. It outlines the domestic coalition argument in detail, explaining why leaders care about public opinion, should want to mobilize broad domestic coalitions of support, and need to persuade doves to support aggression in order to achieve this goal. The chapter presents hypotheses for each step of the argument and contrasts its implications against the conventional wisdom that humanitarian claims are either limited or problematic and best studied in the context of humanitarian interventions.

Chapter 4 turns to the demand side of the domestic coalition argument, providing evidence that there are traditional doves who can be uniquely persuaded by humanitarian appeals. The chapter uses national survey experiments to illustrate that no single justification can convince all members of the public. Isolationists are generally skeptical of military interventions. Hawks and doves, however, can both be persuaded to support military action, but the former respond to all justifications while the latter behave like wary warmongers (Keller 2003), fully joining domestic coalitions only when humanitarian explanations are present. The highest possible support from doves and, as a result, the broadest internationalist coalition creates a demand for humanitarian justifications in security crises.

Chapter 5 explains the restraint in presidential speech patterns, using survey experimental data to explore whether humanitarian justifications empower leaders to manipulate the public. It argues that humanitarian appeals are both more powerful and less problematic than conventional wisdom expects because the same individuals who respond to these claims also limit their effectiveness. Doves pay close attention to information about humanitarian goals and withdraw their support for intervention if the humanitarian claims appear insincere. Where Chapter 4 shows that the support of doves is the benefit to be gained from humanitarian appeals, Chapter 5 demonstrates that political backlash from the same individuals cautions leaders against stretching claims too far. Hawks offer a similar backlash in response to insincere security justifications, which means that instead of making the public easier to manipulate, broad domestic coalitions expand opportunities for accountability.

Chapter 6 then shows that presidents' savvy use of humanitarian claims is intentional—while academics often overlook the power of humanitarian explanations, leaders have recognized the political benefits for decades. The chapter uses original archival research to explore the development of White House communication strategies in two cases: the 1991 Persian Gulf War, representing a security intervention, and the Clinton administration's policy towards Bosnia from 1993 to 1995, representing a humanitarian intervention. The Gulf War case evaluates and establishes the validity of the argument, providing evidence that domestic political incentives shaped

White House communication strategies in an actual case of intervention. The Bosnian conflict then establishes the scope of the argument, revealing that the domestic coalition logic remains relevant in cases of humanitarian intervention. Investigating communications memos, speech drafts, and other primary sources from the archives, the chapter sheds light on how leaders perceive public opinion, understand the importance of humanitarian justifications, and acknowledge the limits of what their speeches can accomplish.

Finally, Chapter 7 concludes by examining the domestic coalition argument in the context of contemporary foreign policy and democratic institutions. Considering statements from additional and more recent US presidents, as well as other world leaders, this chapter shows that the pattern of humanitarian justifications is not US-specific and continues to hold in the face of growing partisan polarization. The power of humanitarian narratives has not declined, even as foreign policy goals shifted and humanitarian interventions became less common. In times of domestic and geopolitical change, humanitarian claims can help maintain democratic accountability by keeping the public engaged in military interventions.

2

How leaders talk about potential interventions

The first step to understanding the power of humanitarian justifications is to establish when and how often they appear in contemporary military interventions. Each existing strand of conventional wisdom about humanitarian justifications, described in Chapter 1, has a different expectation for the pattern by which humanitarian claims appear in a president's speeches. If the rational public explanations are right, humanitarian appeals are of little domestic use to the White House when security justifications are available. In this case, there will be few speeches that use humanitarian claims outside of the context of potential humanitarian interventions where credible security justifications are unavailable. Alternatively, the regular overuse of humanitarian claims—with presidents making no distinction between humanitarian and security crises—would reflect warnings about an emotional public that is easily swayed by graphic depictions of suffering and presents an obstacle to prudent foreign policy (Kennan 1993; Robinson 2011).

This chapter uses an original dataset of US presidents' justifications for potential interventions from 1990 through 2013 to take this first step (Maxey 2020), illustrating the pattern of humanitarian appeals across different types of crises and multiple presidential administrations. It reveals a surprising pattern of justifications that does not fit easily within either existing explanation. Presidents use humanitarian justifications more often than the rational public views expect—these claims appear in the majority of speeches about both humanitarian *and* security crises—but exercise more restraint than the emotional public perspectives anticipate, taking care to keep the emphasis of the speech on the primary impetus for action. This pattern highlights the importance of understanding humanitarian justifications, demonstrating that they are a common tool used across administrations to facilitate foreign policies with grave consequences. It also establishes the need for a better explanation of how protecting foreign civilians influences the relationship

Doves into Hawks. Sarah Maxey, Oxford University Press. © Oxford University Press (2026).
DOI: 10.1093/9780197832738.003.0002

between the president and the public, which accounts for both the perceived demand and restraint in humanitarian appeals.

I begin by outlining evidence that presidents are concerned with public support and that White House communication strategies help persuade the domestic audience—justification patterns thus offer a glimpse into how presidents think they should talk about military interventions to mobilize sufficient public support. I then introduce and validate the dataset of public justifications for potential military interventions before describing the pattern of humanitarian claims and comparing it to security justifications. The findings show that the pattern of justifications in White House speeches is consistent with both incentives for humanitarian claims and caution about their misuse. This pattern holds across different presidential administrations and political parties. Evidence that presidents are cautious about misuse also extends to security justifications. The conclusion brings together the implications of this pattern of justifications and uses it to motivate the domestic coalition argument that is presented in Chapter 3.

The strategic use of White House communications

The claim that presidents take public opinion seriously and craft speeches to mobilize domestic support is well established in both scholarship and practice. In their study of how presidents collect information about and attempt to shape public opinion, Druckman and Jacobs (2015, 13) show that "Before modern presidents speak publicly, private White House polling has often pinpointed the particular topics, words, and framings that resonate with existing attitudes in order to increase the probability of changing public opinion in desired ways." The White House's vast investment of time and resources in polling the public reflects an executive understanding that presidential power is "anchored in the ability to rally public support" (Druckman and Jacobs 2015, 21). Moreover, this expansive polling apparatus is calibrated to monitor not only the general public mood, but also "politically valued segments of the electorate" (Druckman and Jacobs 2015, 11).

Presidents and their staffs also acknowledge their strategic approach to communicating with the public. In the build-up to the US invasion of Iraq in 2003, George W. Bush asserted that "We lead our publics" (Woodward 2004, 296). Preparing for the Gulf War more than a decade earlier, George H. W. Bush's communications team went a step further, outlining the full range of legitimate justifications for action and choosing which to use in presidential speeches based on anticipated public reactions:

> There is a spectrum of justifications for our current military operation in the Middle East that ranges in persuasiveness from the most persuasive reason: that we are upholding world peace and the rule of law by standing up to naked aggression; to the less persuasive (though legitimate) argument that we are protecting America's vital interest in preserving the flow of oil from the Persian Gulf region to the rest of the world. This latter argument will be attacked as a materialist rationale: we are asking American boys to die for oil and cheap gasoline. [...] Therefore, we urge that wherever possible our arguments should be marshalled around the most compelling reason: world peace/rule of law. (Pinkerton 1990)

Consistent with these examples, the justifications used in official speeches shape the relationship between the president and public support for military action. When the White House correctly identifies and uses persuasive justifications, public support for military action increases, and leaders can pursue intervention with fewer political risks. Alternatively, if the White House miscalculates and chooses a justification strategy that divides the public, support will be difficult to come by, and the political costs of action will increase. The justifications the White House chooses to communicate with the public about a particular crisis thus offer insight into what the executive branch thinks is the best way to mobilize the domestic audience and gain support for military action. These elite assumptions about public opinion have political and policy consequences, regardless of their accuracy.[1]

Capturing justifications for potential interventions

Understanding how White House communication strategies attempt to make the case for military action requires data that can capture both opportunities for official justifications and the type of justifications used. To this end, I created a dataset of all 801 national addresses given by a US president

---

[1] See, for example, Kull and Destler's (1999) account of the effects of elite misperceptions about public isolationism. In Chapter 6, I use archival materials to match the pattern of justifications presented in this chapter to the stated objectives of White House administrations.

from 1990 to 2013 that reference a potential case of intervention and represent an opportunity for the leader to justify action (Maxey 2020). Using this dataset, I evaluate the pattern of security and humanitarian justifications across cases that respond primarily to humanitarian and security crises. This section outlines the criteria used to construct the dataset, beginning with the categories of possible justifications and then turning to the definition of a potential intervention.

Categories of justifications

I define justifications as the public and overt rationale presidents use to convince the domestic audience that military action is legitimate, necessary, and worthy of support. As discussed in Chapter 1, in contemporary foreign policy, leaders have two options for justifications that can provide a solely legitimate reason for action: security rationales or humanitarian rationales. Security justifications reference threats to the safety of the US domestic population or to US national interests. Such justifications make the case for how intervention would benefit the United States. Humanitarian justifications, by contrast, refer to the welfare or protection of foreign civilians and explain how intervention would benefit citizens of the target state. Security and humanitarian justifications are not mutually exclusive. Presidents can combine claims within a single speech and change the emphasis they place on different justifications over the course of an intervention.

Although not capable of providing a legitimate reason for intervention on their own, leaders also occasionally evoke a third, ideological category of justifications. Ideological justifications reference the promotion of democratic institutions and US values. They are distinct from humanitarian justifications because their focus is on building representative institutions instead of providing civilians with protection from harm. Similarly, they are separate from security justifications because ideological claims consider the long-term prospects for regional stability rather than imminent threats to US interests. For the sake of thoroughness, I include ideological justifications in the content analysis and present descriptive data for this category. The descriptive analysis confirms that ideological claims make up a minor proportion of presidents' justifications for military action and are not a prominent part of communication strategies.

Identifying cases of potential intervention

The first step in creating a dataset of presidential justifications for military action is to identify cases of potential intervention where leaders had the opportunity to explain their foreign policy decisions. Examining only speeches about military interventions that took place would introduce bias by selecting on the success of the justification strategy—cases that ended in the use of force had sufficient public consent for the president to take the risks associated with military action. Alternatively, building a dataset around all global crises would include cases where the White House never considered active engagement and thus did not need to build a domestic coalition of support.

To avoid these pitfalls, I created a list of potential military interventions that includes only cases with an increased likelihood of military hostilities (Wilkenfeld and Brecher 1984) and sufficient public attention to warrant an official statement. The starting point for this list is all cases included in either the UCDP Armed Conflict (Pettersson and Wallensteen 2015) or the Militarized Interstate Dispute (MID) datasets (Palmer et al. 2015). I combine crises from these two sources because UCDP provides good coverage of low-level internal conflicts but omits a number of conflicts that originated with international threats. The MID data, by contrast, captures international crises but omits states' threats against their own citizens. Together, these two sources offset each other's limitations and provide a comprehensive list of intra- and interstate crises for the 1990 to 2013 period.

The resulting list of crises captures cases with the potential to warrant a US response—it reflects instances where something was wrong or unstable in another country. The next step is to further narrow this list down to cases in which the US paid attention and considered some form of a coercive response. Leaders are most concerned with how to justify their foreign policy to the public when they are considering some form of observable action. For a broad time period and a wide range of cases, it is not possible to know which crises leaders privately considered.[2] Instead, I assume that when coercive action is placed on the table—by the White House itself or by pressure from other groups—the president will bring the issue to the public's

---

[2] Archival records and process tracing better facilitate this type of analysis within single cases. Chapter 6 complements the quantitative analysis offered in this chapter with qualitative case studies of US action in the Gulf War and Bosnia.

attention at an early stage.[3] A public reference is thus both a precondition for a justification strategy and a sign the White House considered the crisis relevant to the US.

I determined which crises received public attention by searching the Public Papers of the Presidents database for references to any of the cases included in the UCDP or MID data. The Public Papers of the Presidents are compiled and published by the Office of the Federal Register (OFR). They contain presidential writings, addresses, and public remarks that were released by the White House Office of the Press Secretary (National Archives 2016). This database offers systematic and comprehensive access to official statements intended for public consumption and is recognized as a credible source of information about presidential rhetoric.[4] Based on statements included in the Public Papers, I defined potential interventions as the subset of crises that met three inclusion criteria: (1) the crisis was mentioned by the president at least once in a public speech or document, (2) the public mention addressed a specific and immediate crisis in detail, and (3) the public mention implied dissatisfaction with the status quo.

Public mention by the president

Before the White House can convince the public to support intervention in a crisis, the public must first know the crisis is happening. Public references are thus the earliest visible sign that the White House is developing a communication strategy for a potential intervention. This first criterion—that the president mentions the crisis in a public statement or document—narrows down the list of cases to those high enough on the foreign policy agenda to require a communication strategy.

Not all crises in the UCDP and MID datasets receive public attention, and an even smaller subset of those publicly referenced is the topic of justifications for action. Instead, I assume that leaders are most concerned about controlling the narrative of a crisis—and therefore most likely address it publicly—when a potential US intervention is on the table. This inclusion criterion acknowledges that parts of the US foreign policy agenda are event-driven (Wood and Peake 1998) and beyond the president's

---

[3] This assumption is not true for cases of covert action, where the White House plans to keep the intervention permanently off the public's radar. Such cases are outside of the scope of this research because, by definition, covert actions do not require public justification, and leaders are not expected to respond to public incentives in the same way. See Carson (2016) and O'Rourke (2018) for the different political dynamics of covert action.

[4] For example, it is one of the main sources for documents included in The American Presidency Project (Woolley and Peters, n.d.).

immediate control. While the White House can raise the profile of a crisis when it intends to act, domestic and international pressure for action also encourage reporters to ask officials for comments on crises they would rather avoid. By searching for public references to a crisis in both presidential speeches and statements, as well as news conferences and exchanges with reporters, I capture the full range of crises that were salient enough to warrant public attention.

References are specific and immediate

Where the first criterion reduced the list of international crises to cases that made it onto the public US foreign policy agenda, the second further condenses the list to crises that received sufficient, detailed attention to warrant potential justifications for action. Requiring that conflicts be referenced specifically and on a short timeframe rules out presidents' tendency to summarize international affairs by quickly mentioning multiple crises. For example, in his remarks at the United States Military Academy Commencement, Clinton (1993) noted, "As we scan today's bloodiest conflicts, from the former Soviet Union and Yugoslavia to Armenia and Sudan, the dynamics of the cold war have been replaced by many of the dynamics of old war." While statements like Clinton's acknowledge the presence of ongoing crises, they serve a broader rhetorical point about the state of the world and do not suggest the United States can or should do anything in response to a specific case.

Clinton's broad reference to multiple crises stands in stark contrast to the Bush administration's detailed account of the situation in Iraq in January 1993, where Press Secretary Marlin Fitzwater (1993) explained, "We continue to keep the situation in Iraq under close scrutiny. We have observed no penetrations by Iraqi aircraft of the No-Fly Zone below 32 degrees north latitude since Wednesday's coalition warning." Unlike the commencement address, this statement identifies the specific source of the concern with Iraq's behavior and commits the US to close and continued attention. Publicly promising to keep a close eye on the situation in Iraq and pinpointing a red line raised the prospect of escalation—and the corresponding demand for justification—in a way that Clinton's simple acknowledgement that there was a conflict in Armenia did not. The second criterion distinguishes between these two types of statements, including Iraq, while excluding Armenia from the list of potential interventions.

Additionally, this criterion requires that the official reference to a crisis is immediate, reflecting either the intensification of an ongoing conflict or a new conflict. This rule most notably excludes statements on the continuation of national emergencies. The dataset includes the initial declaration of a national emergency with respect to the target state but omits continuations in the absence of evidence that the crisis was substantively heightened relative to the previous year.

Dissatisfaction with the status quo

The final step in transforming the list of global crises into a list of potential interventions is to identify cases in which the US considered a coercive policy response. As the Clinton (1993) quote in the previous section highlights, presidents can acknowledge an ongoing conflict without indicating that US involvement is necessary or appropriate. The third criterion ensures that the official reference raised the possibility of a future US action that would require justification. I consider expressions of dissatisfaction with the direction or status quo of the conflict—often combined with a statement of the White House's preferred outcome—to signal the potential for coercive action. I operationalize dissatisfaction by looking for statements that do two things: (1) identify an outcome towards which the US would like the target state to move, often using language such as "we urge" or "we call on," and (2) reference a possible US response with phrases like "we must not permit" or "all options are on the table."

This criterion does not include commitments to work with or offer support to the government of the target state. Support stands in contrast to coercive action and makes action without the consent of the target state less likely.[5] I also exclude references to target states with nuclear capabilities, even if they meet the three criteria, assuming that nuclear deterrence prevents a direct military intervention from being feasible in such cases. The resulting list includes forty-six crises that the public was aware of, that White House communications considered, and for which coercive action was plausible. Using this list of potential interventions, I then collect data on the White House's choice of justifications in each case.

From crisis to justification

I next collected all national addresses that mentioned the target state of the potential intervention in the relevant year. Importantly, national addresses represent a much smaller subset of the official documents that I used to

---

[5] Action without the consent of the target state is a key component of standard definitions of military intervention (Finnemore 2003).

classify potential interventions. There are many cases of potential intervention that do not appear in national addresses or receive any type of justification. The process described above uses the widest possible range of documents—from responses to questions, to reports to Congress, to procedural memoranda—to determine whether a crisis made it onto any part of the public foreign policy agenda. In evaluating justifications, I narrow the focus to statements crafted specifically and intentionally to persuade the domestic audience. Presidents make statements to and for many different audiences, but national addresses are the context in which justifications that reflect a premeditated communication strategy designed to build a domestic coalition are most likely to appear.

A focus on national addresses

I define national addresses as any prepared statement given by the president in an official capacity that either: (1) was given from the White House, or (2) explicitly identified the nation as a whole as the immediate audience. This definition excludes the non-prepared portions of news conferences and the question-and-answer portions of exchanges with the press, as well as remarks given on the campaign trail or at fundraisers that appeal to an explicitly partisan audience. It also leaves out proclamations and memos to Congress that are written rather than spoken communications. I expect the rhetorical style used in spoken communications to be different than the language used to meet reporting requirements and that these written reports primarily target elites in Congress instead of the general public.

Statements that fall within the boundaries of this definition include State of the Union addresses, weekly radio addresses, the prepared portions of news conferences, and statements in response to breaking news. The resulting sample contains 801 national addresses given by George H. W. Bush, William Clinton, George W. Bush, and Barack Obama covering the twenty-four years from 1990 to 2013. These speeches hold constant the intended audience, as well as factors such as audience partisanship and location that could influence leaders' choice of justifications. For example, how a Republican president addresses donors at a campaign dinner in a red state responds to a different set of incentives than speeches written to persuade the nation as a whole.[6] Focusing on national addresses and

---

[6] Vice versa for a Democratic president.

excluding campaign remarks helps standardize the audience that leaders need to convince and the incentives set by their preferences. Limiting the sample to prepared remarks also ensures that the justifications used are intentional and reflect a political message the White House wanted to communicate. These are the speeches in which the White House's understanding of the benefits and limits of humanitarian claims are most likely to appear.

Developing a dictionary of justifications

Working from the collection of national addresses, the next step is to determine whether and how leaders justified each potential case of intervention. To this end, I created a dictionary of terms associated with security and humanitarian justifications for action.[7] The terms in this dictionary were based on hand-coding of justifications in a random sample of 120 speeches (five from each of the twenty-four years included in the study). The manual coding created a list of words associated with each category of justification. I then searched for those words in the full sample of speeches and calculated how often each term correctly identified the relevant justification. Phrases that consistently and correctly identified the relevant justification were included in the final dictionaries for each category. The humanitarian dictionary includes words like "atrocity," "inhumane," "defenseless," "massacre," and "oppression." The security dictionary includes phrases such as "disarm," "harbor," "provocation," "aggression," and "sovereignty."

Next, I imported the final dictionaries into the Yoshikoder content analysis program (Lowe 2015) and used them to measure the number of times a president offered each type of justification in a national address about a potential intervention. This process creates a new dataset with counts of security and humanitarian justifications for potential interventions. The unit of analysis in this dataset is a national address that references a potential intervention. The key dependent variables, discussed in more detail in a later section, are: (1) whether each speech included humanitarian justifications and, (2) how much emphasis the president placed on humanitarian justifications relative to security justifications.

---

[7] I also created a dictionary of terms associated with ideological justifications. To give a comprehensive picture of how presidents talked about post-Cold War interventions, the frequency of ideological justifications is presented in Figure 2.2. These claims are not included in the main analysis, however, because they are relatively rare and cannot provide solely legitimate justifications for military action.

The benefits and limits of automated content analysis

Automated content analysis—in this case, using the Yoshikoder program to locate and count references to different justifications—is invaluable for systematically examining patterns in presidential speeches about military action over time. The volume of text in presidential speeches over multiple administrations makes comprehensive hand-coding infeasible. Applying and drawing conclusions from automated content analysis, however, requires strong assumptions.

Most significantly, content analysis assumes a stable communication process in which words have the same meaning every time they are used. For example, presidential references to "communism" or "containment" evoked vital US national interests and alluded to specific policies during the Cold War, casting the need for action in existential security terms. In the post-Cold War and war on terror eras, these terms more often capture references to institution-building or regime change in states with communist legacies. To understand patterns in how leaders explain interventions, it is first important to make sure words are consistently associated with the same justification category over the time period of interest.

I follow Krebs' (2015, 301) suggestion for limiting concerns about dramatic changes in meaning by "analyzing a narrower range of texts—from a single or relatively homogeneous set of speakers, from a relatively short time span, from a single country—and by generating search-terms and coding rules based on a context-sensitive reading of select texts and secondary literature." In the analysis, I focus on four presidents of a single country over a twenty-four-year period. This time period is broad enough to include a variety of potential interventions and changes in presidential administrations and political parties. It is narrow enough to hold constant the balance of power and the relative US position in the international system. This focus reduces concerns about major rhetorical shifts or changing points of reference. The four administrations included had access to similar toolkits of justifications and addressed voting publics with shared historical experiences. As a result, leaders looking to mobilize public support during this period are expected to use similar phrases that carry similar meaning across both administrations and potential interventions.

The norms surrounding military intervention are also stable across this period (Crawford 2002; Evangelista and Shue 2014; Finnemore 2003). Vitally, this means that humanitarian justifications were consistently capable of providing an accepted rationale for action. Changes in the use of these justifications across interventions do not reflect changes in their overarching international legitimacy.

By building dictionaries inductively based on manual coding, I further ensure that the resulting dataset reflects a stable communication process. I selected each term included in the dictionaries based on a context-sensitive coding of speeches from across the twenty-four-year period. This process is able to catch and account for subtle changes in meaning over time, confirming that the terms are exclusively associated with their assigned category of justification.

The use and emphasis of justifications

Existing accounts of justifications and public opinion differ in terms of their expectations for when humanitarian claims will be present in presidential speeches and when leaders will rely on humanitarian rationales as the primary reason for action. Distinguishing between the *use* and *emphasis* of justifications is thus key to the empirical analysis. If the rational public expectations are correct, presidents will use humanitarian justifications in their speeches about potential humanitarian interventions because other rationales are not available. In cases of potential security interventions, by contrast, leaders will leave out humanitarian claims because they are unnecessary for bolstering public support. I measure the *use* of security and humanitarian justifications based on whether words associated with a given justification category appear in the speech at all. This measure captures the presence or absence of a particular type of justification and appears in the dataset as a binary variable. *Use* takes the value of one if the relevant speech includes at least one word associated with the justification category and is otherwise zero.

The emotional public perspective, by contrast, expects presidents to use humanitarian justifications widely across different types of crises and be willing to overstate the importance of humanitarian concerns in security cases to eliminate public constraints. I use a measure of *emphasis* to reflect the relative prominence of a justification category within a single speech and to capture instances of overstating—i.e., using as the primary justification a rationale that does not match the type of underlying crisis—either humanitarian or security justifications. I create the *emphasis* variable based on the percentage of total justifications in a speech that fall within a given category. For example, to calculate the emphasis placed on humanitarian rationales in a specific speech, I divide the number of humanitarian justifications by the total number of humanitarian and security justifications in the speech. Measuring *emphasis* as a percentage of justifications has two benefits. First, recognizing that presidents often combine justifications, this measure offers a way to determine which justification provided the primary explanation for action. Second, dividing by the number of total justifications accounts for variation in the length of speeches and the propensity of some presidents to talk more than others. The percentage measure thus helps standardize *emphasis* and offers a more accurate illustration of the pattern of justifications across presidents.

Types of crises

Whether a potential intervention addresses a humanitarian or security crisis generates different expectations for the use and emphasis that presidents place on humanitarian justifications. I follow Finnemore (2003, 53) in defining humanitarian interventions as "deploying military force across borders for the purpose of protecting foreign nationals from man-made violence." This definition is also consistent with Wheeler's (2000, 34) distinction between "the ordinary routine abuse of human rights that tragically occurs on a daily basis and those extraordinary acts of killing and brutality that belong to the category of 'crimes against humanity.'" The latter can include genocide, state-sponsored mass murder, mass population expulsions, and state breakdown, "such as in the Somali case, which led to famine and a collapse of law and order" (Wheeler 2000, 34).[8] I label crises as humanitarian if they include dramatic and increasing threats to foreign civilians. Crises that include the short-term escalation of egregious human rights abuses are the cases where military action, should it materialize, would fall within the bounds of the humanitarian intervention definition.

By contrast, security interventions are defined by the coercive use of military force across borders to protect US national security, vital strategic

---

[8] Similarly, Jentleson and Britton (1998, 399–400) define humanitarian intervention policy objectives as "the provision of emergency relief through military and other means to people suffering from famine or other gross and widespread humanitarian disasters."

interests, or the safety of the American people. This view of security interventions is in line with discussions of realist foreign policy goals, such as
preserving the territorial integrity, homeland security, and regional hegemony of the US, as well as responding to violations of sovereignty and
containing rising powers (Drezner 2008, 55). Potential interventions in this
category can include acts that Jentleson and Britton (1998, 397) consider foreign policy restraint—"coercing an adversary engaged in aggressive actions
against the United States, its citizens, or its interests"—or attempts at internal
political change, where military force aims to engineer change in another
country's government or is "an effort to overthrow a government considered an adversary." Consistent with these existing definitions, I label security
crises as those that include dramatic and increasing threats to the US or its
vital national interests. These are crises that, should they escalate to military
action, would fall within existing definitions of security interventions.

In practice, the same features that make the pattern of presidential justifications worthy of study also make crises difficult to characterize. Most cases
of violence involve some combination of security and humanitarian threats.
I approach this challenge by applying Jentleson and Britton's (1998) classification of interventions based on primary policy objectives to the underlying
crisis. I consider the factor that escalated or intensified in the period imme-
diately preceding the crisis to reflect the primary policy objective of the
potential intervention. If a factor was present over a longer period of time but
did not dramatically change in the short-term, it can provide a secondary
rationale but is unlikely to account for why the White House considered
intervention at that moment (instead of taking action when the problem first
appeared).

For example, while Saddam Hussein had a long record of human rights
abuses, his treatment of the Iraqi people did not change dramatically prior
to the 2003 US invasion. Instead, the intervention followed an escalation
in concerns about Iraq's compliance with UN resolutions and a flawed but
increasing focus on the risk that Hussein was developing and interested in
trafficking weapons of mass destruction. The 2003 Iraq case is thus classified
as a security crisis rather than a humanitarian crisis.

Critically, I classified a crisis as primarily security or humanitarian using
coverage of the event that is separate from and prior to the president's first
address. Using prior coverage means that how I label the crisis is not determined by the success or failure of White House communication strategies.
This approach avoids the risk of a tautology—that the reason for action

depends on the justification for action—by ensuring the classification of events precedes any official justifications. Crises that media coverage primarily discussed in terms of cross-border aggression, regional stability and spillover violence, attacks on oil and economic resources, terrorist attacks, or the devolution of power to terrorist groups are coded as potential security interventions. Crises that news stories presented primarily in terms of refugees, starvation, forced migration, attacks on civilians or civilian areas, human rights violations, or threats to civil liberties are classified as potential humanitarian interventions.

Opportunities for justifications

The resulting dataset includes speeches and justification counts from forty-six distinct conflicts that took place in thirty-one different countries. Of these cases, eight ultimately ended in a military intervention, while thirty-eight remain cases of non-intervention that were settled or sustained without escalating to the use of force by 2013. Humanitarian crises make up the majority of both potential and realized interventions during this period—twenty-five of the thirty-eight cases of non-intervention and five of the eight cases of intervention were sparked by intensifying concerns about humanitarian conditions.

Unsurprisingly, presidents spent the most time talking about cases that ended in military action. These cases of intervention require ongoing justifications and benefit from increased public salience, unlike cases of non-intervention for which too much attention can create public pressure for escalation. Of the 762 speeches that uniquely addressed a single crisis,[9] 29 percent were about non-interventions, while 71 percent made the case for interventions that ultimately took place. Speeches about interventions also included more explanations for action, offering on average 6.7 justifications compared to 4.9 justifications in speeches about non-interventions.

There are notable cases of non-intervention that push against this trend, such as Iran, Sudan (Darfur), Myanmar, and Syria, each of which was

---

[9] A small number of speeches—thirty-nine of the 801—justify multiple cases of potential intervention. For clarity and to avoid any bias in interpreting the results, from this point forward, I drop these thirty-nine speeches from the analysis. The results are robust to the inclusion of all 801 speeches.

the subject of ten or more national addresses.[10] Statements about Iran reflect ongoing tensions surrounding their role in the region and their potential development of a nuclear program. Speeches about Sudan highlight the genocide in Darfur beginning in 2003, Myanmar focuses on human rights, and Syria captures concern about Assad's use of chemical weapons following the Arab Spring protests. Consistent with these prominent examples, speeches about non-interventions disproportionately discussed humanitarian crises, which made up 54 percent of statements about non-interventions and only 21 percent of speeches about interventions. This distribution of speeches does not say anything about the types of justifications leaders used to explain US action in each case—the task of the next section—but it does suggest that humanitarian crises are more likely to be met with verbal condemnations and options short of force.

The overall distribution of speeches, illustrated in Figure 2.1, highlights the time and effort US presidents devote to publicly justifying potential interventions. On average, post-Cold War presidents gave thirty-three national addresses per year that mentioned potential interventions. There are a total of 762 national addresses that reference a unique case of potential intervention during the 1990 to 2013 period, 628 of which include at least one justification for military action.[11]

All presidents thus had ample opportunity to publicly justify their foreign policy decisions, but there is variation between administrations and across time in both the quantity of public statements and number of justifications for action. This variation largely tracks the number of crises and actual interventions in each time period. As the top panel of Figure 2.1 shows, George H. W. Bush gave the fewest speeches, while George W. Bush gave the most speeches of any president included in the dataset. This pattern has face validity, reflecting the fact that George H. W. Bush was president for only one term. By contrast, George W. Bush's two terms included the first attack on US soil since Pearl Harbor and the initiation of major military operations

---

[10] Syria is coded as a non-intervention because military action was not underway by the end of 2013, and because the actions that ultimately took place were to address ISIS—a distinct conflict from the concerns about Assad using chemical weapons that were the focal point of Obama's attention during the period included in the dataset.

[11] There are 134 speeches (of the 762 referencing a unique case) that referenced a potential intervention but did not justify action with a phrase included in the security or humanitarian dictionaries. Many of these speeches mention the potential intervention briefly, without justification, but a small subset justify intervention using terms included in the ideological dictionary. The frequency of ideological justifications is reported in Figure 2.2.

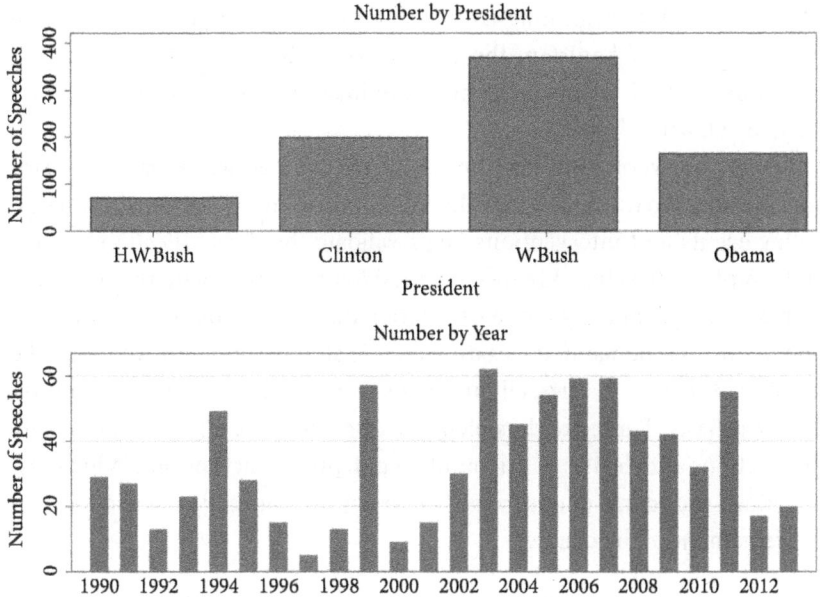

Figure 2.1 Distribution of national addresses

in Afghanistan and Iraq. Between these two extremes, Clinton and Obama gave comparable numbers of speeches about potential interventions, with Clinton addressing the public marginally more often. Again, this is unsurprising given that the data collection concluded one year into Obama's second term.

The distribution of speeches across presidents also corresponds with the number of active US military interventions at a given time. Reasonably, while there are always multiple potential interventions on the table, presidents spend the most time addressing the public when a military action is underway. A closer look at the bottom panel of Figure 2.1 reveals that the years with the highest number of speeches map onto incidents of major US intervention. In the 1990s, the largest number of national addresses were given in 1999 and 1994, respectively. The spike in attention in 1999 corresponds with US involvement in NATO airstrikes in Kosovo. Similarly, 1994 witnessed the escalation of US involvement in Bosnia, intervention in Haiti, and highly publicized but unmet calls for intervention to halt genocide in Rwanda. This pattern holds throughout the 2000s. The number of speeches increases steadily following the terrorist attacks of September 11, 2001, peaking in 2003 as the US justified continuing operations in

Afghanistan while beginning its invasion of Iraq. After surge strategies in both Iraq and Afghanistan, the number of addresses declined, with the exception of 2011 when the Obama administration conducted Operation Odyssey Dawn in Libya.

Taken as a whole, the distribution of national addresses supports two conclusions. First, the fact that this distribution maps onto major foreign policy events and interventions helps validate the data collection process and sample of speeches. As expected, presidents were particularly concerned with providing a public rationale for action during periods of major military operations that demanded sustained public support. Second, although the number of speeches varies, all presidents communicated with the public on a regular basis. There are thus plenty of opportunities for leaders to justify their actions and decisions surrounding potential interventions. Which justifications presidents choose when these opportunities arise is the focus of the remainder of the chapter.

Patterns of justification

Within each speech, leaders have a choice of justifications. Figure 2.2 shows how many times each year presidents chose to use humanitarian, security, or ideology statements in their speeches about potential interventions. The pattern of justifications highlights the importance of both humanitarian and security rationales. Humanitarian claims are consistently present across the post-Cold War period and were at times the most used justification for action, especially during the 1990s. In fact, presidents used at least one humanitarian claim in 59 percent of their national addresses on potential interventions.

The prevalence of humanitarian justifications also travels across party lines. Of the 762 national addresses, 340 were given by Democratic presidents and 422 by Republican presidents. Humanitarian claims appear in the majority of speeches given by members of both parties—56 percent of the speeches by Democratic presidents and 62 percent of speeches by Republican presidents. This relatively even distribution of humanitarian justifications across partisan divisions helps rule out the possibility that Republican presidents face stronger incentives to use humanitarian claims to appear more moderate, while Democratic presidents should limit their

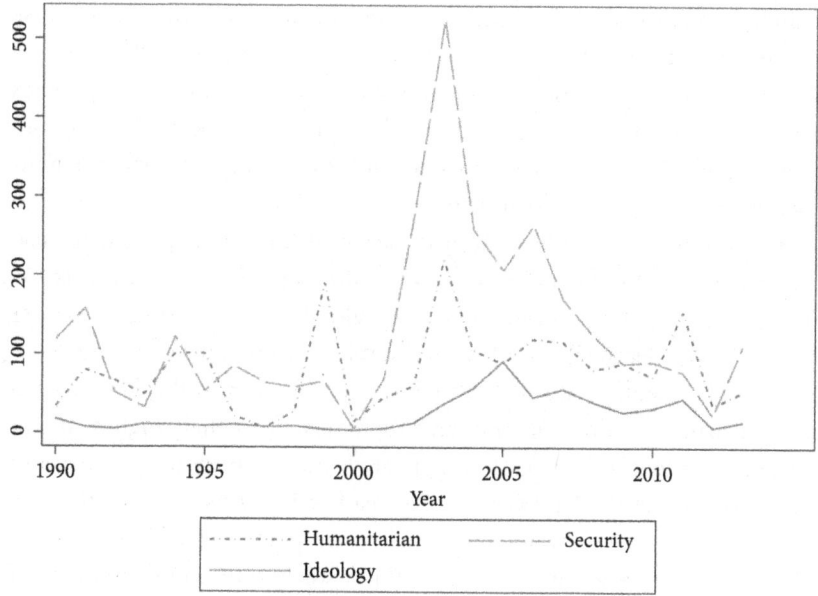

Figure 2.2 Count of justifications by year

humanitarian appeals to avoid appearing weak on defense (Trager and Vavreck 2011). The pattern of justifications instead suggests that presidents from both parties believe there are benefits to talking about humanitarian concerns.

References to national security appear in 66 percent of all speeches about potential interventions. Like humanitarian justifications, security claims also appear in the majority of speeches given by members of both parties. Democratic presidents used security explanations in 59 percent of their speeches and Republican presidents in 72 percent. The distribution of humanitarian and security justifications across party lines shows that neither rationale is limited to a single party. Caution is warranted, however, in linking these specific percentages to general partisan tendencies—there are multiple variables, including external threats and attacks like 9/11, that could confound the effects of presidential partisanship on justification choice in this data.

Additionally, both humanitarian and security justifications are present across cases of non-intervention and intervention but are more common when the conflict ultimately involves military action. Of the speeches that include humanitarian justifications, 72 percent were associated with a case of intervention (326 of 452 documents) and 28 percent with a case of non-intervention (126 of 452 documents). The distribution of speeches that include security justifications is identical: 72 percent addressed an intervention (366 of 505 documents) and 28 percent addressed a non-intervention (139 of 505 documents).

In addition to security and humanitarian justifications, presidents also occasionally used ideological explanations to make the case for action. As Figure 2.2 shows, the prominence of ideological justifications increased over time, but falls decisively short of the number of humanitarian and security appeals. Ideological justifications peaked in 2005 as the US engaged in reconstruction efforts in Iraq and Afghanistan. At their highest point, however, ideological justifications appeared in a minority of speeches and accounted for less than a quarter of the justifications used to make the case for potential military action. These claims are part of presidents' rhetorical toolkit, but they are neither a central nor solely sufficient component of White House communication strategies.

Beyond the context of humanitarian interventions

The pattern of presidential statements in Figure 2.2 confirms that humanitarian justifications are common and persist over time. They are an important part of White House communication strategies and worthy of attention. This yearly pattern is not enough, however, to capture variation in justifications across contexts. To this end, I next compare the *use* and *emphasis* of justifications across security and humanitarian crises.

Are humanitarian justifications used in security crises?

While humanitarian justifications are most often studied in the context of humanitarian interventions, presidential speech patterns reveal that this limitation does not exist in practice. Of the 762 speeches in the dataset that address a unique crisis, 233 include a discussion of a humanitarian crisis and 529 mention a security crisis.[12] The results presented in Table 2.1 show that presidents' use of humanitarian justifications extends well beyond

---

[12] As noted above, Tables 2.1 and 2.2 include only the 762 speeches that uniquely justified a humanitarian or security crisis. The results are robust to the inclusion of all 801 speeches. A related discussion of use and emphasis appears in Maxey (2020) using a different coding scheme.

Table 2.1 Justification used by crisis type

	Humanitarian crises	Security crises
Humanitarian justifications	158 (68%)	294 (56%)
Security justifications	133 (57%)	372 (70%)
No justifications	42 (18%)	92 (17%)
Total	233	529

Note: Counts and percentages sum to more than the total (or 100 percent) because speeches can include both humanitarian and security justifications.

cases of potential humanitarian interventions. As expected, humanitarian justifications appear in the majority (68 percent) of speeches about humanitarian crises, but presidents also used humanitarian claims in the majority (56 percent) of their speeches about security crises. Presidents' common use of humanitarian rationales is contrary to the expectations of the rational public perspective and challenges the assumption that such rhetoric only has power in the context of humanitarian interventions. Instead, the widespread presence of these justifications highlights the importance of better understanding how humanitarian claims operate in security crises.

The pattern of justifications in Table 2.1 also shows that humanitarian appeals do not eliminate the relevance of security justifications. Instead, the pattern of security justifications is the other side of the same coin. Unsurprisingly, presidents used security justifications in the majority of their speeches (70 percent) about security crises. They also, however, included security justifications in 57 percent of their speeches about humanitarian crises. The frequent use of security and humanitarian justifications across different types of crises demonstrates that presidents' public appeals often combine these two rationales. This overlap raises the question: are humanitarian and security rationales presented as equals?

When are humanitarian claims the primary justification for action?

Focusing on the emphasis presidents place on humanitarian justifications in different situations helps answer this question and sheds light on whether the White House views security and humanitarian claims as interchangeable. For each speech, I calculate the relative emphasis placed on humanitarian and security rationales by dividing the number of each type of justification by the total number of justifications in that speech. To create Table 2.2, I then calculated separate means of emphasis for speeches that referenced humanitarian versus security crises. The result is the average emphasis presidents placed on humanitarian or security justifications in each speech, by crisis type.

When the speech addressed a humanitarian crisis, on average, humanitarian claims made up 62 percent of the justifications offered by the president. Humanitarian justifications were the primary explanation for action in these addresses. Security justifications received less emphasis, on average, accounting for 38 percent of the official justifications in a given speech. The pattern of emphasis shifts when the speech instead addressed a security crisis. When talking about potential security interventions, humanitarian appeals made up slightly more than a third of the justifications for action. Presidents instead placed the primary emphasis on security explanations, using these claims as 66 percent of the justifications in their speeches, on average.

The stark difference in emphasis between humanitarian and security crises suggests that leaders evoke humanitarian concerns in security crises strategically, rather than as often as possible. They exercise restraint in their justification strategies, distinguishing between the primary impetus for action and additional, available explanations. This restraint means that outside of the context of humanitarian crises, presidents deploy humanitarian rationales as a secondary justification for military action. This pattern of restraint is contrary to the expectations of the emotional public perspective. The same caution appears in presidents' emphasis of security justifications. Security explanations are the primary rationale for action in security crises, but their emphasis is reduced and they serve as secondary justifications in humanitarian crises. While presidential speech patterns suggest the White

Table 2.2 Average emphasis of justifications by crisis type

	Humanitarian crises	Security crises
Humanitarian justifications	0.62 (0.37)	0.34 (0.35)
Security justifications	0.38 (0.37)	0.66 (0.35)
N	191	437

Note: Table reports the mean percentage of each type of justification in speeches that contain at least one justification. Standard deviations reported in parentheses.

House believes both humanitarian and security justifications are useful across crisis contexts, the patterns also suggest that administrations are cautious about over-using justifications that do not match the primary impetus for action.

Conclusion

Where the first chapter offered examples of humanitarian justifications in high-profile security interventions, this chapter demonstrated that the power of humanitarian claims is not limited to prominent cases. Instead, the broader pattern of justifications is consistent with a White House communication strategy that recognizes the domestic power of humanitarian claims. Communications teams, however, also appear to understand that more is not always better when it comes to using humanitarian statements to persuade the public. Leaders included humanitarian appeals in the majority of their speeches about security crises, showing that humanitarian claims are not limited to cases of humanitarian intervention and should be studied in a broader range of contexts. Presidents also, however, avoided overstating humanitarian appeals, using them as a common but secondary justification in security crises.

Chapter 2 illustrated this pattern of humanitarian and security appeals by using an original dataset of US presidents' justifications for potential military interventions from 1990 to 2013. I outlined the development, verification, and application of this dataset in four steps. First, I identified crises with the potential to become targets of US military intervention and official justifications for action. I then classified each potential case of intervention based on whether it responded primarily to a security or humanitarian crisis. Second, I collected all national addresses that referenced at least one case of potential intervention. Focusing on national addresses and excluding non-prepared, written, or campaign remarks holds constant the intended audience. It also ensures the remarks are intentional rather than off the cuff and reflect a communication strategy the White House designed for public presentation. In the third step, I developed dictionaries of phrases associated with security, humanitarian, and a less common category of ideological justifications. The final result of this process is a dataset of every national address from 1990 to 2013 that referenced a potential intervention. The dataset includes measures of whether a given speech *used* humanitarian or security justifications at all and of the relative *emphasis* placed on each category of justification.

Fourth and finally, the chapter used this dataset to illustrate how justifications are distributed across time and administrations. The overall pattern of justifications reveals that humanitarian claims are common features in national addresses across the post-Cold War period. For significant parts of the 1990s, humanitarian appeals were in fact the most used justifications for action. Humanitarian justifications are thus a regular and important feature of contemporary US foreign policy for presidents from both parties and are worthy of attention.

Beyond demonstrating that humanitarian appeals are widespread and worthy of study, Chapter 2 also showed that the pattern of presidents' humanitarian justifications defies the expectations of existing explanations. For a rational public focused primarily on protecting its own interests while limiting costs, presidents' frequent use of humanitarian justifications in security crises makes little sense. For an emotional public driven by humanitarian impulses, the prevalence of humanitarian claims is expected, but the limited emphasis leaders place on these justifications in security crises is puzzling. The limitations of these existing approaches highlight the need for a theory of justifications that can strike a middle ground, accounting for both the perceived demand and restraint that appears in presidential statements.[13] The domestic coalition theory presented in the next chapter takes on this challenge.

---

[13] Moving forward, I use the language of demand and restraint to describe the pattern of justifications, assuming that a White House concerned with public support uses humanitarian claims because they meet a perceived public demand and avoids overusing these same claims because public opinion provides a reason for restraint. Chapter 4 formally demonstrates that a public demand for humanitarian justifications exists, Chapter 5 confirms the risk of public backlash that provides a reason for restraint, and Chapter 6 establishes that the White House has both incentives in mind when developing its justification strategy for military interventions.

3

Justification strategies for broad domestic coalitions

Humanitarian justifications bring to mind cases of humanitarian intervention, such as US action in Somalia in 1992 where George H. W. Bush asked the nation to: "Imagine 7,000 tons of food aid literally bursting out of a warehouse on a dock in Mogadishu, while Somalis starve less than a kilometer away because relief workers cannot run the gauntlet of armed gangs roving the city. [...] It's now clear that military support is necessary to ensure the safe delivery of the food Somalis need to survive" (G. H. W. Bush 1992). In this context, the power of humanitarian claims is to legitimate the protection of civilians when no other security or economic interests are at stake (Finnemore 1996, 154). Efforts such as the Responsibility to Protect aim to institutionalize and strengthen this power as a means of preventing mass atrocities in the future (Bellamy 2006; ICISS 2001).

Helping to prevent mass atrocities is normatively desirable and important in its own right, but both proponents and skeptics of humanitarian intervention still view humanitarian rationales as suboptimal in terms of providing effective justifications for military action. While humanitarian appeals can help mobilize public support for action in extreme cases, humanitarian crises are generally "far removed from the everyday lives of American voters" (Hildebrandt et al. 2013, 250). As a result, countries that carry out humanitarian interventions "must be sensitive to inevitable opposition from domestic constituencies" (Western and Goldstein 2011, 58). In other words, the power of humanitarian claims is expected to be limited. Leaders may rely on humanitarian appeals when credible links to the national interest are not available, but when national security is at stake, talking about the safety of Americans is the more compelling way to move public opinion. All else equal, this conventional wisdom expects leaders to have little reason to include humanitarian justifications when talking about security crises.

As Chapter 2 showed, these conventional expectations—that the power of humanitarian justifications is limited to cases of humanitarian intervention

Doves into Hawks. Sarah Maxey, Oxford University Press. © Oxford University Press (2026).
DOI: 10.1093/9780197832738.003.0003

and that security claims are the most effective justifications for military force—do not reflect the way US presidents actually communicate the need for military action to the domestic audience. Rather than relying on humanitarian claims as a last resort, the speech data in the previous chapter revealed that presidents evoked humanitarian rationales for every intervention, as well as the majority of potential interventions, in the post-Cold War period. This pattern includes cases such as the 2001 US invasion of Afghanistan, where the national security interests involved in responding to a terrorist attack on US soil offered credible and popular justifications for the use of military force. Yet, despite the direct and obvious threats to US national security, from the earliest stages of the intervention, Bush accompanied announcements that he had "called our military into action to hunt down the members of the Al Qaida organization who murdered innocent Americans" with promises that "We care for the innocent people of Afghanistan" who would join the rest of the world in saying "Good riddance" to the Taliban government (G. W. Bush 2001b).

Why do leaders consistently spend their time and political capital offering humanitarian rationales for interventions like Afghanistan where there are obvious national security interests at stake? And, if humanitarian claims are useful across crises, why do leaders exercise restraint when evoking them in security cases? The answer, I argue, is that humanitarian claims are powerful in more ways and have more nuanced implications for democratic accountability than the conventional wisdom recognizes. Their power stems from the political benefits humanitarian narratives generate among the domestic audience. Namely, humanitarian appeals have the unique ability to convince individuals who are ordinarily doves to become temporary hawks, broadening the domestic coalition of support for military action. By building a diverse domestic coalition that includes doves and hawks, leaders also increase opportunities for accountability, which explains why they exercise restraint rather than overstating either humanitarian or security justifications.

In this chapter, I outline a theory of domestic coalitions that identifies the political incentives behind the pattern of demand and restraint described in Chapter 2. I argue that leaders respond to these incentives with communication strategies that expand their leeway for action while minimizing the risk of political backlash. These domestic political benefits explain the consistent presence of humanitarian claims in security crises and demonstrate the full power of humanitarian narratives. The domestic coalition approach establishes that humanitarian appeals are necessary to build public support, even when US security is at stake. Highlighting this overlooked aspect of humanitarian justifications improves our understanding of the domestic politics of international security, the power of leaders, and what it takes to sell intervention to the public.

The assumption that public opinion and domestic political incentives are relevant to foreign policy decisions is not a given. Historically, scholars and practitioners argued that foreign policy was best left to the professionals—the public was too inattentive and too impulsive to exert a consistent or positive influence on policy decisions in the short term (Holsti 1992 for a description of this critique; Kennan 1984). With these concerns in mind, the chapter begins by outlining why public opinion matters for foreign policy and how presidential communications simultaneously shape and are constrained by public attitudes. Because domestic constraints on the use of force are not static, public support determines the executive's leeway for action. This dynamic incentivizes presidents to broaden the domestic coalition of support rather than settle for a simple majority. The benefits of expanding the domestic coalition in turn create a need for humanitarian justifications—without these claims, potential support is left on the table and the domestic coalition is difficult to sustain.

To understand why humanitarian narratives are necessary to broaden domestic coalitions, the chapter then addresses three related questions: (1) Who responds to humanitarian appeals? (2) Do humanitarian justifications undermine accountability for military action? (3) Do leaders recognize the power and limits of humanitarian claims? I compare the domestic coalition theory's answers to these questions with alternative explanations and then outline a multi-method research design that complements the speech data presented in Chapter 2 by evaluating the theoretical expectations at the individual and intervention levels.

Why public support matters

Unlike domestic policy decisions, the stakes of foreign policy can appear far removed from people's day-to-day lives. For example, where tax reforms affect individuals' pocketbooks, changes in foreign aid or diplomatic strategy are more likely to fly under the public's radar. As a result, early models of public opinion expected the public to be inattentive and ill-informed on matters of foreign policy (Almond 1950; Lippmann 1922). Even today, with increased access to information and 24/7 news coverage, the mass public often lacks the capacity to locate foreign policy threats on the map (Dropp, Kertzer, and Zeitzoff 2014; Quealy 2017).

When threats become salient and military action is on the table, however, the public tunes in to foreign policy decisions (Aldrich, Sullivan, and Borgida 1989; Western 2005). More importantly, in the aggregate, the public's preferences appear relatively prudent (Jentleson 1992; Jentleson and Britton 1998; Shapiro and Page 1988). In general, the public prioritizes missions that appear legitimate and likely to be successful (Eichenberg 2005; Gelpi, Feaver, and Reifler 2009) and prefers interventions that minimize casualties and financial costs (Gartner 2008; Geys 2010; Kreps 2018). These preferences exert a helpful influence on foreign policy that constrains US leaders in the face of risky operations.

Presidents' concern with public attention and attitudes stems from key features of democratic institutions. Elected leaders who conduct unpopular interventions ultimately risk their own reelection or the reelection of members of their own party (Tomz, Weeks, and Yarhi-Milo 2020). Incumbent presidents focused on reelection must balance this political risk with the importance of demonstrating strong leadership, which can create unexpected incentives for hawkish behaviors like military intervention (Friedman 2023). Beyond elections, unpopular decisions also tighten institutional constraints, making it more difficult to pursue other items on the White House's political agenda (Gelpi and Grieco 2015; Tomz and Weeks 2013). This risk of political punishment in the absence of public consent is a defining aspect of democratic governance that affects foreign policy in myriad ways, including when and how well states initiate and fight wars (Reiter and Stam 2002; Russett 1993; Valentino, Huth, and Croco 2010).

The benefits of broad coalitions

Political coalitions take many different forms, from the electoral coalitions needed to cross winning vote thresholds for legislative seats, to the coalitions of lawmakers necessary to pass legislation, to coalition governments. In his theory of political coalitions, Riker (1962) expects participants to create minimum winning coalitions, based on the logic that larger coalitions decrease the value for each member. His theory focuses on elite coalitions in which, "typically some part of the authority-possessing group comes together in alliance to render a decision binding on the group as a whole and on all who recognize its authority" (Riker 1962, 12). Building on this definition, his model shows that, "In n-person, zero-sum games, where side-payments are permitted, where players are rational, and where they have perfect information, only minimum winning coalitions occur" (Riker 1962, 33).

In contrast to Riker (1962), I use the language of coalitions to highlight the White House's goal of bringing together different public constituencies to support a common cause: military intervention. Such domestic coalitions of public support for military action diverge from Riker's (1962) definition and assumptions—and thus the implications of his model—in important ways. Unlike elections or legislative votes, there is not an objective, predetermined threshold at which the executive "wins" public consent for intervention. Additionally, credible side payments are more difficult to make to the public compared to elites, and the domestic benefits of military action do not neatly fall within the boundaries of zero-sum games. Most notably, the public's losses or gains from military intervention are generally non-excludable goods. Riker's (1962, 39) logic is based on the assumption that "When a coalition includes everybody, the winners gain nothing similarly because there are no losers." In other words, larger coalitions carry less value for each participant because the higher the number of coalition members, the smaller the proportion of the spoils of victory each individual receives. The same is not true for public support for military action. For example, the fact that 88 percent of Americans supported US military action in Afghanistan in October 2001 (Newport 2001) means neither that national security gains were felt less by each supporter nor that the benefits to the Bush administration were spread more thinly than if 51 percent of the public offered its support.

Instead, in the context of public support for military action, I expect leaders to benefit from building the broadest and strongest domestic coalitions possible. The incentives for expansive coalitions stem from the political and policy benefits of popularity, as well as the frequent, often dramatic, decline in support for action that takes place over the course of an intervention. Politically, with the public on their side, presidents gain leverage in their negotiations with other politicians and are better equipped to navigate domestic obstacles to the use of force (Kriner 2010). In the US context, Congress represents a particularly important domestic obstacle. The institutional powers granted to Congress allow members to impede military action by restricting the available funding, demanding the withdrawal of US troops, and holding hearings to gather and publicize relevant information (Howell and Pevehouse 2005; Kriner 2010). Presidents recognize congressional constraints, initiating fewer major military operations when they anticipate congressional opposition (Howell and Pevehouse 2005). After military action is initiated, opposition from Congress also affects the duration and scope of interventions (Kriner 2010, 36–37).

The magnitude and breadth of public support shapes the political incentives of members of Congress. In the realm of foreign policy, legislators' own electoral concerns generally incentivize them to delegate authority to the White House—avoiding culpability for major decisions with unpredictable long-term consequences—and serve as a largely reactive institution (Canes-Wrone, Howell, and Lewis 2008). As a result, members' willingness to express their dissent or obstruct intervention decisions depends on whether they see "strategic opportunities" to do so (Kriner 2010, 38; Schultz 2003, 110). The presence of these strategic opportunities in turn depends on public support. Kriner (2010, 244) captures this dynamic, noting that, "Even for members of Congress with latent partisan incentives to challenge the president, the benefits of doing so are smaller and the potential risks are higher when the president remains strong in the polls." In other words, the more public support leaders can marshal, the fewer congressional obstacles they will expect to encounter and the easier it will be to implement their desired foreign policies. Gaining public consent for military interventions also helps leaders pursue their domestic policy agenda, both by maintaining incentives for cooperation and compromise among legislators and by keeping foreign policy controversies off the legislative docket, leaving room to promote other goals (Gelpi and Grieco 2015).

The domestic leverage that presidents gain from public approval incentivizes leaders to build broad coalitions of support for military action (Maxey 2020). If supporters represent a single constituency or party, elites in the opposition party have more reason to join their voters in expressing dissent to help strengthen their party brand (Kriner and Shen 2014). Alternatively, with a broad coalition that expands the depth and breadth of potential supporters, the incentives for members of Congress to block or vocally oppose the president dissipate because taking a stand against the White House is contrary to the position of many voters in their own district. By including hawks and doves in domestic coalitions, leaders appeal both to traditional opponents of military action and across parties. The links between policy agendas, congressional deference, and public opinion means that presidents benefit from a broad domestic coalition of support for military action, even if people do not vote based on foreign policy outcomes.[1]

Moreover, broad coalitions help interventions remain popular for a longer period of time, providing a safeguard against the erosion of support that takes place over the course of an intervention. In the early stages of interventions, multiple factors—from the leader's information advantage, to changes in media coverage and elite opposition, to patriotism and unified national identities that stem from external threats (Baum 2002; Baum and Potter 2008; Brody 1991; Mueller 1973)—converge to create a favorable environment for bolstering public support. As the intervention continues, however, the costs of action become more salient at the same time that the president loses their near-monopoly over information about the crisis and the initial rally of support dissipates (Baum and Groeling 2010; Brody 1991).

This decline appears across post-Cold War US interventions, from controversial cases—such as the invasion of Iraq in 2003—to conflicts that began with almost universal support like the 2001 invasion of Afghanistan. When US forces invaded Iraq in March 2003, Gallup public opinion polls showed that 75 percent of respondents voiced their support by reporting that the US action was not a mistake (Dugan 2015).[2] By October 2003, "not a mistake" responses had dropped to 59 percent, and by June 2004, they became the minority view that included only 44 percent of respondents. Similar Gallup polls focused on the US invasion of Afghanistan showed that support began from a much higher baseline but eventually eroded, albeit more slowly than in the Iraq case (Brenan 2021). In 2001, only 9 percent of respondents viewed the intervention as a mistake, compared to 89 percent who said it was not a mistake.[3] The percentage of respondents in the "not a mistake" category

[1] The extent to which foreign policy preferences influence individuals' vote choice is the subject of ongoing debate. Tomz, Weeks, and Yarhi-Milo 2020, for example, find that foreign policy preferences have a substantive and significant effect on how people choose between presidential candidates, even when accounting for partisanship and domestic policy positions. Friedman (2023), on the other hand, finds that people are more likely to vote for candidates with a reputation for strong leadership, even if the candidate implements otherwise unpopular foreign policies. By identifying multiple channels through which leaders have reason to be concerned with public opinion, this section demonstrates that the domestic coalition argument does not hinge on the outcome of this debate.

[2] The question asked, "In view of the developments since we first sent our troops to Iraq, do you think the United States made a mistake in sending troops to Iraq, or not?"

[3] The question asked, "Thinking now about U.S. military action in Afghanistan that began in October 2001, do you think the United States made a mistake in sending military forces to Afghanistan, or not?"

began to decline after 2002, dropping to 72 percent by 2004, and becoming the minority view ten years later in 2014. Both declines in support were also echoed in Bush's approval ratings, which peaked at 90 percent approval at the beginning of the Afghanistan intervention in September 2001, had fallen to 57 percent by February 2003, rose to 71 percent with the invasion of Iraq in March 2003, and dropped to 49 percent by March 2004 (Gallup 2009).

Preventing or delaying this erosion of support is an important and stated goal of the White House, even in shorter interventions like the 1991 Gulf War. In a review of internal polling on the Persian Gulf from February 1991, George H. W. Bush's campaign staff noted that "Initially, the questionnaire had one stated objective: to determine what real time event or events caused public support for the President and the war effort to decline" (Steeper 1991b). After the initial invasion began, the goal of the polls evolved to serve the additional purpose of identifying, "what event or factors might cause public support for the President and the war effort to decline. The reason for adding this purpose is the obvious one that the Administration might be able to do something to avoid the problem or nip it in the bud" (Steeper 1991b, emphasis in original). In this same memo, Bush's polling team outlined an additional reason the White House is concerned with maintaining broad coalitions of public support: they are reinforcing. Listing "national strife" as a factor that could trigger an erosion of support, the memo explained that "If the public perceives that most Americans support the war, their support should remain stable" (Steeper 1991b).

When only a narrow majority or segment of the public backs military action during the early stages of an intervention, the benefits of public support will erode quickly as the costs of action, concerns about failure, and dissenting voices become more salient. By strengthening coalitions beyond this minimum, leaders do what they can to guard against declining public support and delay any political backlash as long as possible. By building broad coalitions across different foreign policy constituencies, leaders strengthen their prospects for maintaining baseline favorability even if one constituency eventually drops out. Additionally, broad coalitions complicate the task of elite opponents and antiwar movements, leaving these actors with fewer easy recruits. Instead of galvanizing public attention or mobilizing existing dissent, broad coalitions push opponents towards the more difficult task of convincing current supporters to flip their existing policy position.

For these reasons, the domestic coalition theory assumes that when it comes to mobilizing approval for military action, presidents have a strong incentive to exceed minimum coalitions and build the broadest possible domestic base of support. Following this incentive, I expect communication strategies to focus on building coalitions across different foreign policy constituencies. Leaders' statements may not always be successful in achieving this goal, but broadening and strengthening support are expected to be consistent political aims. When leaders are not able to build a broad coalition, they maintain the ability to pursue military action, but the intervention will carry dramatically higher political costs than would otherwise be the case. The relevance of justifications and other tools for mobilizing the domestic audience thus depends on how much they help leaders expand coalitions of support.

The influence of presidential speech

The presence or absence of public consent shapes the political costs of military action. Leaders anticipate public preferences, and the prospect of domestic backlash sets political boundaries around acceptable policy options. Leaders are not, however, powerless in the face of these domestic constraints. Instead, they have access to a vast communications apparatus and hold institutional advantages that provide the White House with multiple tools for managing public perceptions. Among domestic actors, presidents have the unique ability to directly and at length address the general public via the media (Nelson, Oxley, and Clawson 1997, 238). The White House can also expect that its messages will receive ongoing coverage and set the terms of debate among political elites (Berinsky and Kinder 2006, 641). Official justifications for intervention are particularly important because they influence how the public evaluates presidents' leadership and policies (Cavari 2012; Druckman and Holmes 2004; Nelson and Oxley 1999).

Official statements operate through a combination of persuasion, framing, and priming to influence public attitudes on a broad range of issues (Chong and Druckman 2007; Druckman et al. 2010; Druckman and Holmes 2004; Nelson and Oxley 1999; Nelson, Oxley, and Clawson 1997).[4] The narrative leaders use to explain a decision makes certain aspects of the situation more prominent in the public mind, encouraging individuals to

---

[4] Persuasion changes the content of individuals' beliefs, framing changes the importance of beliefs used to evaluate a given issue, and priming changes the accessibility of considerations used in this evaluation (Nelson et al. 1997; Nelson and Oxley 1999).

use these criteria to evaluate the policy or to change the content of their beliefs altogether (Druckman et al. 2010; Nelson, Oxley, and Clawson 1997).

While presidential statements are always important, their influence is amplified at the beginning of military interventions because leaders hold information and first-mover advantages (Baum and Groeling 2010; Baum and Potter 2008; Kernell 1997, 194; Western 2005, 14). In this context, messages from the president are the public's first cue that a crisis could require a military response. The content of these presidential messages—including justifications for why action is necessary and legitimate—dominates the early stages of the intervention because many elites cannot access classified information and do not have political incentives to challenge what the White House says (Baum and Groeling 2010). In this low-information environment, the president's early statements provide the framework for evaluating the intervention and set the terms of any debate that follows (Krebs and Lobasz 2007). Presidents' justifications are powerful enough to both bolster support for action and help leaders manage the costs of backing down, as long as "the president explains the logic behind the decision to withdraw to the public and that logic seems plausible" (Levendusky and Horowitz 2012, 327).

Over the course of a military intervention, both elites and the public eventually gain access to information from non-White House sources and consensus among elites plays a more important role in maintaining public support (Berinsky 2007; Guisinger and Saunders 2017). Even as presidents lose their monopoly over information, however, they continue to benefit from providing the first account of the intervention. Cavari (2012, 337) shows that, because presidents speak first, they "generate a momentum of public support" that has lasting effects on public attitudes. Early frames also provide a focal point for media coverage and are reiterated as the target of later opposition. As a result, they stick in the public mind, even when they are discredited. For example, even in the face of elite dissent and the well-publicized absence of weapons of mass destruction, significant portions of the US public continued to hold misperceptions about the 2003 war with Iraq that matched George W. Bush's initial justifications (Kull, Ramsay, and Lewis 2003, 571, 579). The persistence of these beliefs and their correlation with support for the intervention demonstrate that presidents' justifications can influence public attitudes in the long run, even in the face of elite dissent and contradictory information.

How humanitarian justifications broaden coalitions

Up to this point, the chapter has outlined two guiding assumptions about the relationship between leaders and public opinion in the context of military action: (1) when it comes to lowering political costs and loosening constraints on the use of force, broader public support is better, and (2) leaders' public justifications for action are an important tool for mobilizing public support. Chapter 2 showed that presidents consistently include humanitarian rationales in their public statements about military action, suggesting that leaders consider humanitarian claims helpful in bolstering public support for security crises. This pattern raises the question: Do humanitarian justifications help presidents broaden the domestic coalition?

The domestic utility of humanitarian claims depends on which individuals they persuade and how these same individuals respond to security justifications. Figure 3.1 illustrates the three possible ways in which support for humanitarian and security justifications could be distributed across the domestic audience. It visualizes the assumptions made by each of the conventional wisdoms outlined in previous chapters—the rational public and the emotional public—and positions the domestic coalition argument as a middle ground between the two. Starting on the left side of Figure 3.1, the rational public model captures the assumption that the constituencies who can be mobilized to support intervention are hawks who will reliably find national security threats sufficiently compelling. A subset of these hawkish individuals may also accept humanitarian explanations for the use of force, but humanitarian appeals are not necessary to gain their support. In this case, security justifications will persuade everyone who can be persuaded and presidents will not gain additional support by adding humanitarian rationales.

Moving to the right side of Figure 3.1, the emotional public model captures an opposing set of assumptions. It expects that the public is generally fixated on humanitarian concerns and will fully respond to humanitarian justifications. Some members of the public may also be concerned with national security, but this is a smaller subset of those who react to humanitarian appeals.

Viewing support for military action as a domestic coalition built across different foreign policy constituencies offers a middle ground between these two sets of expectations. Instead of one group of individuals who all respond to the same justifications, there are at least three distinct constituencies

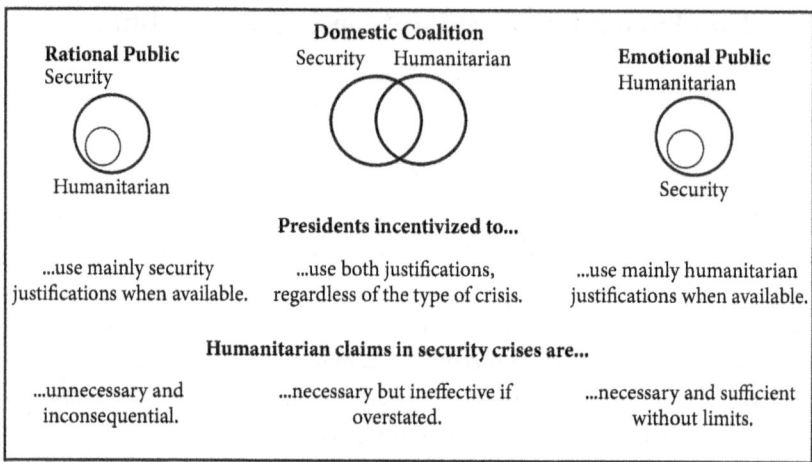

Figure 3.1 Public preferences for justifications

Note: Figure 3.1 illustrates alternative assumptions about who responds to humanitarian claims. Starting on the left, the rational public model captures the assumption that individuals who react to humanitarian justifications are a fully included subset of the group that responds to security justifications. Moving to the far right, the emotional public model captures the opposite assumption that all individuals who respond to security justifications are a subset of the humanitarian group. The domestic coalition model exists in the literal and figurative middle position. It visualizes the assumption that the domestic audience consists of three types of individuals. Some respond primarily to security justifications (isolationists), others to humanitarian justifications (doves), and others to either justification (hawks). The circles illustrate the presence or absence of overlap in the justifications that resonate with different groups but are not directly proportional to the size of the relevant group within the domestic audience.

that make up public attitudes towards military action. In the center of Figure 3.1, the domestic coalition model illustrates how disaggregating the public changes the incentives for White House communication strategies. There is still a group that responds strongly to security justifications, with a subset of members who also accept humanitarian appeals (hawks). Where the domestic coalition logic diverges from the rational public model, however, is in its recognition that the domestic audience also includes a group of individuals whose support is maximized only when humanitarian rationales are present (doves). The existence of this group, and the possibility of convincing them to join domestic coalitions of support, explains why presidents include humanitarian justifications in their speeches about security crises. Without humanitarian claims, this group's support will not reach its full potential and, as a result, the domestic coalition will not be as broad as possible.

Unlike the emotional public model, the domestic coalition model also implies that presidents have an incentive to consistently offer security justifications for action, even in cases that respond to primarily humanitarian crises.[5] Security justifications are necessary to maximize the support of individuals who are skeptical of humanitarian goals but can be persuaded to support military action when US national interests or safety appears at stake (isolationists). The argument thus helps make sense of the full range of domestic incentives behind justifications for the use of force.

In the empirical chapters that follow, I include information about the pattern and resonance of both humanitarian and security justifications. The focus of the theory and analysis, however, remains on establishing the domestic power of humanitarian justifications. I maintain this focus because while the importance of security rationales is well-documented (Gadarian 2010; Herrmann, Tetlock, and Visser 1999; Malhotra and Popp 2012; Western 2005), humanitarian justifications are underestimated in the context of security crises and their implications for democratic accountability remain unclear.

Persuading hawks and doves

Who are the people in these three foreign policy constituencies and why do they react differently to humanitarian claims? Answering this question requires a more nuanced approach to the traditional hawk versus dove distinction in foreign policy attitudes. At the most basic level, hawks and doves are separated by their views of military force. Public opinion polls commonly present the two categories as opposites, anchored in strong statements about whether the use of force is ever warranted, most emblematically, "If you had to choose, would you describe yourself as a hawk, that is someone who believes that military force should be used frequently to promote U.S. (United States) policy, or as more of a dove, that is someone who believes the U.S. should rarely or never use military force?" (CNN/Time Magazine 2003). From this simplified perspective, hawks like war and doves do not. Convincing doves to support military action should thus be an uphill battle and one that is unlikely to result in a sustainable mobilization of domestic approval.

This narrow definition of hawks and doves struggles to make sense of the fact that many doves—like the wary warmongers from Chapter 1—are often

---

[5] An additional incentive for security justifications stems from concerns about public backlash if justifications stray too far from the impetus for action and appear insincere. Discussed in greater detail later in the chapter, all three constituencies contribute to concerns about insincerity.

willing to support the use of military force under the right circumstances. To capture the justification strategies most likely to create these right circumstances and convince different constituencies that military intervention is necessary, I define doves and hawks based on what people in each group want, not just what they want to avoid. I do so by building on the priorities associated with well-established foreign policy orientations: cooperative internationalism, militant internationalism, and isolationism (Holsti 1979; Hurwitz and Peffley 1987; Kertzer et al. 2014; Mandelbaum and Schneider 1979; Rathbun et al. 2016; Wittkopf 1990).

For doves, this expanded definition means focusing on individuals who prioritize using cooperative methods to achieve other-regarding goals.[6] Doves' combined preference for diplomacy and other-regarding goals means they hold priorities consistent with cooperative internationalism (Holsti and Rosenau 1990; Kertzer et al. 2014). Because of these underlying preferences and their connection to the individualizing moral foundations that focus on harm and care, as well as fairness and reciprocity (Kertzer et al. 2014), doves are most likely to support policies that emphasize common interests, global goods, and human rights. The skepticism of military force that is traditionally associated with doves reflects this constituency's relatively lower level of militant internationalism. Recognizing that doves question the efficacy of military force while also holding preferences *for* other-regarding objectives suggests that the concern about foreign civilians raised by humanitarian justifications may be enough to convince doves to override their skepticism and support intervention under the right conditions.

For hawks, traditional definitions remain insightful because they already focus on the policies this group prefers. Hawks are high in militant internationalism, which emphasizes "the importance, effectiveness, and/or desirability of using force to reach foreign policy objectives" (Kertzer et al. 2014, 830). In terms of what those objectives should be, hawks prioritize military strength, resolve, and competitiveness. The militant internationalism underlying hawks' preferences is also rooted in moral foundations, but in this case, in the binding foundations (Kertzer et al. 2014)—emphasizing the

---

[6] This expanded definition is also consistent with work on hawkish and dovish tendencies among political elites, which classifies leaders and policies as dovish based on their prioritization of diplomacy, cooperation, and common interests (Kreps, Saunders, and Schultz 2018, 482; Mattes and Weeks 2019, 57; 2022, 960). Hawkish leaders and policies, on the other hand, are associated with a reputation for prioritizing conflict, competition, and military strength.

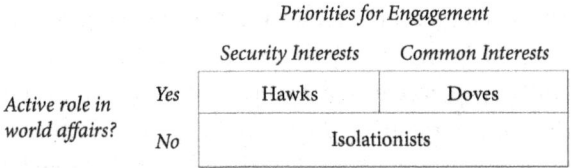

Figure 3.2 Foreign policy constituencies

protection of the ingroup and loyalty, authority and respect, and purity and sanctity—which resonate with conventional national security objectives like safeguarding one's own country from external threats.

An additional benefit of defining doves and hawks based on their broader foreign policy priorities is that it becomes possible to separate both groups from a third constituency of isolationists. Tolerating sustained international engagement is a precondition for an individual to offer reliable, lasting support for military action. Internationalists—both doves and hawks—support active engagement, while isolationists do not (Kertzer 2013).[7] The policies isolationists prefer exist predominantly in the realm of domestic versus foreign policy (Iyer et al. 2012) and are difficult to link to military interventions. Internationalists are thus the more efficient target audience for official justification strategies and, at a minimum, building a broad domestic coalition of support for military action means appealing to the priorities of both doves and hawks. Figure 3.2 summarizes the criteria used to separate these three foreign policy constituencies.[8] In the section that follows, I outline the justification strategies most likely to maximize support among each group.

Who responds to humanitarian justifications?

Dividing the domestic audience into foreign policy constituencies helps assess different justification strategies by answering two key questions: (1) Who is an effective target audience for White House communications? (2) How do the members of this audience respond to humanitarian claims?

---

[7] There are many reasons to doubt the existence of "true" isolationists in any sizeable number (Braumoeller 2010; Nincic 1997; Urbatsch 2010). The goal here is to capture individuals who are predisposed, at the time of a given crisis, to resist policies that require sustained international engagement.

[8] Maxey (2020) makes a similar argument but focuses instead on cooperative internationalists and militant internationalists. Doves and hawks capture the more politically salient distinction and clarify that individuals can hold high levels of both militant and cooperative internationalism.

First, the relevant target audience for White House communication strategies is made up of individuals who can plausibly be convinced to offer support for military interventions. Military intervention, as it is defined in Chapter 1, demands large-scale, high-risk, and often lasting involvement in the affairs of another country. A tolerance for sustained US engagement in international affairs is thus necessary for an individual to offer support for military action that extends beyond the initial rally period. Given their baseline belief that the US should not seek active engagement in international affairs, isolationists are not a reliable source of support for military intervention—a particularly intense form of engagement. Increasing isolationist sentiment could make leaders think twice about proposing intervention, but once military action is on the table, presidents have little incentive to craft messages that appeal directly to these unreliable members of the domestic coalition. When isolationists do support the use of force, it is often because they perceived vital US national interests to be at stake. Any effect that humanitarian claims have on these individuals' support is likely to be negative because humanitarian rationales appeal to broader, other-regarding interests that are the opposite of minding one's own business in international affairs.[9] Taken as a whole, the content of isolationists' foreign policy preferences and the fact that they represent a small subset of the domestic audience mean they do not create a demand for humanitarian justifications. The first hypothesis captures the expected response from isolationists:

H1: *Adding humanitarian justifications to security justifications does not significantly increase support among isolationists.*[10]

Instead, the key target audience for official justifications for military intervention is made up of internationalists who have a baseline preference for sustained engagement with the world. Because they share a belief that the US should be actively involved in addressing international problems, both

[9] While pacifists who fall into the isolationist category may be focused on other-regarding goals, their definitional opposition to military force means there is no justification that can persuade them to support military intervention.

[10] Importantly, the absence of significance is not the same as the presence of null effects (Rainey 2014). I expect to find no evidence that humanitarian justifications positively shift support among—and thus are primarily designed to target—isolationists, which is in line with the domestic coalition logic that these individuals are not the key incentive behind justification strategies. With this standard of testing, however, it remains possible that humanitarian justifications exert a non-zero effect on isolationists' attitudes. The same logic applies to hypothesis two's expectations for hawks.

hawks and doves can often be persuaded to support intervention. As a result, both groups contain potentially reliable members of the domestic coalition. This potential support makes it worthwhile for the White House to develop communication strategies that resonate as strongly as possible with as many internationalists as possible.

After identifying internationalists as the target audience for presidential appeals, the question then becomes: How do different internationalist constituencies respond to security and humanitarian claims? If there is no clear difference in how hawks or doves react based on the presence of humanitarian claims, humanitarian appeals will carry little weight in security interventions—consistent with the rational public assumptions in Figure 3.1. If, instead, either group reacts more strongly when humanitarian appeals are present, humanitarian justifications are critical for broadening domestic support.

I first turn to the individuals who behave as the rational public model expects: hawks. Hawks exemplify militant internationalist policy preferences, viewing international engagement as important and military power as the primary means of US foreign policy. In terms of foreign policy priorities, members of this group are expected to focus on the pursuit of traditional national security goals for which military force offers an effective and appropriate response. Security justifications appeal to hawks' preferences for both the means and ends of foreign policy, presenting the safety of the US and protection of its interests as the reason for engagement, while also proposing that the use of force is a necessary and effective way to achieve these goals. As a result, when presidents offer security justifications for an intervention, support from hawks is reliable.

Hawks also respond to humanitarian justifications. Humanitarian frames shift attention from national security goals to the protection of foreign civilians but maintain a focus on military force as the tool that can effectively resolve the crisis. Because hawks believe that the US should be engaged in solving international problems and view force as an effective tool of foreign policy, I expect them to be generally supportive of military interventions, regardless of how they are justified.

What makes hawks distinct from their dovish counterparts is the fact that their support can be maximized with security justifications alone. In security crises, adding a humanitarian explanation to the security narrative will do little to raise levels of support among this group—they were already convinced. If these individuals were the only segment of the public to respond to humanitarian claims, humanitarian appeals would be uninfluential in security crises. The expectation for how hawks respond to the presence of humanitarian justifications in security crises is summarized in hypothesis two:

H2: Adding humanitarian justifications to security justifications does not significantly increase support among hawks.

Doves also believe that the US should play an active role in solving international problems. Reflecting their cooperative priorities, doves are distinct from hawks because they prefer the use of diplomatic means to provide other-regarding or common goods. Critically, there is a tension between doves' policy priorities and their preferred tools of foreign policy—diplomacy alone is sometimes insufficient to save others from egregious harm. It is this tension that makes doves persuadable members of the domestic coalition and humanitarian justifications key to maximizing their support.

Doves' diplomatic priorities make them generally skeptical of the use of military force. Their focus on other-regarding goals means that national security justifications do not reliably provide a good enough reason to override this skepticism. As a result, even in the context of security crises, speeches that rely on security justifications alone leave the support of some persuadable doves on the table. By adding humanitarian justifications to their rationale for security interventions, however, presidents evoke concerns about both national security and the wellbeing of others. Referencing the welfare of foreign civilians resonates with doves' cooperative priorities— in this case, civilian protection—and offers a more persuasive reason to override their skepticism and support military intervention. As a result, I expect doves to evaluate military interventions more positively when the White House narrative includes humanitarian appeals. These are the individuals for whom the presence of humanitarian appeals makes a substantive difference. I expect doves' maximized support to be the benefit that presidents gain from adding humanitarian justifications to speeches about security crises. In other words, the domestic benefits of humanitarian justifications are their ability to persuade as many doves as possible to join the domestic coalition. These expectations make up hypothesis three:

H3: Adding humanitarian justifications to security justifications significantly increases support among doves.

Taken as a whole, the interaction between presidential justifications and different foreign policy constituencies helps clarify why the White House has domestic incentives to include humanitarian rationales in speeches about security crises. While hawks will be satisfied by the security explanation and isolationists will not reliably respond to either explanation, there is a subset of dovish individuals whose support is maximized only when humanitarian rationales are present. When presidents add humanitarian explanations to their security justifications, these traditional doves become temporary hawks, making it possible to build a broad domestic coalition of support for intervention.

Are doves politically important?

If the full support of doves is the benefit presidents gain from using humanitarian justifications, the next question becomes: Are doves a large enough part of the US population to matter? If doves made up only a small segment of the US public, their preferences might be of little interest to the White House. Instead, multiple measures of dovishness and cooperative preferences show that doves play a lasting and prominent role in US public opinion. First, Chicago Council surveys from 1974 to 2015 regularly asked respondents to choose which issues they viewed as very important goals for US foreign policy. Consistent support for different clusters of goals maps onto the preferences held by each of the three foreign policy constituencies. Hawks prioritize the national interest and goals related to military dominance such as "strengthening countries who are friendly towards us" and "protecting the interests of American business abroad." Doves prioritize other-regarding goals that provide a global good and rely on diplomacy more than force, for example, "combating world hunger" and "strengthening the United Nations." Isolationists are people who agree with the statement, "it will be best for the future of the country if we stay out of world affairs."

Using information collected from thirteen waves of these surveys, Figure 3.3 shows the average percentage of respondents who thought the policies associated with hawkish, dovish, and isolationist priorities were "very important" for foreign policy. Because priorities were non-exclusive— a respondent could label every goal as "very important"—the surveys provide imperfect measures of the number of doves who exist at any moment in time. Despite this limitation, Figure 3.3 clearly shows that the cooperative

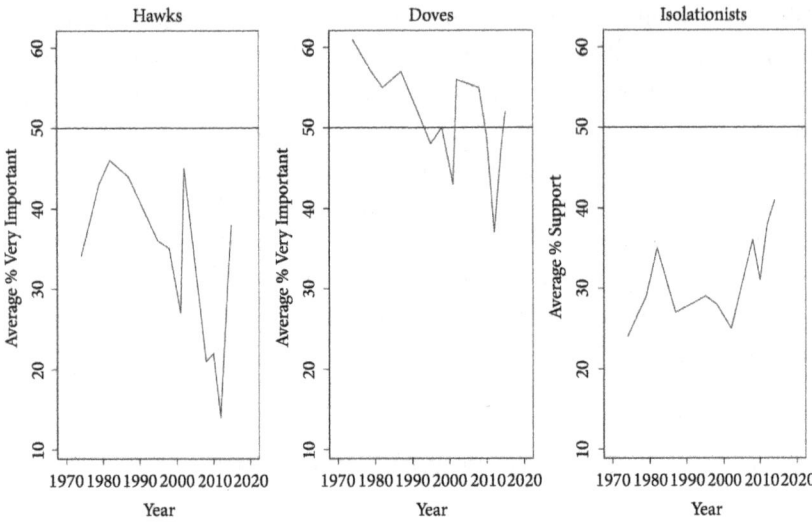

Figure 3.3 Very important foreign policy goals

Note: Based on the data from the Chicago Council Survey, 1974–2015. The first cell reports the average percentage of respondents for whom militant (hawkish) policies were very important, the second cell the average percentage for whom cooperative (dovish) policies were very important, and the third cell the percentage that supported the isolationist statement.

policies associated with doves are prioritized and common among the US domestic audience. When leaders make speeches that appeal to doves, they emphasize policies that a majority of the public has supported for over four decades. Dovish policies are also consistently prioritized by a higher percentage of respondents than hawkish policies or the isolationist statement. Developing appeals that can convince doves to support military action is therefore politically valuable and worth the White House's effort.

To further bolster the claim that these constituencies make up distinct, non-negligible portions of the US domestic audience, I turn to poll questions that forced respondents to choose whether they identify as a hawk or dove.[11] Figure 3.4 reports the percentage of respondents who were

[11] The limitation of these questions is that the forced-choice polls simplify doves and hawks into opponents and supporters of military action and do not directly account for isolationist priorities. However, the fact that these polls support the same conclusion as the Chicago Council data provides more concrete evidence that these constituencies exist and matter. Because of these limitations, the experimental chapters introduce an alternative measure of hawks and doves which more closely matches the theoretical concepts outlined in the previous section.

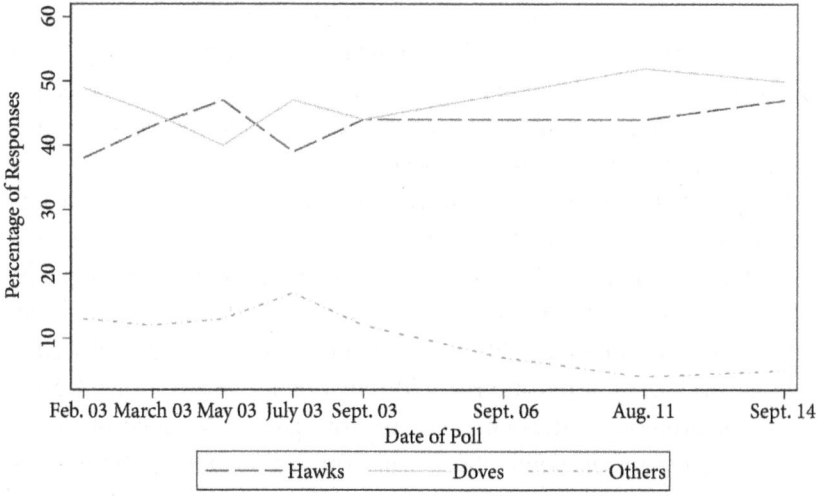

Figure 3.4 Percentage of hawks and doves in public opinion polls

Note: Figure reports responses to forced-choice poll questions included in the Roper Center iPoll database which asked whether individuals described themselves as more of a hawk or a dove. Questions were asked with varying frequency between February 2003 and September 2014. Other responses include don't know, no opinion, and not sure.

self-reported hawks or doves for all questions in the Roper Center iPoll database that met three criteria: (1) they contained the word "hawk" or "dove," (2) they forced respondents to choose one category or the other, and (3) they did not explicitly link dovish or hawkish identities to a specific conflict. Consistent with the Chicago Council measure, both hawks and doves again appear as non-negligible constituencies capable of incentivizing elite rhetoric.

Are leaders accountable for humanitarian claims?

Up to this point, the domestic coalition logic suggests that humanitarian claims are powerful political tools. When leaders effectively combine security and humanitarian justifications, they stand to gain a major political benefit: the broad support of an internationalist coalition that enables military action and loosens constraints on executive decision-making. A public that can be persuaded by humanitarian justifications, however, might also react strongly to any humanitarian crisis. As the emotional public model warns, these strong reactions can become problematic if they create domestic pressure for leaders to take risky action for purposes that do not serve the national interest (Snyder 1991). A domestic audience that pressures leaders to add humanitarian claims may also create pressure for mission creep or overreach in the service of humanitarian concerns.

The fact that domestic coalitions depend on strategically chosen justifications also raises concerns about the White House's ability to manipulate the public at will. The risk is that presidents will use humanitarian justifications to "bamboozle" the public "into supporting strategic aims at odds with their own interests rightly understood" (Goddard and Krebs 2015, 11). Humanitarian justifications could thus provide a cover for interventions that promote strategic national security goals but would otherwise be unpalatable to the public. Such concerns are heightened by the vast communications apparatus available to the White House (Druckman and Jacobs 2015). Drawing on public opinion polls and a wealth of information about public reactions to different frames, presidential speeches are crafted to emphasize what the public wants to hear. Leaders who strike the right balance between security and humanitarian claims could thus be able to remain popular and avoid accountability for their foreign policy decisions. From this view, the prevalence of humanitarian claims could be a sign of an emboldened executive and weak public constraints on the use of force.

Fortunately, a closer look at the characteristics of doves—as the individuals whose support is maximized in the presence of humanitarian claims— assuages concerns about these worst-case scenarios. As discussed earlier in this chapter, doves are defined by their focus on other-regarding, common problems and by a preference for achieving foreign policy goals through diplomatic ends. This preference for diplomatic ends makes doves skeptical of the use of military force. The group's focus on other-regarding goals makes them particularly attentive to the presidents' use of humanitarian claims and to the humanitarian consequences of military action. When there is reason to doubt the sincerity of the president's humanitarian appeals, this doubt increases doves' skepticism and decreases their support towards military action.

Additionally, doves are politically engaged.[12] Doves are therefore likely to be exposed to media coverage or elite debates that cast doubt on the

---

[12] Chapter 4 provides empirical support for this engagement.

president's humanitarian claims. If leaders try to stretch humanitarian claims too far—overstating their importance, attempting to create humanitarian crises where none exist, or using them while causing harm to civilians—the White House risks political backlash from the same group that humanitarian justifications are intended to persuade. The implication is that the same group of individuals that creates a demand for humanitarian justifications also limits their misuse. Rather than weakening constraints on the use of force, by engaging doves on issues they care about, humanitarian claims create an additional opportunity to hold leaders accountable for what they say.

Hawks are also engaged and pay attention to politics. Unlike doves, however, their main focus is on the security rationale for action. Hawks create the risk of political backlash that holds leaders responsible for their security statements. Leaders' efforts to mobilize a broad coalition of internationalists thus have a counterintuitive side effect—diverse coalitions amplify opportunities for the public to hold leaders accountable. The importance of avoiding perceptions of insincerity among both doves and hawks helps explain why, despite their incentives to use humanitarian justifications in security crises, leaders still assign the most emphasis to the security rationale. While focusing on a different type of decision, the requirement that justifications appear sincere is consistent with Levendusky and Horowitz's (2012, 333, 327, 334) finding that presidents can talk their way out of audience costs, but only if the reason for backing down "makes sense," "seems plausible," and ultimately proves to be the right decision. Both their account and the domestic coalition argument show that justifications are powerful tools but are not without limits.

Isolationists, on the other hand, offer limited support for military interventions only in cases where narrowly defined US national security interests are at stake (Herrmann, Tetlock, and Visser 1999). Because of this focus, I expect isolationists to respond negatively to the misuse of security justifications. I also expect, however, that isolationists are subject to a floor effect in terms of support. The fact that isolationists' tolerance for sustained military engagement is low to begin with means that the room for their support to decline further—and its substantive implications for the domestic coalition—is limited.

The common thread across these constituencies is the expectation that individuals respond primarily when the justifications that match their core preferences are challenged. Hypothesis four and its components summarize these expectations for each foreign policy constituency:

H4: When the preference-consistent justification is challenged, support decreases among the relevant group.

H4a: Challenging humanitarian justifications decreases support among doves.

H4b: Challenging security justifications decreases support among hawks.

H4c: Challenging security justifications decreases support among isolationists.

Does the White House care about coalition building?

In its strongest form, the domestic coalition argument expects that presidents' speeches follow the pattern of demand and restraint described in Chapter 2 because White House communication strategies intentionally use humanitarian justifications to persuade doves, with the goal of broadening domestic coalitions of support for military action. Patterns of justifications can be directly observed in public speeches, but understanding the intention behind different justifications requires a closer look at the process through which speeches are developed. Official presidential addresses reflect careful planning and collaboration between multiple actors on the White House's domestic and foreign policy teams. Presidents also rarely give national addresses that focus on only one topic. In this regard, examining documents from planning meetings, staff memos, and comments on speech drafts offers insight into whether the White House was concerned about building a domestic coalition at all and whether humanitarian claims were part of its strategy to achieve this goal. Examining the process of speech development also sheds light on the extent to which the White House is concerned with overstating humanitarian claims and provoking backlash.

In the context of developing communication strategies, the domestic coalition logic has two expectations. First, that the justifications used to explain military action to the public are developed primarily with the domestic audience in mind. While communications teams may take care not to offend or create problems with the international audience or other political elites, their main goal will be to choose the wording most likely to bolster and maintain domestic public support. The vast polling apparatus available to the White House and lessons from past interventions about what the public is willing to tolerate will inform these discussions. Second, presidents and their staffs are expected to know that the US public is made up of individuals with diverse opinions about what foreign policy should look like. Based on this knowledge, the White House will recognize that appealing to individuals with different views is important for building and maintaining broad public support. Together, these expectations lead to hypothesis five:

H5: When developing the communication strategy for a military intervention, leaders and their staffs primarily aim to persuade the domestic audience. They recognize that this audience is made up of different foreign policy constituencies that must be brought into a coalition of support.

What about partisanship?

Partisan identities—whether an individual identifies as a Democrat or Republican, and how strongly—influence foreign policy attitudes through multiple channels (Brutger 2021; Lee 2022; Heaney and Rojas 2011; Trager and Vavreck 2011). In terms of understanding public incentives for and reactions to humanitarian justifications, partisanship could be relevant in three main ways: by undermining the relevance of foreign policy preferences, by changing individuals' acceptance of official justifications, and by influencing partisans' willingness to hold members of their own party accountable.

Are foreign policy preferences still relevant in a polarized world?

The first way in which partisanship could influence the domestic coalition argument is by making the foreign policy predispositions that shape individuals' hawkish or dovish priorities less relevant. This risk stems from the fact that increasing ideological and affective polarization makes partisanship a more central part of individuals' social identities (Mason 2018). Partisanship's relevance for understanding humanitarian justifications is tempered, however, by evidence that attitudes towards the use of military force are some of the most likely to remain bipartisan and resist polarization (Kertzer, Brooks, and Brooks 2021; Maxey 2021a; Tama 2024). Especially in moments of international crisis, leaders are able to appeal to the national identity, making partisan identities less central drivers of public reactions to presidential statements (Levendusky and Horowitz 2012, 325).

One reason for this resistance stems from the fact that foreign policy issues in general—and attitudes towards military intervention especially—do not divide neatly along the left–right ideological spectrum.[13] Critically, this complexity appears in elite and public attitudes, as well as in the activity of advocacy groups (Tama 2024, 70). Instead of dividing into polarized camps, individuals lack clear assumptions about the partisan type associated with many traditional foreign policy issues (Kertzer, Brooks, and Brooks 2021, 1765, 1770). As a result, even in contemporary interventions where the effects of increasing polarization are most likely to be felt, the use of force is commonly met with bipartisan or cross-partisan support (Tama 2024).

As I will show in Chapter 4, the distribution of foreign policy preferences in this book's survey data is consistent with existing accounts of cross-partisanship, suggesting that divisions within parties are as important as the differences between them. While a majority—69 percent—of Democrats are doves, 21 percent are hawks and 10 percent are isolationists. Among Republicans, the split is even more pronounced, with no single constituency including a majority of party members: 49 percent are hawks, 38 percent are doves, and 13 percent are isolationists. Knowing an individual's party identity is informative but not sufficient to know how they approach decisions about the use of force. In the context of the domestic coalition argument, this cross-partisanship means that neither party can afford to ignore the foreign policy preferences of doves. Even for Republican presidents primarily interested in appealing to their base, humanitarian justifications can help strengthen the relevant coalition of support.

Within interventions, there is also reason to think that the effects of humanitarian rationales will be the most resilient to polarization. In related work (Maxey 2021a, 817), I show that even in the highly polarized political environment surrounding the 2016 presidential election, there is no partisan gap in how Democrats and Republicans respond to humanitarian justifications. Moreover, the partisan gap that exists in responses to security justifications—with Republicans reporting higher support than Democrats—did not increase as affective polarization rose over

---

[13] Milner and Tingley (2015) reach similar conclusions, focusing instead on the low distributional consequences of military interventions.

this time period. Only when experimental manipulations directly primed affective polarization were attitudes towards security justifications affected. Even under these artificially intense conditions, responses to humanitarian justifications remained stable in the face of rising polarization. One factor behind this bipartisan stability is evidence that humanitarian explanations are uniquely capable of evoking a sense of moral obligation among members of both parties (Kreps and Maxey 2018, 1832–1833).

Partisanship undoubtedly plays a critical role in contemporary politics and if current polarization trends continue to intensify, the implications for US credibility and the future of the liberal world order are significant (Myrick 2022; Schultz 2017). In the context of the domestic coalition argument, however, partisanship does not replace the role that foreign policy constituencies play in explaining why presidents consistently add humanitarian justifications to their statements about security crises. Instead, evidence that military interventions and humanitarian claims resist polarization makes it even more important to understand why this justification strategy consistently and effectively mobilizes support from members of both parties.

Presidential partisanship

A second line of argument suggests that while partisanship is not sufficient to understand which justifications resonate with different groups, it can still have a significant effect on people's willingness to listen to justifications from different leaders. Democrats are likely to be more supportive of justifications that come from a Democratic president, while Republicans are more likely to doubt these justifications and vice versa. Such partisan differences in reactions to elite rhetoric are consistent with research on elite cues, which expects that individuals gathering information about foreign policy give more weight to statements that come from their own political party (Berinsky 2009; 2007).

Guisinger and Saunders (2017), however, find evidence of significant variation in reactions to elite cues across foreign policy issues. Their analysis shows that partisan cue seeking mainly characterizes issues that are already polarized. For issues which resist polarization, the public is more likely to respond to cues from either party as primarily informational (Guisinger and Saunders 2017, 434). It remains the case that partisans may never respond as strongly to leaders from the opposing party as they would to a copartisan president. In the relatively less polarized context of military interventions, however, non-copartisan doves are still open to receiving some information from the leader. The domestic coalition contention is that these opposing-party doves are more likely to respond positively to the information they do receive when humanitarian justifications are present. For example, a Republican president can improve the relative strength of support for intervention among dovish Democrats by adding humanitarian justifications to their security claims—even if this support will never be as high as it is among Republicans.

Beyond altering the public's response to elite cues, an additional partisan argument suggests that the president's partisan affiliation changes their justification incentives. This argument builds on evidence that presidents who act against-type gain more credibility and leeway for their actions (Kreps, Saunders, and Schultz 2018; Mattes and Weeks 2019; Trager and Vavreck 2011). If humanitarian claims are in line with assumptions about how Democratic leaders act and talk, humanitarian statements could be seen as more credible when made by Republicans because they counter expectations. Republican presidents would thus face a stronger incentive to include humanitarian justifications in their speeches about security interventions to appear more moderate and dovish than they otherwise are.

The muted relationship between humanitarian uses of force and partisan types challenges this logic. The same aspects of humanitarian rationales that make them appealing to doves and hawks also mean that these justifications are relatively against-type for presidents from both parties (Maxey 2021a). The fact that humanitarian justifications can be framed as either a hawkish or dovish policy—because they combine a hawkish policy tool with a dovish rationale—is in line with Kertzer, Brooks, and Brooks' (2021) finding that most individuals do not associate the deployment of troops for humanitarian purposes with a particular partisan type. These characteristics also mean that adding humanitarian justifications to statements about security crises can help leaders avoid the issue-image trade-offs that Friedman (2023) identifies as a key foreign policy goal for presidential campaigns. Humanitarian justifications for security crises send a hawkish signal of strong leadership by making the case for military intervention. They also help communicate that the leader exercised good judgment by using force only when necessary to protect others.

To the extent that leaders have incentives to use humanitarian justifications to signal an against-type action, these incentives do not clearly differentiate between Republican and Democratic leaders. In Chapter 6, I consider against-type signaling as an alternative explanation in more detail, showing that official conversations about humanitarian justifications stemmed from concerns about appealing to different segments of the domestic audience rather than the president's reputation for hawkish or dovish behavior.

Holding copartisans accountable

Finally, a third area in which partisanship warrants attention is its ability to weaken public accountability for the misuse of justifications. The domestic coalition argument expects that, all else equal, doves will hold presidents accountable for their humanitarian claims, while hawks are concerned with the misuse of security justifications. Partisan loyalty suggests that all else is rarely equal and individuals' willingness to hold leaders accountable may apply only to members of the opposing party.

Existing evidence shows that this concern is warranted, but not straightforward—there is important variation between parties. In related work (Maxey 2021b), I find that members of both parties respond negatively when leaders provide misinformation about their reasons for military intervention. The limits of accountability, however, appear among Republican respondents who learn that a Republican president has stretched the truth. In this context, Republican copartisans not only fail to punish the leader, the magnitude of their support for the intervention actually increases. The same is not true among Democrats, who maintain their willingness to punish even copartisan presidents for misleading statements about military action.

In the context of the domestic coalition argument, these previous findings imply that Republican presidents likely have the most leeway to misuse humanitarian justifications. Republican presidents still face backlash from Democratic doves, which can substantially weaken their domestic coalitions, but they have a better chance of avoiding punishment from members of their own party. Democratic presidents, on the other hand, are not well-positioned to avoid backlash from doves in either party and thus have reason to be especially cautious about stretching humanitarian appeals too far.

In Chapter 6, I further explore these dynamics in the George H. W. Bush administration's justifications for the Gulf War and the Clinton administration's communication strategy towards Bosnia. The cases demonstrate that even Republican presidents worry about cross-partisan backlash against the misuse of humanitarian claims. It remains possible, however, that growing polarization has weakened this form of accountability over time—a trend I consider in more detail in the concluding chapter.

Alternative explanations

The domestic coalition argument explains the use of humanitarian justifications in security crises by connecting the incentives set by different foreign policy constituencies among the public with White House communication strategies. It is, however, only one way of looking at the world. In addition to the against-type logic outlined above, alternative explanations for why presidents use humanitarian claims can be grouped into two categories: (1) those that focus on domestic actors other than the public as the source of incentives for humanitarian claims, or (2) those that focus on factors outsides of domestic politics. This section outlines each alternative explanation in turn.

The domestic coalition argument assumes that presidents are concerned with building support for military action among the domestic public. Beyond members of the public, however, leaders are also concerned with gaining the support of—or at least avoiding vocal opposition from—other political elites, ranging from bureaucrats and political appointees within the administration to members of Congress and other publicly recognized experts. Elites can impose political costs on leaders and limit their freedom to act (Saunders 2024). Presidents thus have an incentive to bargain with key players within the administration to reduce the political risks associated with military action (Saunders 2015, 467). From this perspective, one alternative explanation for the prevalence of humanitarian claims is that the demand for their presence stems from the preferences of political elites. In this case, the pattern of justifications used in presidential speeches would reflect concessions to advisors or an effort to win over Congress instead of or in addition to the general public. Presidential speeches could appeal to both political elites and the public at the same time—there are doves and hawks in both audiences and these explanations are not mutually exclusive. The pattern of justifications in presidential speeches, however, shows that even when the advisors surrounding the executive change, humanitarian claims are still present. Presidents from both parties, advised by very different groups of experts with very different views of the US national interest and role in the world, have consistently come to similar conclusions about how to publicly present military action. Elite pressures from within the administration may be key to the decision to pursue military action in the first place or shape policy changes over the course of an intervention, but they are less likely to drive leaders' public communication strategies.

Beyond the domestic audience, leaders could also choose justification strategies based on how they resonate with the international audience. The international audience can include foreign leaders and diplomats, international organizations, and publics in other countries. Support from this broadly defined international community plays an undeniably important role in carrying out military action. With international support, leaders can turn to other countries to help share the personnel and financial burdens of intervention, while also boosting the intervention's legitimacy (Grieco et al. 2011; Kreps 2011; Thompson 2006). Humanitarian justifications evoke concerns consistent with the international norms that facilitate humanitarian interventions. Appealing to these norms could help leaders explain how the intervention reflects the "basic rules of the system about what action is permitted and where the boundaries of sovereign control lie" (Finnemore 2003, 2). From this perspective, the international audience instead of the domestic public could set the incentives that encourage leaders to include humanitarian claims in their explanations for military action. If the international audience is the target of humanitarian justifications, these claims would be especially likely to appear in speeches when the intervention is facing international dissent or when leaders are trying to build multilateral coalitions to carry out the operation. Again, the consistency with which leaders include humanitarian rationales in speeches about security-driven interventions presents a challenge for the international alternative. Humanitarian claims appear in speeches even when international support is locked in and the initial mission is relatively unilateral (Kreps 2011). For example, as Chapter 1 outlined, George W. Bush provided a humanitarian rationale for the US invasion of Afghanistan despite widespread international support and the fact that NATO had already invoked Article 5—the statement of collective defense that affirms an attack against one ally is considered an attack against all members of the alliance—only 24 hours after the terrorist attacks of September 11. Similarly, George H. W. Bush relied on humanitarian claims during the 1991 Persian Gulf War even after gaining the approval of the United Nations in the form of resolutions focused on security concerns.

The first two alternative explanations offer different audiences whose preferences could incentivize presidents to offer humanitarian justifications for security crises. The domestic coalition argument expects the US public to be the main target of presidents' humanitarian appeals; however, it is not in direct competition with evidence that elite or international audiences also matter. Presidents may decide to use humanitarian justifications in service of building a broad domestic coalition, while also acknowledging that humanitarian appeals are helpful for persuading domestic elites and the international audience. In other words, the difference in these explanations is a matter of primacy. Showing that the domestic public is the primary target audience for the justifications used in national addresses matters because it is the White House's concern with this audience that makes public accountability relevant and generates the argument's implications for democracy.

By contrast, the third alternative explanation directly contradicts the logic of the domestic coalition argument. This alternative suggests that the justifications presidents use to explain military action are not strategic choices intended to persuade a target audience. Instead, the explanations the White House offers for its actions could be motivated primarily by the realities of the conflict. Over time, evolving human rights norms have increased the attention states pay to how civilians are treated during war (Crawford 2014; Evangelista and Shue 2014). During the same period, the US pursued counterinsurgency strategies in Afghanistan and Iraq that emphasized winning the "hearts and minds" of local populations (Department of the Army 2014). Both of these trends mean that the wellbeing of foreign civilians is more likely to be seen as relevant to operational success, even in the context of security-driven interventions. From this perspective, presidents might include humanitarian justifications as part of their rationale for security interventions simply because it is true that humanitarian objectives are part of the military strategy.

The logic of this third alternative is limited in its ability to explain presidents' consistent use of humanitarian justifications across and within missions where humanitarian objectives varied. For example, although it may not be surprising that George W. Bush relied on humanitarian claims in Iraq in 2003 as US forces pursued nation-building objectives, it is not clear why George H. W. Bush used humanitarian justifications in the early stages of the 1991 Gulf War. In this conflict, humanitarian explanations are present long before the US launched Operation Desert Storm, despite the fact that the initial military objective focused on removing Iraqi forces from Kuwait—a goal that did not require "hearts and minds" or nation-building. Following this operation, the US did pursue humanitarian objectives as part of Operation Provide Comfort, but the pattern of justifications over time does not neatly map onto this shift in strategy. Additionally, this alternative does not explain leaders' expressed concerns with public backlash against insincere justifications. In a reality where humanitarian claims reflect actualized humanitarian efforts, presidential rhetoric is sincere by definition and there is no risk of stretching the claim too far.

In sum, none of the three alternative explanations map neatly onto the pattern of humanitarian justifications for security crises identified in Chapter 2. To test these alternatives more directly, Chapter 6 uses two case studies of post-Cold War interventions to demonstrate that presidents choose justifications strategically and that neither political elites nor the international community is the primary target audience for humanitarian appeals. Instead, the case evidence supports the domestic coalition argument. White House communications teams talk about using humanitarian appeals to persuade doves among the domestic public and work to avoid backlash from key groups.

Humanitarian claims across levels of analysis

The domestic coalition argument creates expectations that exist at three different levels of analysis. Chapter 2 illustrated the pattern of humanitarian claims at the level of presidential speeches, revealing evidence of perceived demand and restraint that warranted further investigation. The remainder of the book takes a multi-method approach to evaluate each set of expectations at the appropriate level. First, the argument anticipates that foreign policy constituencies will respond differently to the combination of humanitarian and security justifications. To evaluate the first four hypotheses, Chapters 4 and 5 use a series of survey experiments that measure changes in how people evaluate interventions based on their foreign policy constituency. The surveys vary the justifications used to explain military action and whether the president's statement matches expert accounts.

Individual attitudes represent the micro-foundations of foreign policy, setting the domestic political incentives to which leaders can then respond.

These incentives do not, however, directly determine leader behavior—leaders retain the agency to choose between different justifications and policy options, even if they carry political costs. The remaining question is: Do presidents use humanitarian justifications as part of an intentional strategy aimed at broadening the domestic coalition of support? The expectations for leaders' intent, outlined in hypothesis five, have implications for the process through which communication strategies are developed. Chapter 6 conducts two case studies—one of the Gulf War and the other of US policy towards Bosnia from 1993 to 1995—using archival materials including speech drafts, poll reports, and internal memos from the George H. W. Bush and William J. Clinton administrations. The Gulf War represents a hard case for the domestic coalition argument because it precedes the humanitarian interventions of the 1990s that demonstrated the legitimacy of humanitarian explanations for military force. The intervention also centered around clearly defined security objectives without a nation-building component. Evidence that the Bush administration viewed humanitarian claims as valuable tools—and also recognized the risk of backlash—increases confidence that the strategic benefits of this rhetoric were also recognized in later interventions. The Bosnian case then establishes the scope of the argument. It illustrates how the domestic coalition remains relevant in response to primarily humanitarian crises and explains why doves support but do not pressure leaders to pursue humanitarian interventions. By examining justifications at these three levels of analysis, the book tests the full causal chain behind the domestic coalition argument and provides a clear picture of the power humanitarian narratives wield in security crises.

Conclusion

This chapter theorized that humanitarian justifications are powerful and necessary tools in contemporary interventions because they broaden domestic coalitions of support for military action. Without humanitarian justifications, presidents leave potential support on the table and increase the risk of public backlash against their foreign policy decisions. This domestic power of humanitarian claims changes how we think about what it takes to sell intervention to the public, showing that security threats alone are not enough.

The chapter detailed the domestic coalition argument, explaining why public support matters, what leaders can do to persuade the public, and how foreign policy constituencies create demands for different justifications. First, I argued that presidents have an incentive to build not only major-ity coalitions but also broad coalitions of public support for military action. Broadening the domestic coalition helps leaders navigate other institutional constraints on the use of force, including making members of Congress think twice about opposing popular White House policies. Presidents anticipate and take public opinion into account when making policy decisions, but they also have a powerful means of persuading the public. Leaders who choose the right justifications are likely to expand the domestic coalition of support.

Next, I explained why choosing effective justifications requires a more fine-grained understanding of public preferences for foreign policy. For the domestic coalition argument to hold, there must be a subset of people in the US public that responds to humanitarian appeals more strongly than security appeals. Considering different foreign policy constituencies made it possible to identify this key group of doves and account for the power of humanitarian justifications. The first three hypotheses outlined expecta-tions for how different foreign policy constituencies react to justifications. I expect doves to offer their highest levels of support only when humanitar-ian claims are present. This group sets the incentive for presidents to include humanitarian appeals in security crises. Chapter 4 tests these hypotheses.

The chapter then considered the risk that humanitarian justifications weaken public accountability for military action. In contrast to warnings that a public responsive to humanitarian appeals will be problematic and easily hoodwinked, I argued that humanitarian justifications can have pos-itive consequences for democratic accountability. Because individuals are most likely to hold leaders accountable for the justifications that match their policy priorities, mobilizing a broad coalition of doves and hawks amplifies opportunities for accountability. Chapter 5 evaluates these expectations.

Beyond public opinion, the domestic coalition argument also has implica-tions for how presidents develop their communication strategies. Chapter 6 shows that presidents' patterns of justifications reflect an intentional White House strategy that takes the domestic coalition seriously. Taken as a whole, the remainder of the book finds strong evidence to support this chapter's domestic coalition expectations across multiple levels of analysis.

4

Demand for justifications

Who responds to humanitarian appeals?

The 9/11 terrorist attacks presented the most direct threat to US national security since World War II.[1] For the American public watching the twin towers fall on live television, the severity and immediacy of this threat was obvious (Gadarian 2014). When George W. Bush gave a news conference at the beginning of Operation Enduring Freedom in Afghanistan, it was no surprise that he talked about military action as "a war against all those who seek to export terror and a war against those governments that support or shelter them," promising that the operation would "drive the terrorists out of their hidden caves and bring them to justice" (G. W. Bush 2001c). Bush's public focus on defending the United States against future terrorist attacks also reflected the international community's view of the intervention—military action was legitimate and authorized based on the right to self-defense outlined in Article 51 of the UN Charter. In short, the 2001 invasion of Afghanistan was as clearly and credibly linked to US security as possible. And, yet, in the same speech, Bush stopped talking about terrorism to focus on foreign civilians, noting "At the same time, we are showing the compassion of America by delivering food and medicine to the Afghan people, who are, themselves, the victims of a repressive regime" (G. W. Bush 2001c).

The presence of humanitarian appeals in a case as extreme and important as Afghanistan highlights the gap between how presidents talk about military intervention—illustrated in Chapter 2—and what studies of public opinion expect to sway the domestic audience. When the US is directly attacked, the military intervention that follows can be presented as necessary to protect the safety of the public's own country and way of life. Leaders who

---

[1] The survey data presented in this chapter and the logic behind the argument and analysis also appeared in *Political Research Quarterly*. Beyond an expansion of the discussion and analysis, the main difference between this chapter and Maxey (2020) is that this chapter focuses on doves and hawks, while Maxey (2020) focused on cooperative and militant internationalism. Doves and hawks facilitate clearer, though closely related, conceptual distinctions.

Doves into Hawks. Sarah Maxey, Oxford University Press. © Oxford University Press (2026).
DOI: 10.1093/9780197832738.003.0004

use this type of security justification make the need for military action specific and proximate (Western 2005, 22). They also encourage the public to rally around their leadership because an external security threat "gives rise to the belief that one's patriotic duty requires the appearance of solidarity" (Brody 1991, 45–46). Leaders who can evoke terrorist threats like the one the US faced in the aftermath of 9/11 will have a particularly strong influence over the public and may even be able to convince people to support hawkish foreign policy decisions that would be unpopular at different times (Gadarian 2010; 2014; Malhotra and Popp 2012).

The US security interests at stake in Afghanistan were not in doubt and alternative explanations were not needed. In this context, critics and humanitarian advocates alike view humanitarian claims as unnecessary. Humanitarian crises are distant from the public's everyday life and do not directly threaten US security or national interests (Hildebrandt et al. 2013, 250). As a result, the public is not expected "to care enough about human rights to invest significant American resources" (McFarland and Mathews 2005, 308) and leaders who rely on these claims should expect inevitable domestic opposition to appear over time (Western and Goldstein 2011, 58). Expectations that the support created with humanitarian appeals will be inferior and short-lived lead critics to warn that these justifications promote overreaching foreign policies which are likely to fail (Mandelbaum 1996, 19). In other words, humanitarian claims are limited in their ability to bolster public support and should be avoided when leaders have other options.

By the time he held his October 2001 news conference, the credibility of Bush's security justifications for intervention in Afghanistan was domestically and internationally accepted. Under these conditions, the rational public accounts cannot make sense of Bush's decision to repeatedly emphasize the wellbeing of Afghanistan's civilians in his early public addresses. Such humanitarian claims appear superfluous. If anything, they seem to raise the political risks of action by creating public expectations that the intervention will improve both US security *and* civilians' lives.

Why, then, did Bush consistently talk about helping the people of Afghanistan as part of US counterterrorism operations? In Chapter 3, I argued that humanitarian appeals are much more powerful than conventional, rational accounts of public opinion expect. This power stems from humanitarian claims' unique ability to turn traditional doves into temporary hawks and broaden the domestic coalition of support. Bush's addition of humanitarian explanations to his speeches about US action in Afghanistan thus reflects his incentive to build and sustain the broadest possible coalition of public support—even in this extreme case, security justifications alone would leave important support on the table.

The domestic coalition theory has expectations both for how presidents communicate and for how the public reacts to elite rhetoric. In this chapter, I focus on public reactions and test individual-level hypotheses about how members of different constituencies view security and humanitarian justifications. Public attitudes set the incentive structure for elected officials and can account for the demand for humanitarian justifications that appeared in Chapter 2. Leaders do not have to act in line with public opinion. If, however, they want to reap the benefits of having the public on their side—from reelection to leverage over Congress—or avoid the political costs associated with opposition, they will measure and attempt to cater to public preferences as much as possible. Examining individual-level responses to different justifications is therefore a necessary step towards establishing a key piece of the domestic coalition argument: Presidents can gain unique domestic political benefits by adding humanitarian appeals to their speeches about security crises.

This chapter uses national survey experiments to capture the effect of adding humanitarian justifications to security explanations, demonstrating that doves make humanitarian appeals worthwhile. Survey experiments are both appropriate for the individual level of analysis and helpful for isolating the influence of different justifications across foreign policy constituencies. Observational data like public opinion polls are specific to the details of each case of intervention, making it difficult to determine which justifications a participant heard. Experimental designs hold these details constant and cleanly vary the presence or absence of humanitarian appeals. For these reasons, I use survey experiments to demonstrate that, all else equal, humanitarian claims are persuasive to the group of people the domestic coalition theory expects. Chapter 6 then considers evidence from actual cases of US intervention to help place these results in a real-world context and evaluate expectations at different levels of analysis.

The results show that humanitarian justifications play a powerful role in contemporary security crises. Adding humanitarian justifications to security explanations does not obviously influence hawks, but it significantly increases the support of doves—the domestic coalition of support is the broadest when humanitarian claims are present. The findings support the book's overarching expectation that leaders benefit from using humanitarian claims even when the US is threatened, and that this benefit comes from persuadable doves. Follow-up analyses reveal that doves' increased support is driven by heightened concerns about foreign civilians that override their skepticism towards military force.

The remainder of the chapter is divided into four parts. First, I review the theoretical expectations for individuals from different foreign policy constituencies and explain why analyzing public opinion is important for understanding the behavior of political elites. I then describe the experimental design, including how individuals are divided into foreign policy constituencies and how the survey vignettes evoke rhetoric used in recent US interventions. Third, I present the main experimental results, examining support for humanitarian claims across subgroups. Finally, I discuss the implications of the results and explain why they raise concerns about democratic accountability which are tackled in Chapter 5.

Theoretical expectations

In Chapter 3, I outlined the reasons presidents care about building public support for military action. With the public on their side, leaders gain a number of benefits. They bolster the reelection prospects for themselves and other members of their party, minimize the risk of opposition from Congress, and guard against over-time declines in approval (Gelpi and Grieco 2015; Kriner 2010; Pevehouse and Howell 2007). Presidents are not required to win over the public before launching a military intervention, but moving forward without public consent dramatically increases the political costs of action and the risk of domestic backlash. In the US context, presidents have information and first-mover advantages that make their national addresses and statements justifying military action effective ways to sell intervention to the public (Baum and Groeling 2010). Before the president makes a public statement, the vast White House communications team carefully gauges how different justifications will resonate with the domestic audience and tailors speeches accordingly (Druckman and Jacobs 2015). Given the importance of public opinion and the attention it receives from the White House, I expect that leaders' common use of humanitarian claims in security crises reflects a belief that this rhetoric is politically beneficial. The goal of this chapter is to show that such a belief has merit.

The expectation that humanitarian appeals are useful tools for swaying public opinion is consistent with growing evidence that attitudes towards military action are linked to moral concerns (Kertzer et al. 2014; Rathbun and Stein 2020; Tomz and Weeks 2013) and can be influenced by moral rhetoric (Post 2023). Moral concerns can include a desire for vengeance and retribution (Liberman 2006; Stein 2015), but often appear as a moral obligation to protect foreign civilians from harm (Kreps and Maxey 2018). By raising humanitarian considerations, leaders encourage the public to think about action in moral terms and also heighten perceptions of the threat posed by the adversary (Tomz and Weeks 2019). The question that remains is whether humanitarian justifications are worthwhile when the US faces a clear security threat.

In Chapter 3, I argued that humanitarian appeals are politically beneficial because they are necessary to build broad domestic coalitions of support for intervention. The unique benefits of humanitarian narratives stem from their ability to evoke a response among a distinct group of individuals—doves—who are not equally persuaded by security explanations. In the experimental context, if the domestic coalition logic is correct, I expect the combination of security and humanitarian justifications to generate the broadest coalition of internationalists because of who humanitarian claims persuade. This combined category captures the effect of adding humanitarian claims to existing security justifications—consistent with the pattern present in presidential speeches in Chapter 2.

This expectation for the effectiveness of humanitarian claims stems from their ability to appeal to different groups of potential coalition members. Foreign policy constituencies capture the intersection of how people think about whether the US should be actively engaged in international affairs, the most important goals of foreign policy, and which tools are most effective for achieving those goals. In Chapter 3, I argued that internationalist doves and hawks are key members of potential coalitions of support for intervention because, unlike isolationists, both groups believe that the US should be actively involved in solving global problems. Hawks view military force as a generally effective tool of foreign policy and so are expected to respond to all justifications for the use of force. Given the choice, doves prefer for the US to rely on diplomacy to help others and will be skeptical of statements that focus only on national security. I expect that adding humanitarian justifications to speeches about security crises is key to persuading doves because the humanitarian claims shift their focus from national security to other-regarding goals that resonate with their cooperative values.

In sum, where conventional accounts of public opinion expect humanitarian claims to be inconsequential in the presence of security claims, the domestic coalition theory expects humanitarian appeals to be the key to broadening support. The power of humanitarian appeals is rooted in their ability to persuade doves, who are otherwise skeptical of military force. The remainder of this chapter uses survey experiments to show how individuals' responses to humanitarian claims vary across foreign policy constituencies. It evaluates the expected responses for each group, which match the first three hypotheses initially presented in Chapter 3:

H1: Adding humanitarian justifications to security justifications does not significantly increase support among isolationists.[2]

H2: Adding humanitarian justifications to security justifications does not significantly increase support among hawks.

H3: Adding humanitarian justifications to security justifications significantly increases support among doves.

How the survey experiments work

I use an experimental approach to capture how individuals from different foreign policy constituencies respond to humanitarian and security claims. This approach makes it possible to maintain control over the information to which participants are exposed, varying only the part of the intervention that is relevant for testing the domestic coalition theory—whether humanitarian and security explanations are present. The benefit of survey experimental methods is that by randomly assigning people to read different statements from hypothetical presidents, the design ensures that any changes in support for the intervention are linked to the content of the president's message instead of other commentary, concerns, or events in the news. This method is thus a good match for figuring out who responds to humanitarian claims and under what conditions. To this end, the chapter prioritizes the internal validity needed to show that doves are more supportive of humanitarian explanations than security claims alone. Chapter 6 then considers the implications of the experimental

[2] To reiterate the note from Chapter 3, the absence of significance is not the same as the presence of null effects (Rainey 2014), but knowing the foreign policy constituencies for which humanitarian justifications make a significant difference is the relevant information for the domestic coalition logic.

results in real-world military actions, testing expectations for how the White House thinks about doves and hawks while designing communication strategies.

The survey samples

The results presented in this chapter are from two survey experiments conducted with two different samples and survey firms. In survey one, I investigate the main treatment effects—whether adding humanitarian justifications to security claims increases the support of doves—with responses from 499 individuals who participated in a national survey fielded through Dynata (formerly Survey Sampling International) in July 2017.[3] With survey two, I examine the mechanisms behind the hypotheses, considering whether humanitarian justifications persuade doves by increasing their focus on helping foreign civilians. Survey two uses a sample of 1571 US adults fielded through Amazon's Mechanical Turk (MTurk) in July 2016. This second experiment also introduces a counterterrorism scenario to demonstrate that the results hold across different types of security crises. MTurk samples are not nationally representative, but are consistently shown to produce treatment effects comparable to national samples (Berinsky, Huber, and Lenz 2012; Coppock 2019; Weinberg, Freese, and McElhattan 2014). I also replicate the main treatment effects with the samples from both experiments to reduce the risk that any findings are an artifact of the particular sample or the time at which the survey was in the field.

Separating doves from hawks

Foreign policy constituencies shed light both on the groups of individuals that leaders can persuade to join domestic coalitions of support and on which justifications will be most effective at bolstering coalition membership. In both surveys, the first step is thus to capture respondents'

---

[3] Using Conrad et al.'s (2017) measure of reading speed, I exclude respondents who spent two minutes or less on the entire survey. Removing speeders reflects a common practice and recognition that time is an indicator of data quality (Berinsky, Margolis, and Sances 2014, 743; Conrad et al. 2017; Malhotra 2008). Limiting the analysis to individuals who spent enough time on the survey to plausibly read the president's statement and receive the treatment increases confidence that any differences between the conditions can be interpreted as an effect of the justifications used.

relevant foreign policy constituency, categorizing individuals as doves, hawks, or isolationists. To avoid post-treatment bias, I divided respondents into foreign policy constituencies with a question asked as part of a series of demographic measures that appeared before the intervention scenarios. To avoid priming responses to the experimental scenario, I used a single-item measure that forced trade-offs between different foreign policy priorities.

The foreign policy constituency question asked survey participants to choose the statement that "Best reflects the role the United States should play in the world" from a list that included an item consistent with each of the three main constituencies. Because my definition of hawks and doves combines their internationalism and militant or cooperative priorities, I selected the statements for each group from Kertzer et al. (2014) based on items highly correlated with index measures of militant and cooperative internationalism. The statement associated with doves said, "It is essential for the United States to work with other nations to solve problems such as overpopulation, hunger, and pollution." Hawks are associated with the statement, "It is important for the United States to maintain a strong military to ensure world peace." I then used the Chicago Council's standard measure for isolationism (Smeltz, Daalder, and Kafura 2014): "It is best for the future of the United States if we stay out of world affairs."

This approach to measuring foreign policy constituencies captures individuals' primary beliefs about the role the US should play in the world using the fewest questions possible. The trade-off associated with the single-item measure is nuance—realistically, each individual holds a mix of views consistent with different goals and this question reflects only the foreign policy goals a person prioritizes when forced to choose. The rationale behind this choice of measure is both theoretical and empirical. Theoretically, the measure allows me to place respondents into three constituencies that capture the logic of the main hypotheses, providing the minimum level of classification needed to understand who can potentially be convinced to join a domestic coalition. Empirically, asking participants to complete an extensive battery of foreign policy-related questions risks priming responses to the intervention scenarios and makes it difficult to confidently interpret the treatment effects. Consistent with the goals of this chapter, this choice of measure prioritizes internal validity, making it possible to isolate the effect of humanitarian justifications on individuals who predominantly take a dovish approach to foreign policy.

Caution is warranted, however, and I take extra steps to confirm the valid-ity of the single-item measure. First, if the single-item measure influences the findings, it biases against the expectations outlined in the domestic coalition theory and serves as a hard test of the hypotheses. For example, because the individuals that I count as doves may also hold beliefs that are con-sistent with hawkishness or isolationism, they should be more likely to be persuaded by security justifications than my argument anticipates. Evidence that doves have a unique reaction to humanitarian claims—even under this relatively blunt classification—increases my confidence that foreign policy constituencies are meaningful and distinct groups which are best mobi-lized by communication strategies that combine humanitarian and security rationales.

Second, in addition to the foreign policy constituency question, exper-iment one also asked respondents to place themselves on a seven-point militant assertiveness scale based on how they thought the US should solve international problems. The low end of the scale represents the dovish belief that the US should "mainly solve problems with diplomacy and interna-tional pressure," using military force only when it is absolutely necessary. Alternatively, the high end of the scale reflects the hawkish belief that diplo-macy and pressure often fail, so the US should "mainly be ready to use military force." If the single-item measure of foreign policy constituencies works correctly, doves should place themselves at the low end of the scale and hawks at the high end. Because isolationists are defined by a desire to avoid solving international problems in the first place, their responses are expected to be less coherent. The survey responses are in line with each of these expectations. Doves reported the lowest level of military assertiveness while hawks reported a level of assertiveness significantly higher than either of the other groups. On average, isolationists placed themselves between the two extremes. As expected, military assertiveness is a significant predictor of being classified as a dove or hawk but is not significantly associated with identifying as an isolationist. The details of this analysis are included in the appendix.

Third, to further validate this measure, I conducted a follow-up survey that included both the single-item measure and a full battery of questions commonly used to capture foreign policy orientations. The results from this follow-up confirm that foreign policy orientation scores are significant pre-dictors of responses to the single-item measure and vice versa. Details of this survey and the results are included in the appendix.

Varying justifications for intervention

After dividing participants into foreign policy constituencies, the survey randomly assigned each individual to read one of three excerpts from a hypothetical president's national address. In these statements, the president explained that military action was necessary using either: (1) security claims, (2) humanitarian claims, or (3) a combination of security and humanitarian claims.[4] When combined with the foreign policy constituency measure, comparing reactions to the justification conditions between groups can determine whether there is a constituency that responds more strongly to calls for intervention when humanitarian appeals are present.

First, all participants read that "Over the last few months, a violent conflict has developed in the country of Numar" and that the US president proposed a military response.[5] The scenario then branched into three different statements based on random assignment to a treatment condition. For participants assigned to the security condition in survey one, the president's address explained that military action would respond to a threat to "the security of the United States, including the American people" posed by a foreign regime that had "invaded its neighboring state and is a threat to the United States." I designed this version of the scenario to reflect an instance of foreign policy restraint—similar to the goals of the Gulf War—where the US intervenes to block or reverse the aggressive actions of another country. This type of scenario evokes security interests without a direct threat to US soil and previous scholarship expects it to be particularly popular among the domestic audience (Eichenberg 2005; Jentleson 1992; Jentleson and Britton 1998).

Foreign policy restraint scenarios do not, however, capture the counterterrorism objectives that defined US interventions after 2001, including high-profile and high-cost operations in Afghanistan. To represent justifications from the war on terror—and confirm that the results are consistent across different types of security threats—the security condition in survey two told participants that the regime in Numar "has created a safe haven for

---

[4] The full text of the survey instrument is included in the appendix.

[5] Using a fictional country maintains experimental control over the assumptions respondents make about the scenario and avoids contamination based on current events. See Brutger et al. (2023) for a discussion of the trade-offs surrounding situational hypotheticality and artificial country names.

terrorists and threatened the United States." The remainder of the scenario, as well as the wording of the humanitarian treatments, is otherwise identical to survey one.

In the humanitarian condition, the president instead claimed that a military response was necessary because the foreign regime posed a threat to "its own civilians, including innocent women and children" and had "killed thousands of its own people and directly targeted civilians." This wording reflects the type of statements leaders make in the context of humanitarian interventions, where protecting civilians is the main impetus for action and links to US security interests are not clear. In other words, this treatment mirrors the context in which humanitarian claims are conventionally expected to be most useful.

Finally, the combined conditions, when compared to the security conditions, capture the effect of adding a humanitarian justification to a security rationale. They include both security and humanitarian justifications. Participants in survey one read a presidential statement that said military action was necessary because the foreign regime posed a threat to "its own civilians and to the security of the United States. It has invaded its neighboring state and killed thousands of its own people." In survey two, the combined condition again used terrorism as the security threat, reporting that Numar "has created a safe haven for terrorists and killed thousands of its own people." These conditions reflect the rhetoric that motivates this book: presidents' common choice to offer both security and humanitarian explanations for action. Determining how different members of the public respond to the statements in this condition—and how their reactions compare to other justification strategies—is the first step towards understanding what presidents stand to gain from talking about humanitarian concerns in the context of security crises.

I crafted the wording used by the hypothetical president from the actual language used repeatedly by Republican and Democratic presidents to justify post-Cold War US military actions in Iraq, Bosnia, Afghanistan, and Libya. Using phrases from past interventions helps increase the external validity of the treatments. The experimental vignettes are the type of the language people are likely to encounter and use to form opinions about real-world foreign policy decisions. This approach also helps ensure that the experimental scenarios follow contemporary rhetorical conventions and norms that cross party lines.[6]

---

[6] See Finnemore (2003) and Krebs (2015) for discussions of how norms and elite discourse can shift over time.

Table 4.1 Justification text used in the survey experiments

	Numar poses a grave threat to...	*It has...*	*The safety of...*
Security (Survey One)	...the security of the United States, including the American people.	...invaded its neighboring state and is a threat to the United States.	...the United States is at stake and we must act.
Humanitarian	...its own civilians, including innocent women and children.	...killed thousands of its own people and directly targeted civilians.	...Numar's civilians is at stake and we must act.
Combined	...its own civilians and the security of the United States.	...invaded its neighboring state and killed thousands of its own people.	...Numar's civilians and the United States is at stake and we must act.

After reading the president's statement, participants also received information about how experts responded to the speech. Chapter 5 will use variation in expert agreement to investigate whether humanitarian claims need to appear sincere to be persuasive. For the analysis in this chapter, I hold the expert information constant—using only the conditions in which experts agreed with the president's account of the conflict—to highlight baseline differences in support that stem from justifications and foreign policy constituencies. Following the details of the scenario, I asked participants to report their support or opposition to the intervention and what actions they would be willing to take to voice their opinion. I also asked a series of follow-up questions, including a manipulation check. Table 4.1 outlines the details of the three treatment conditions from experiment one.

The political relevance of internationalists

The domestic coalition argument expects the benefits of humanitarian claims to stem from their unique ability to maximize support among doves. Winning over doves is only important, however, if this group constitutes a politically relevant segment of the US public. I consider groups to be politically relevant if they represent a non-negligible proportion of the population—large enough to tip the balance of an election, for example—and show signs of political engagement—being willing to take actions like voting that could influence elections or approval of the president.

How many doves are in the survey samples?

The past Chicago Council surveys and public opinion polls, presented in Chapter 3, offer initial evidence that dovish policy preferences are common among the US public and remain relatively high over time. The measure of foreign policy constituencies included in this chapter's surveys more directly captures people who are predominantly doves and confirms that these individuals make up a sizeable part of the domestic audience. Based on responses to the foreign policy constituency question outlined above, 53.5 percent of participants in the national Dynata survey chose the dove statement as their primary view of how the US should engage with the world. By comparison, 33.3 percent of respondents identified with the hawk statement and 13.2 percent chose the isolationist option. The percentage of doves in this sample is in line with the average number of Chicago Council Survey respondents who selected the dovish policies as "very important" foreign policy goals. The comparability of these two alternative measures helps validate the appropriateness of the single-question measure in this context.

More importantly, regardless of the measure used, doves easily pass the non-negligible threshold. When a constituency reflects over half of the domestic audience, leaders concerned with strengthening public approval have a clear incentive to appeal to these views—to do otherwise would leave a substantial amount of potential support on the table. The distribution of different constituencies also highlights the benefits of building coalitions across internationalist views. With both doves and hawks onboard, presidents have a coalition that includes a strong majority of the US public and enables them to reap the political benefits of broad support. Adding isolationists to the coalition is both a more difficult task—because their baseline preference is for the US to stay out of international affairs—and has a more marginal effect on the overall level of support.

Are doves politically active?

Responses to follow-up questions about voting and political action show that doves are not only a sizeable group, they are also likely to put their numbers to political use. The majority of both doves and hawks reported voting in the previous election. The proportion of these internationalist voters is also significantly higher than isolationists.[7] Although self-reported voting is almost certainly inflated, the relative differences between internationalists and isolationists are informative. Because both internationalist groups vote in relatively high numbers, leaders concerned about elections have an incentive to appeal to hawks and doves when explaining their foreign policy decisions.

Another follow-up question asked participants to select any actions they would be willing to take to show their support or opposition to military action. The actions included posting on social media, signing a petition, writing a letter to the editor, contacting a member of Congress, participating in a rally, or "none of the above." On average, doves were the most willing to take action. They also reported a significantly higher willingness to act than hawks.[8] This heightened willingness to act extends to the more time-intensive activities such as participating in rallies. As in the case of voting, self-reports may overestimate the baseline number of actions an individual would actually take. The differences between groups, however, suggest that doves have a high propensity to act relative to other members of the domestic audience.

Partisan distributions

A closer look at each group reveals that doves and hawks, as well as isolationists, have distinct distributions of party identification and other demographic characteristics. Examining these differences makes it easier to understand how foreign policy constituencies overlap with other domestic constituencies that leaders may want to appease. Most notably, it highlights the interaction between partisanship and foreign policy constituencies in constructing domestic coalitions.

First, in terms of party identities, Figure 4.1 shows the partisan composition of each foreign policy constituency (top row), as well as how foreign policy constituencies are distributed within each political party (bottom row). Starting with doves, a majority—60 percent—identified as Democrats, while 23 percent identified as Republicans and 17 percent as independents. Presidents focused on persuading doves with humanitarian justifications

---

[7] Throughout the remainder of the analysis, all statistically significant differences are assessed at the $p < 0.05$ level unless otherwise noted.

[8] The full results from this analysis are included in the appendix.

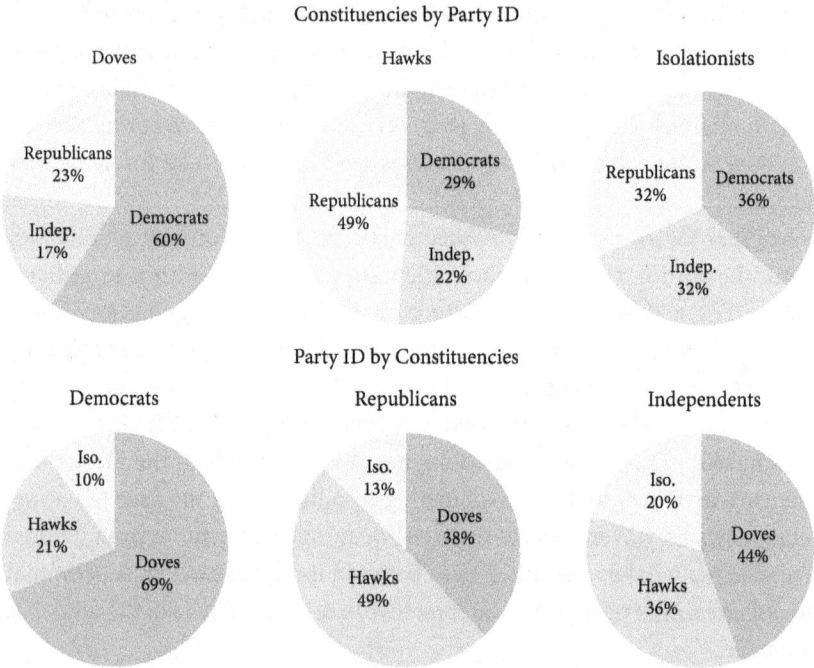

Figure 4.1 Distribution of constituencies and party identifications

are thus especially well-positioned to convince Democrats, but their communication strategies will also appeal to a number of Republicans and independents whose support would otherwise be left on the table.

Hawks, on the other hand, hold more varied party identities. The plurality of hawks—49 percent—are Republicans, while 29 percent are Democrats and 22 percent are independents. Isolationists reported the most even distribution of party identities, with roughly one-third identifying as Republicans, Democrats, and independents. This distribution of isolationists is consistent with existing evidence that the group is event-driven and rooted in distinct, potentially libertarian, moral foundations (Iyer et al. 2012; Kertzer 2013; Kertzer et al. 2014). Overall, the top row of Figure 4.1 shows that there are connections between foreign policy constituencies and party identities, but all foreign policy constituencies have cross-partisan membership.

The bottom row of Figure 4.1 then flips the focus, examining what percentage of each party is made up of different foreign policy constituencies. This distribution of foreign policy preferences across parties sheds light on the incentives that Democratic and Republican presidents have to use humanitarian justifications to appeal to persuadable doves. Democrats have the clearest concentration of foreign policy constituencies, with 69 percent falling into the dove category, compared to 21 percent who are hawks and 10 percent who are isolationists. For Democratic presidents, persuading doves is critical even if the White House's primary focus is on mobilizing its base. Humanitarian justifications are not only relevant for persuading Democrats, however, they are also well-positioned to resonate with the 38 percent of Republicans and 44 percent of independents who identified as doves.

For Republican presidents, appealing to hawks is key to mobilizing a near-majority (49 percent) of their voter base. These leaders can get further with security justifications alone compared to Democrats. Without appealing to doves, however, even Republican presidents leave over a third (38 percent) of their own party's support weaker than it would otherwise be. Alternatively, when Republican presidents persuade doves by adding humanitarian justifications to their security rationales, they strengthen support from copartisans, reach out to 44 percent of independents, and dramatically increase the potential for a bipartisan coalition with Democrats. Critically, these distributions show that while Democratic and Republican presidents will mobilize different combinations of in- and out-party members, both have political incentives to use humanitarian justifications.

Beyond partisanship, doves, hawks, and isolationists also vary in terms of gender, political ideology, and education. Doves included the highest proportion of women: 57 percent compared to 53 percent of hawks and 44 percent of isolationists. Doves were also significantly more liberal than either hawks or isolationists, whose political ideologies were not significantly different from each other. Finally, doves reported significantly higher levels of overall education compared to hawks.

Results from survey one: How justifications influence support

Unsurprisingly, security justifications are effective at mobilizing the domestic audience, receiving support from 64 percent of people in survey one and 54 percent of participants in survey two. Humanitarian justifications alone can also raise support from a majority of respondents. In the aggregate, 58 percent of participants in survey one and 59 percent in survey two supported the intervention when the president only talked about protecting foreign civilians. When used in isolation, the relative ranking of humanitarian and security justifications varied between the surveys—security-only justifications were more popular in survey one and humanitarian-only justifications were more popular in survey two. In both cases, however, the combination of humanitarian and security justifications generated the highest level of support. Adding a humanitarian rationale to the security justification raised support to include 70 percent of respondents in survey one and 62 percent of respondents in survey two.[9] While the combined justifications are the most popular across surveys, the more interesting story appears when examining how different constituencies react to the addition of humanitarian claims. Disaggregating responses reveals that leaders' main domestic political incentives for using humanitarian justifications in security crises stem from how these claims mobilize doves, changing the way in which they view the use of military force.

Who sets the incentive for humanitarian appeals?

For the domestic coalition logic, it is not enough to examine aggregate views of justifications. Instead, capturing the political benefits of humanitarian claims demands a closer look at who responds to these appeals and their role in broadening coalitions of support. The results from survey one confirm the validity and importance of this approach. Evaluating responses based on foreign policy constituencies provides a clearer picture of how humanitarian claims shape public opinion and explains why leaders have incentives to include humanitarian appeals in their justifications for security crises. Using the measure of foreign policy constituencies described in earlier sections, Figure 4.2 reports the average support for each type of justification among hawks, doves, and isolationists. These results offer the most direct test of hypotheses one through three.

Compared to both groups of internationalists, isolationists offered generally lower support for military intervention. The average levels of support from isolationists are reported in the right-hand panel of Figure 4.2. Support among isolationists is the highest in the security-only condition where 61 percent of respondents approved of military action. Compared to hawks,

[9] The differences between the security-only and combined justifications do not reach conventional levels of significance.

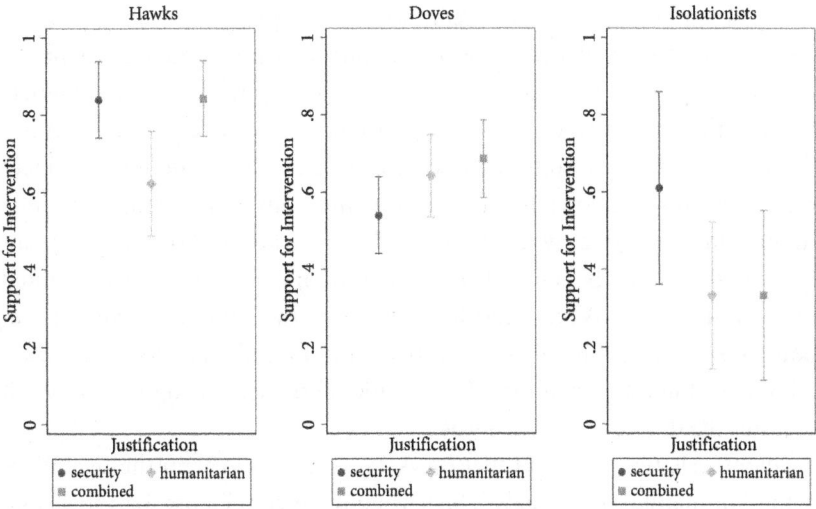

Figure 4.2 Support by foreign policy constituencies

Each panel shows support for intervention divided by foreign policy constituencies. The first panel shows results for hawks, the second for doves, and the third for isolationists. Within each panel, point estimates report the average level of support for security, humanitarian, and combined justifications, moving from left to right.

isolationists support security-driven action in significantly smaller proportions. This pattern of support is consistent with past evidence that isolationists are mobilized by direct threats to a narrowly defined national interest (Herrmann, Tetlock, and Visser 1999). It is also in line with the domestic coalition argument that even if both respond to security justifications, isolationists are not as reliable members of coalitions as hawks.

Hypothesis one expected that adding humanitarian justifications to security justifications would not significantly increase support among isolationists. This expectation is borne out in the experimental evidence, which shows that the presence of humanitarian claims instead significantly decreased support among isolationists. In both the humanitarian-only and combined justification conditions, only 33 percent of isolationists were willing to support military action. This proportion of support is the lowest of any group. Isolationists' opposition to humanitarian claims provides clear evidence that this group does not set an incentive for leaders' humanitarian rhetoric. If isolationists were key members of domestic coalitions of support for intervention, presidents would be incentivized to avoid humanitarian claims altogether and the use of these claims in security crises would be counterproductive.

The apparent disconnect between isolationists' preferences and presidential rhetoric aligns with the domestic coalition logic mentioned in Chapter 3, which expects leaders to view isolationists as less central coalition members because they are both unreliable supporters and relatively small in number. In the aggregate results, incorporating isolationists' preferences reduces support for justifications that include humanitarian claims while increasing support for security-only justifications. Their inclusion thus helps account for why the added benefits of humanitarian appeals are relatively muted in the full sample. While presidents may lose the support of some isolationists by offering humanitarian justifications for military action, they gain a broader domestic coalition of internationalists. Capturing this trade-off requires the disaggregated analysis.

Hypothesis two expected that hawks also cannot explain the incentives behind humanitarian appeals. The left-hand panel of Figure 4.2 shows that a majority of hawks supported military action across all types of justifications. This group's support was the highest when security justifications were present and—consistent with hypothesis two—support did not significantly increase when leaders combined humanitarian and security appeals. Instead, in both the security and combined categories, 84 percent of hawks approved of intervention. Support included a significantly smaller proportion of this group when the president offered only humanitarian justifications, but even this relatively less popular condition still evoked support from 62 percent of hawks.

The overall pattern of support among hawks suggests that leaders hoping to mobilize domestic approval can expect hawks to respond to multiple different justification strategies. While security claims maximize the support of this group, a solid majority of hawks are willing to back intervention regardless of the justifications used. Hawks are not opposed to the inclusion of humanitarian justifications, but they do not provide an incentive for leaders to add such claims to speeches about US security.

Instead, as the domestic coalition argument and hypothesis three expect, it is doves who set the political incentives for humanitarian claims. Presented in the middle panel of Figure 4.2, doves are the least supportive of military action when it is justified only in security terms. When the president's speech exclusively explained the need for action as a response to security threats, 54 percent of doves supported intervention. Adding a humanitarian claim to this security rationale significantly increases support, consistent with hypothesis three. By using combined justifications, the hypothetical president gained almost 15 additional percentage points of support, persuading 68.6 percent of doves. While doves' support is the highest in the combined conditions, it is also high and not statistically different when the hypothetical president relied on exclusively humanitarian claims.

Taken as a whole, the pattern of doves' support helps explain why presidents commonly add humanitarian justifications to their explanations for security crises, in line with the speech data from Chapter 2. Given that doves make up a non-negligible and active segment of the US domestic audience, leaders have an incentive to include humanitarian claims and maximize doves' support for intervention. It is this task that makes humanitarian claims necessary and politically powerful.

Results from survey two: How humanitarian claims maximize support

The results from survey one support the domestic coalition argument, showing that how an individual responds to justifications depends on their foreign policy constituency. Additionally, the findings confirm the expectation that humanitarian claims are necessary to maximize the support of doves. But what is it about humanitarian appeals that bolster doves' support? Survey two addressed this question by asking participants to report their reasoning and assumptions about the different justification scenarios.

Raising concerns about foreign civilians

The domestic coalition logic asserts that doves react more strongly to humanitarian justifications because these rationales focus on the other-regarding aspects of intervention—protecting foreign civilians. An other-regarding focus resonates with doves' underlying values and preferences, helping to overcome any lingering skepticism these individuals feel about the use of military force. To gauge whether humanitarian justifications change what participants think about when deciding to support military action, the survey asked, "Which of the following did you think about most in your decision to support or oppose the military action?" The response options included: whether or not action would protect civilians in Numar, whether or not there was a threat to US national security, whether or not failing to act would make the US appear weak, and whether or not action would help uphold international standards.[10]

Responses to this question do not offer a direct test of causal mechanisms, but they can shed light on how the presence of humanitarian justifications shifts what people think about when deciding to support an intervention. If humanitarian claims increase support by allowing doves to think about intervention in other-regarding terms, this group's reported concern with protecting civilians should be higher when humanitarian appeals are present. Responses to this question also address the risk that by talking about humanitarian concerns, leaders distract other groups from the more persuasive security considerations. If the presence of humanitarian claims decreases concerns about security threats among hawks, this would be evidence that caution is warranted.

Figure 4.3 illustrates the effect of humanitarian justifications on reported concerns about protecting civilians and threats to US national security. The point estimates reflect the difference in average reported concerns between the security-only and combined justification conditions. This comparison captures the effect of adding a humanitarian appeal to a security justification. In other words, Figure 4.3 highlights the constituencies for which humanitarian claims make people think about civilians and security threats more or less than they would if only security justifications were used.

When presidents add humanitarian claims to security justifications, Figure 4.3 shows that they shift perceptions among doves without significantly changing hawks' focus on security threats. Doves are, in fact, the only group whose considerations change significantly when humanitarian claims are added to security justifications. In the presence of a humanitarian appeal, doves thought significantly more about civilians and less about security threats compared to the security-only condition. Combining humanitarian and security justifications thus changes doves' minds in the direction and for the reason the domestic coalition argument expects. At the same time, this combination of justifications does not significantly change how

---

[10] In the remainder of this section, I focus on differences in concerns about civilians and threats to US national security between the security and combined treatment conditions because these differences are most closely in line with the theoretical expectations. Analyses of the humanitarian-only conditions, as well as concerns about US strength and upholding international standards, are included in the appendix.

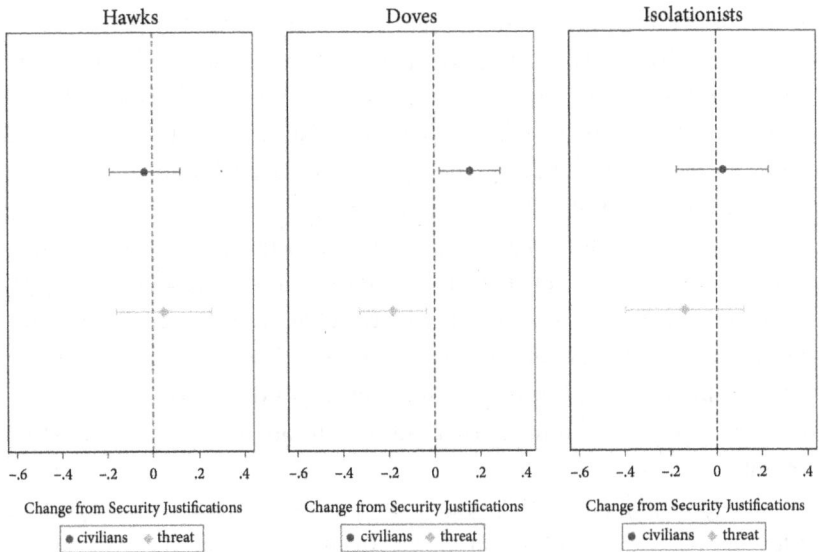

Figure 4.3 Reasons for support

The figure reports the effect of adding humanitarian justifications to security justifications (i.e., the combined treatment compared to the security treatment) on reported concern with civilians and security threats by foreign policy constituencies.

hawks or isolationists think about the intervention. Adding humanitarian justifications to security claims does not distract the individuals who find security appeals more persuasive.

Raising expectations of humanitarian outcomes

So far, the experimental results provide clear evidence that humanitarian claims resonate with doves. Humanitarian appeals allow these individuals to focus on other-regarding goals, without distracting hawks or isolationists from the security aspects of the intervention. The highest possible support from doves thus sets a clear incentive for presidents to add humanitarian claims to their speeches, even when US security is at stake. Do leaders take any political risks by drawing attention to the needs of civilians?

One potential unintended consequence of humanitarian justifications is that these claims raise the bar for success. By drawing attention to the plight of foreign civilians, humanitarian appeals could lead the public to assume that the intervention will make civilians' lives better. I evaluate this potential consequence by asking survey participants, "If the US takes military action in this case, how likely do you think each of the following outcomes will be?" The listed outcomes included "Civilians in Numar will be safe" and "The US will be more secure," with response options displayed as a four-point scale ranging from "very unlikely" to "very likely."

Humanitarian claims significantly and consistently increased participants' assumptions that civilians in Numar would be safe when the intervention ended. Among participants who read only security justifications for action, 36 percent thought civilians' safety was likely. When the scenario added a humanitarian claim, 58 percent of respondents expected civilians to be safe, and in the humanitarian-only condition, the number rises to 64 percent.

Looking within different foreign policy constituencies, two important patterns appear. First, adding humanitarian appeals to security justifications significantly increases doves' expectation that civilians will be safe by 14 percentage points.[11] The magnitude of doves who are confident that civilians will be safe, however, remains relatively low across conditions—35 percent in the security condition and 49 percent in the combined conditions thought it was likely that the intervention would have positive humanitarian outcomes. These tempered expectations are in line with doves' overarching skepticism of military force as a policy tool. Humanitarian claims may convince these individuals to give intervention a chance, but doves' support does not reflect a fundamental change in their view that military action is often ineffective. Chapter 5 builds on this pattern, further evaluating how the skepticism of doves places limits on the misuse of humanitarian claims.

Second, for hawks, the change in expectations is dramatic. Only 44 percent of hawks expected civilians to be safe when they read security justifications, but expectations almost double when a humanitarian claim is added to include 86 percent of this group. Unlike doves, hawks believe that military force can effectively achieve humanitarian goals. The effect of combined justifications on hawks' expectations for humanitarian outcomes also reflects their baseline focus on security goals—the prospect of protecting civilians is only salient when explicitly mentioned. Among this group, the addition of

---

[11] This change is statistically significant at the p < 0.10 level.

humanitarian claims raises the expectation that civilians will be protected without changing their focus on security threats as the main impetus for action.

Even among isolationists, humanitarian claims increased assumptions that civilians would be safe by over 15 percentage points compared to statements that only included security justifications. For individuals from all foreign policy constituencies, hearing the president talk about foreign civilians creates an expectation that civilians will be safe when the intervention ends. This assumption exists even when individuals' support for intervention is not rooted in the importance of protecting civilians from harm. In reaping the benefits of humanitarian appeals, leaders also raise the bar for success and take on the risk of future political costs.

This risk is heightened by evidence that humanitarian claims raise expectations of humanitarian outcomes without reducing expectations that the intervention will improve US security. When asked whether the US would be more secure after the intervention, 64 percent of respondents in the security condition and 60 percent of respondents in the combined condition reported that improved security was likely. This view is not moderated by foreign policy constituencies—majorities of both doves and hawks expected security to improve.[12] Expectations of security are marginally lower among isolationists, with 42 percent reporting that intervention would be likely to make the US more secure.

Are the results robust?

Did the participants in these surveys pay enough attention to understand the justifications for action? How can we be sure that it is the presence of humanitarian justifications that increases doves' support and not some other factor? How well do the results from these experiments travel to other scenarios? I take three steps to answer these questions: (1) examining how well people remembered what the hypothetical president said, (2) showing that humanitarian claims do not change people's assumptions about the costs or difficulty of the intervention, and (3) demonstrating that the pattern of support in survey one also exists for terrorist threats

[12] When only humanitarian justifications are used, expectations are significantly lower. In the humanitarian-only conditions, 44 percent of respondents thought improved security was likely, including 55 percent of hawks, 36 percent of doves, and 50 percent of isolationists.

like those presented in survey two. First, in survey one, 66 percent of participants correctly remembered the justifications the president used, and in survey two, 75 percent remembered correctly. Second, there is no indication that respondents' perceptions of intervention difficulty—measured in terms of prospective success, military casualties, and cost—are significantly higher when the hypothetical president combined security and humanitarian justifications. Third, the main results from survey one can be replicated with survey two, using a different sample and a different security scenario. The details of all three robustness checks are included in the appendix. Together, these checks increase confidence that the experiments capture meaningful differences in doves' support for military action and that these differences are linked to the presence of humanitarian justifications.

Conclusion

In this chapter, I used experimental methods to verify the domestic coalition theory's explanation of the demand for humanitarian justifications in security crises: that it is doves who set an incentive for presidents to talk about foreign civilians. The chapter affirmed this claim in three steps. First, for the preferences of doves to matter, doves must be a politically important constituency that is needed for coalition-building. Across both surveys—and consistent with the Chicago Council surveys from Chapter 3—more than half of the respondents are doves. It is not a stretch, then, to view doves as a sufficiently large domestic group to warrant White House attention. In addition to their numbers, doves are also politically active and include groups otherwise important to electoral coalitions. Whatever their preferences, doves are a politically relevant group whom presidents are well-advised to persuade. This constituency thus has the potential to set meaningful incentives for the use of humanitarian claims.

Second, the chapter turned to the question: Who responds to humanitarian appeals? By varying whether participants read humanitarian justifications, security justifications, or a combination of the two and analyzing support across different foreign policy constituencies, the survey experiments provide a clear answer. Doves are the individuals who respond most strongly to humanitarian claims for military action, even when security justifications are also present. Hawks are supportive of military action across the board and isolationists offer support only when US security alone is at stake. Maximum support from doves is the political benefit leaders stand to gain by adding humanitarian claims to their speeches.

Third, having affirmed both the political relevance of doves and their unique sensitivity to humanitarian appeals, the chapter examined how humanitarian claims change the way individuals think about interventions. For doves, humanitarian appeals make it possible to think about intervention in other-regarding terms focused on protecting foreign civilians. These concerns resonate with the values and predispositions behind their cooperative preferences. By contrast, as long as a security justification was present, hawks and isolationists remained focused on eliminating security threats—adding humanitarian appeals to appease doves does not distract other groups from the security interests at stake. Across all foreign policy constituencies, however, humanitarian justifications did increase expectations that civilians would be safer by the end of the intervention. Increased expectations were most dramatic among hawks, consistent with their view of military force as an effective way to address problems. Notably, a minority of doves expected interventions justified in humanitarian terms to make civilians safer. Humanitarian claims temporarily override but do not eliminate doves' skepticism about the utility of military force as a policy tool.

In short, Chapter 4 highlights the unique benefits of humanitarian justifications. Only these claims can maximize the support of doves, who are a politically important group. This heightened support is necessary to build the broadest possible domestic coalition and presidents thus have a domestic incentive to include humanitarian claims in speeches about security crises. Does the power of humanitarian justifications mean leaders who use them wisely can manipulate public opinion at will? If strategically placed humanitarian claims allow leaders to broaden support and circumvent domestic constraints on military action, they could pose a threat to democratic accountability. Chapter 5 tackles these concerns directly with additional survey experiments that vary the perceived sincerity of humanitarian appeals.

5

Reasons for restraint

Broader coalitions create broader accountability

The power of humanitarian justifications resides in their ability to build the broadest possible domestic coalitions of support for military action. These benefits are desirable in the context of necessary, legitimate military interventions where leaders need help explaining the importance of action to the public. In more questionable cases of intervention, however, the domestic benefits of humanitarian appeals raise red flags about leaders' ability to manipulate public opinion and use humanitarian concerns as a pretext for illegitimate action. Nowhere were the potential risks of misused humanitarian claims more on display than in the US invasion of Iraq in 2003.

When George W. Bush (2002a) first listed Iraq as part of the "axis of evil" in 2002, he added the claim that "This is a regime that has already used poison gas to murder thousands of its own citizens, leaving the bodies of mothers huddled over their dead children" to his assertion that "Iraq continues to flaunt its hostility toward America and to support terror." References to Saddam Hussein's treatment of civilians were a common feature in official statements leading up to the US invasion of Iraq in March 2003. In fact, Bush (2002d) often included accusations that "Hussein's regime continues to support terrorist groups and to oppress its civilian population" in the same sentence, listing "supporting terrorist groups, repressing its own people, and pursuing weapons of mass destruction" as the combined reasons that the regime presented "a grave and gathering danger." Humanitarian justifications remained part of the administration's communication strategy throughout the duration of the war. After the intervention began, humanitarian appeals asserted that the Iraqi people had been liberated and claimed that had the US failed to act, "Iraq's torture chambers would still be filled with victims, terrified and innocent. The killing fields of Iraq, where hundreds of thousands of men and women and children vanished into the sands, would still be known only to the killers" (G. W. Bush 2004).

Doves into Hawks. Sarah Maxey, Oxford University Press. © Oxford University Press (2026).
DOI: 10.1093/9780197832738.003.0005

As it became clear that Iraq did not possess weapons of mass destruction and the security rationale for the invasion was faulty at best, human rights advocates rang alarm bells about the role that humanitarian arguments played in mobilizing support for US action. Chief among their concerns was that by evoking humanitarian claims as a false pretext for a questionable intervention, the Bush administration had eroded the future credibility of humanitarian appeals (Bellamy 2004). Gareth Evans (2004) outlined the logic behind this fear, noting "to the extent that the invasion was based on Saddam Hussein's record of tyranny over his own people [...] we have seen almost choked at birth what many were hoping was an emerging new norm of justifying intervention on the basis of the principle of 'responsibility to protect.'" The concern was not that the Bush administration lied about Saddam Hussein's past record of human rights abuses—which was well-documented—but that threats to civilians in Iraq did not intensify prior to the intervention, making it difficult to credibly claim that a supreme humanitarian emergency was the impetus for action (Wheeler 2000). Evans and others worried that evoking humanitarian concerns in this context would undermine future US attempts to mobilize the international community in response to mass atrocities. Inaction in the face of genocide in Darfur seemed to confirm these fears (Bellamy 2005).

On the surface, the experimental evidence from Chapter 4 also seems to confirm the worst-case scenario highlighted by critics of the US invasion of Iraq—that leaders who understand the strategic importance of humanitarian claims are emboldened to initiate and avoid accountability for military action. Assessing this risk requires a closer look at whether humanitarian appeals gain knee-jerk support from doves, regardless of the justification's credibility. To fully capture the implications of the experimental results for cases like the Iraq war, in this chapter I tackle the question: Is the power of humanitarian claims the power to deceive?

I argue that the answer is no. Instead, doves impose important limits on the effectiveness of humanitarian justifications that both facilitate democratic accountability and avoid the worst-case scenario raised in the aftermath of the Iraq war. Hawks impose similar limits on the effectiveness of security justifications. As a result, leaders who successfully mobilize broad coalitions of public support also increase opportunities for public accountability. This increased accountability explains the restraint in presidential justifications uncovered by Chapter 2. It also means that powerful humanitarian appeals are less problematic than critics initially feared.

The remainder of this chapter provides experimental evidence that there are public incentives for leaders to make sure that their justifications appear sincere and that these incentives limit how far presidents can stretch the truth. First, I outline the link between deception and democratic account- ability, reviewing theoretical expectations for how foreign policy constituen- cies influence the way individuals respond to misused humanitarian and security claims. Next, building on the surveys in Chapter 4, I present addi- tional experiments that vary the perceived sincerity of a president's humani- tarian and security justifications for military action. The results confirm that diverse domestic coalitions bolster democratic accountability, with doves both incentivizing *and* limiting the use of humanitarian appeals. Hawks and isolationists, by contrast, react more strongly to the misuse of security justifications. Including multiple groups in the domestic coalition expands opportunities for accountability—the support that good communication strategies mobilize is not a blank check.

The results are also sanguine in their implications for managing the risk of humanitarian pretext that appeared after the Iraq war. The survey experiments demonstrate that the misuse of humanitarian appeals does not significantly undermine public support for addressing future mass atrocities. Moreover, individuals are not willing to blindly accept humanitarian expla- nations for illegitimate interventions. Consistent with prominent apologies, policy changes, and the growth of an antiwar movement in the later stages of the Iraq war (Heaney and Rojas 2015), humanitarian concerns cannot sus- tain a coalition of support when the credibility of the broader operation is in question. The chapter concludes by discussing what these findings imply for democratic accountability for the use of force, finding room for optimism.

Deception and democratic accountability for military action

A key feature of democratic institutions is their ability to hold leaders accountable for what they say and do. The existence of a free press and marketplace of ideas offers checks on the credibility of leaders' claims and increases the likelihood that efforts to mislead the public will be exposed (Baum and Potter 2015). Reports of falsehoods both activate and amplify congressional dissent, providing the public with additional elite cues about the prudence of a decision (Berinsky 2007; Guisinger and Saunders 2017). When evidence of deception reaches the public, voters are expected to respond by withdrawing their support for the policy in question and by punishing the leader via lower approval and trust. The risk of public punishment—for both the president's election prospects and ability to pursue their domestic agenda (Gelpi and Grieco 2015; Kriner 2010; Tomz and Weeks 2013)—makes leaders think twice about lying and constrains their leeway for action.

In theory, these democratic institutions should be able to limit leaders' reliance on different types of misinformation, ranging from outright lies and deceit to the more common practice of spin and "crafted talk" (Jacobs and Shapiro 2000, 50). Schuessler (2015, 8) defines deception as "deliberate attempts on the part of leaders to mislead the public about the thrust of official thinking." Deceit can thus include tactics of blame-shifting—present in cases like the Gulf of Tonkin incident—where presidents "do their best to conceal the fact that they are actively considering war while seeking out provocations that shift the blame for hostilities onto the adversary" (Schuessler 2015, 3–4). It can also include overselling, exemplified by the case of Iraq 2003, where leaders inflate the level of threat "to convince the public that the stakes are high enough to justify the use of force" (Schuessler 2015, 3–4). Maxey (2021b) arranges these different forms of misinformation along a spectrum ranging from truth to spin to deceit and finds that the public reacts negatively to being misled to any degree.

Despite widespread recognition that misinformation plays a role in the domestic politics of military action, scholars disagree on the extent to which leaders can stretch the truth and get away with it. From the more optimistic, liberal institutionalist perspective, democratic institutions increase the risk of exposure to such an extent that even if leaders are "motivated to deceive in order to provide themselves more freedom of action in foreign policy," they will ultimately be "deterred from engaging in deception, especially deception over high salience matters like the initiation of war" (Reiter 2012, 595). Alternatively, if the public is ill-informed and unconcerned with foreign policy, deception appears both more effective and lower in risk. From this view, "It is reasonably easy for policymakers to lie to their publics" and, because policymakers can manipulate both the content and flow of information, "most people will be inclined to trust what their leaders tell them unless there is hard evidence that they are being deceived" (Mearsheimer 2011, 58). The middle ground in this debate contends that while political costs constrain leaders who would mislead the public, the extent to which these costs are prohibitive varies across outcomes and individuals.

As long as the operation is a success, the potential costs of deception are moderate enough for leaders to accept (Schuessler 2015). The political implications of these costs also depend on the president's party identification and electoral coalition—Republican presidents primarily concerned with their base have the most leeway for deception (Maxey 2021b).

While this chapter does not further adjudicate this debate, it is relevant for two reasons. First, the domestic coalition argument and experimental evidence from Chapter 4 identify an additional domestic incentive for deception: the necessity of humanitarian justifications for building broad coalitions of support for military action. The importance of these justifications means that leaders face domestic pressure to make a humanitarian case, even if one does not credibly exist. In response to this pressure, they have an incentive to stretch the truth of the impetus for military action. Second, evidence that deceptive rhetoric can—at least under some circumstances—help mobilize support for military action establishes the feasibility of concerns about humanitarian pretext. Deception in the context of humanitarian appeals carries additional negative consequences because it also threatens the future development of humanitarian intervention norms (Bellamy 2004; Evans 2004). The plausibility and gravity of these consequences depends on whether presidents who offer insincere humanitarian appeals are still able to build and sustain broad domestic coalitions of support.

Defining deceptive justifications

When applied to justifications for military action, "true" statements are difficult to classify. Interventions are almost always motivated by multiple concerns and objectives, giving communications teams many potential true statements from which to choose. For example, in the build-up to the Gulf War in 1991, George H. W. Bush's communications staff outlined a "spectrum of justifications" that ranged from rebuking aggression in the interest of world peace to maintaining access to oil (Pinkerton 1990). The administration ultimately chose to emphasize world peace and the rule of law, not because a speech about oil would be false, but because it gave the undesirable impression that the US was asking its soldiers to die for economic gain. Choosing to talk about one driver of intervention instead of another is strategic but not deceptive.

Instead, I reserve the term deception for cases in which the White House's public justifications are *perceived* to diverge from any true driver of military action. Perceptions of deceit can stem from justifications that overstate the importance of a particular factor or from justifications that create an impetus for action where one does not exist. In the context of humanitarian justifications, I distinguish between: (1) humanitarian claims that are overstated to bolster support for an intervention with a different but legitimate purpose, and (2) humanitarian appeals used to provide cover for an intervention which could not be legitimately justified on other grounds. Legitimate in this case refers narrowly to the two reasons force can be justified in line with both international law and the norms of the international community (Finnemore 2003): self-defense and threats to international peace and security, including humanitarian crises.

In the former "different but legitimate" category, presidents overstate the centrality of helping civilians in an intervention that is otherwise legitimate but driven by national security concerns. The leader appeals to human rights abuses that are realistic but may have taken place in the past or continued at a steady pace for a long period of time. Neither the humanitarian claim nor the underlying rationale for intervention is false, but humanitarian concerns are overstated, misplaced, and thus potentially perceived as insincere.[1] Speech drafts from the Gulf War, discussed in more detail in Chapter 6, demonstrate that the Bush administration anticipated perceptions of insincerity and backed away from referencing Saddam Hussein's past use of chemical weapons against his own citizens to explain the US intervention (McNally and Simon 1990). If Bush had instead insisted that the main reason for US participation in the Gulf War was to protect Iraqi civilians, this would exemplify the different but legitimate category.

Alternatively, the "different and illegitimate" category reflects the use of humanitarian appeals to make the case for an intervention that was not primarily driven by a humanitarian crisis and that could not be justified on other grounds. This category is designed to capture the worst-case scenario described in studies of humanitarian pretext—that because almost every country has some history of human rights abuses, the public resonance of humanitarian justifications could give leaders an effective cover

---

[1] Sincerity reflects the extent to which leaders are perceived to mean what they say. Credibility reflects the extent to which leaders' statements appear plausible given the history and other facts of the situation. I use these terms interchangeably. See Maxey (2021b) for evidence that the public evaluates mistakes and intentional misinformation in the same way.

for interventions that would not otherwise be considered legitimate. There are a wide range of illegitimate motivations for military action, from the personal to domestic political benefits to aggression. Personal motivations are consistent with critiques of the 2003 Iraq War, which focused on the number of George W. Bush administration members who were also present for the Gulf War, accusing these officials of wanting to finish the job or get revenge for Hussein's assassination attempt on George H. W. Bush in 1993 (Frontline 2014; R. Johnson 2002; J. Stein and Dickinson 2006). Domestic political benefits are consistent with the logic of diversionary war and cases like Clinton's 1998 bombing of alleged terrorist targets in Sudan and Afghanistan in the build up to his impeachment trial (Oakes 2012, 1). Aggression is exemplified by Putin's failed attempts to use accusations of genocide and humanitarian disaster to create a pretext for invading Ukraine in 2022 (Berg 2023; Pomeranz 2022; Reid 2022). In the experimental scenarios that follow, I focus on the misuse of humanitarian justifications as a cover for illegitimate interventions that primarily serve the president's own political agenda. While it is only one of many illegitimate motivations, this scenario captures a common form of pretext that is feasible to the members of the US public who completed the survey.

This distinction between the misuse of humanitarian justifications in legitimate and illegitimate interventions is key to understanding the threat that deceptive humanitarian claims pose to democratic accountability and the future development of humanitarian norms. If misleading humanitarian claims bolster support only for interventions that are otherwise legitimate, they give leaders an additional tool for navigating domestic constraints on the use of force but do not change the broader pattern of military engagement—there still needs to be some credible rationale for an intervention to take place. Alternatively, if deceptive humanitarian claims allow presidents to pursue and avoid punishment for interventions that could not otherwise be justified, the threat of humanitarian pretext raised during the Iraq war is valid and cause for significant concern.

To capture this distinction, the survey experiments described later in this chapter vary both expert agreement with the president's justifications and the legitimacy of the underlying intervention. The information that casts doubt on statements from the White House and builds perceptions of deceit comes from other actors in the democratic marketplace of ideas including political elites and the media, as well as civil society groups.

Theoretical expectations: Deception in the domestic coalition

Deception, like justifications, resonates differently across foreign policy constituencies. Across constituencies, I expect that the same factors that drive an individual's support for intervention will also generate the most backlash when they appear to be misused. Doves are thus expected to be most sensitive to the misuse of humanitarian claims, while hawks and isolationists will be more sensitive to misinformation surrounding security rationales. As a result, a broad coalition of support creates more opportunities for democratic accountability to work. While examining variation across constituencies and justifications, I pay particular attention to how individuals react to the misuse of humanitarian appeals for two reasons. First, these justifications are the subject of historical concerns about an overly emotional, permissive public. Second, they are the target of contemporary critiques related to the potentially negative side effects of the Responsibility to Protect and other humanitarian intervention norms.

Accountability for humanitarian statements

In Chapter 3, I identified doves as the members of domestic coalitions who are sensitive to other-regarding concerns and skeptical of military force. This combination of concern and skepticism makes doves uniquely responsive to humanitarian appeals. Chapter 4 confirms that humanitarian claims are necessary to maximize support from this group. Humanitarian explanations persuade doves in ways that security justifications cannot because encouraging these individuals to think about civilians helps override their skepticism towards the use of force—intervention may not work, but if it could save lives, it is worth a try.

Because the prospect of helping civilians is central to doves' support for military action, I also expect that their support will decrease when the sincerity of humanitarian claims is in doubt. Without an other-regarding lens for the intervention, there is no counterpoint to doves' skepticism towards military force and leaders will have a difficult time keeping this group in the domestic coalition. Their interest in helping civilians also means that doves are attentive to information about humanitarian developments and likely to notice elite accounts that contradict the president on these terms.

Evidence from Chapter 4 that doves are willing to take political action to express their opinions makes it plausible that a drop in this group's support will translate into active opposition, creating political problems for the president. In the Iraq case, these are likely the individuals who supported the war in 2003 but mobilized against it by 2008 (Heaney and Rojas 2015).

In short, a president who stretches humanitarian justifications too far in a security crisis—either by overstating their centrality or using them as a cover for illegitimate action—risks substantial backlash from the same group these claims persuade. The central role doves play in forming broad domestic coalitions means that losing their approval carries significant political risks for leaders. By imposing political costs, doves' role in the domestic coalition creates a deterrent against humanitarian pretext. The experiments that follow demonstrate that the risk of backlash from doves is credible. Chapter 6 then shows that presidential speeches exercise restraint and avoid stretching humanitarian appeals too far because the White House anticipates and is deterred by potential backlash from this group.

Accountability for security statements

Does doves' focus on humanitarian statements mean that leaders can instead use deceptive security rationales? If doves were the only members of the domestic coalition, presidents would have more leeway to misuse security justifications, but these individuals are only one part of the equation. Instead, the importance of building a broad internationalist coalition means that leaders also need the support of hawks and, to a lesser extent, isolationists. I expect these two groups to provide accountability for security justifications.

Where doves focus on other-regarding concerns, hawks have a baseline belief that military force is an effective way to achieve foreign policy goals. Chapter 4 shows that even when humanitarian claims are present, hawks remain focused on the importance of protecting US national security. Isolationists are unlikely coalition members, but also focus on security objectives, consistent with evidence that they support intervention only in the face of direct threats to the national interest (Herrmann, Tetlock, and Visser 1999). By the same logic outlined for doves, I expect both hawks and isolationists to pay the most attention to information about the security objectives of an intervention, including areas in which elite accounts contradict the president's security rationales. While insincere humanitarian claims do not change how these groups evaluate the intervention, evidence of insincere security explanations leads hawks and isolationists to question and lower their support for military action. Leaders who misuse security justifications should expect backlash primarily from these two groups.

As introduced in Chapter 3, the link between foreign policy constituencies and reactions to the misuse of different justifications generates hypothesis four and its components:

H4: *When the preference-consistent justification is challenged, support decreases among the relevant group.*

H4a: *Challenging humanitarian justifications decreases support among doves.*

H4b: *Challenging security justifications decreases support among hawks.*

H4c: *Challenging security justifications decreases support among isolationists.*

Deceptive justifications in the survey experiments

This chapter uses an experimental approach to capture how members of different foreign policy constituencies respond to the misuse of humanitarian and security claims. When it comes to capturing reactions to deceptive claims, an experimental approach is both helpful and necessary. If accusations of misleading the public carry high political costs, presidents may anticipate and intentionally avoid these costs, making it difficult to capture public backlash in observational data. Experimental methods avoid this form of selection bias (Tomz 2007, 822) and make it possible to isolate and identify any public disincentives that may stop presidents from stretching humanitarian claims too far. Chapter 6 then turns to cases of intervention to evaluate whether leaders recognize and adhere to these public constraints.

Survey two, initially introduced in Chapter 4, is designed to test hypothesis four and its components. The survey varies both the justifications the president used to make the case for intervention and the extent to which experts provided information that contradicted official statements, raising the possibility of deceit. I fielded this survey to 1512 US adults using Amazon's Mechanical Turk (MTurk) in July 2016. As previously noted, MTurk samples are shown to produce treatment effects comparable to national samples (Berinsky, Huber, and Lenz 2012; Coppock 2019; Weinberg, Freese, and McElhattan 2014). Additionally, Chapter 4 validates this specific MTurk sample by using it to replicate the main results from the national survey. The results confirm that the survey produces comparable and meaningful treatment effects. The measures of foreign policy constituencies and other demographic questions remain the same and are described in detail in Chapter 4.

Varying levels of deceptive claims

The survey begins by assigning participants to read excerpts from a hypothetical president's national address. As before, the president explains that "Over the last few months, a violent conflict has developed in the country of Numar" and then makes the case for a US military response. The text of this address is randomized so that participants read about one of the three rationales for military action: security, humanitarian, or a combination of the two. The security claims reference a terrorist threat, described in Chapter 4's discussion of the survey.

Following the president's address, the survey presented participants with information from experts who either publicly agreed with or disputed the official justifications for military action. In the *true* conditions, experts agreed with the president's stated rationale for the conflict and the scenario does not evoke perceptions of deception. In the following conditions, the content of expert disagreement captures two levels of deceptive justifications based on whether the intervention is ultimately considered legitimate or illegitimate. The first type of deception, referred to as the *different but legitimate* conditions, captures cases in which experts challenge the leader's main rationale for action, but maintain that the "real" reason for intervention is legitimate. For example, participants assigned to humanitarian justifications and the different but legitimate condition read that "After the President's address, most experts publicly disputed the President's reasons for intervention. They thought that, instead of concern for civilians, the real motivation for the US action was to protect US security."

The second type of deception, captured by the *different and illegitimate* conditions, reflects a president who tries to make the case for intervention where no legitimate reasons for action exist. These conditions most closely approximate concerns about humanitarian pretext—that leaders could use humanitarian appeals to initiate interventions for which there is no legitimate underlying rationale. Participants assigned to both humanitarian justifications and the different and illegitimate condition read that, "After the President's address, most experts publicly disputed the President's reasons for intervention. They thought that protecting Numar's civilians was a story to cover up the President's own political agenda." The three justification conditions and deception conditions are fully crossed to produce the ten treatments described in Table 5.1 below.

Table 5.1 Experimental conditions for survey two

After the President's address, most experts...

	Security	*Humanitarian*	*Combined*
True	(1)...publicly agreed with the President's reasons for intervention. They, too, thought US action would protect US security.	(2)...publicly agreed with the President's reasons for intervention. They, too, thought US action would protect Numar's civilians.	(3)...publicly agreed with the President's reasons for intervention. They, too, thought US action would protect Numar's civilians and US security.
Different but legitimate	(4)...publicly disputed the President's reasons for intervention. They thought that, instead of concern for US security, the real motivation for the US action was to protect Numar's civilians.	(5)...publicly disputed the President's reasons for intervention. They thought that, instead of concern for civilians, the real motivation for the US action was to protect US security.	...publicly disputed the President's reasons for intervention. They thought that, instead of concern for [(6) civilians/(7) US security], the real motivation for the US action was to protect [(6) US security/ (7) Numar's civilians].
Different and illegitimate	(8)...publicly disputed the President's reasons for intervention. They thought that protecting US security was a story to cover up the President's own political agenda.	(9)...publicly disputed the President's reasons for intervention. They thought that protecting Numar's civilians was a story to cover up the President's own political agenda.	(10)...publicly disputed the President's reasons for intervention. They thought that protecting Numar's civilians and US security was a story to cover up the President's own political agenda.

The design of this survey also makes it possible to evaluate whether offering multiple explanations for intervention reduces the risks of deception. In addition to broadening the domestic coalition, providing both humanitarian and security justifications for military action makes it possible for the leader to tell "half-truths." The logic here is that as long as one part of the justification remains true, the consequences of misusing the other justification are reduced because the president still mostly told the truth. Identifying the level of deception at which public backlash kicks in helps clarify its implications for democratic accountability and assess the risk of humanitarian pretext. To this end, I further divide the deception treatments in the combined justification conditions into three groups: (1) experts confirm the security explanation but cast doubt on the humanitarian justification, (2) experts confirm the humanitarian explanation but cast doubt on the security justification, or (3) experts cast doubt on both the security and humanitarian justifications. These categories correspond to conditions six, seven, and ten in Table 5.1.

Why experts?

Justifications for military action are ripe for deception because, given the president's information advantage, there is a high burden of proof required to demonstrate that an intervention did not respond to a stated goal. This information imbalance also makes it challenging to design accurate and valid experimental manipulations. Providing survey participants with smoking gun evidence that the president intentionally lied about the impetus for intervention would be unrealistic in this context and undermine the experiment's external validity. For example, even in the case of Iraq 2003—the intervention most subject to accusations of deception in recent history— the extent to which the Bush administration knew beyond a shadow of a doubt that Saddam Hussein did not possess weapons of mass destruction and the magnitude of their intent to mislead the public remain topics of debate.

Explicitly telling participants that the experts' account of the intervention is accurate and that the president's claims are false is also problematic. Scholars point to the public's inherent trust in the White House to handle issues of national security as a key factor that creates a permissive environment for deception (Mearsheimer 2011; Western 2005, 17). Trust in the president is thus an important potential mediator of the relationship between perceived deception and support. Given this relationship, directly telling participants who to trust would be both unrealistic and risk biasing the results.

Instead, the survey gives participants information about presidential and expert opinions and allows individuals to decide who to trust. The experiment uses information about expert opinions to cast doubt on the president's account because this is the mechanism through which studies of democratic constraints expect institutions to deter deception. The presence of a free press, combined with media coverage of interventions that amplifies elite cues, exposes attempts to mislead the public (Baum and Potter 2015; Berinsky 2007; Reiter 2012; Saunders 2015). Hearing that there are alternative explanations or ulterior motives for the intervention then causes individuals to reevaluate their support. Presenting survey participants with the president's justification for action alongside the response and alternative account of experts reflects this hypothesized democratic process.

The scenario also tells participants that "most experts" publicly agreed with or disputed the president's explanation for military action. Experts come in many different forms and the public trusts the expertise of individuals for different reasons (Lupton and Webb 2022). Presenting an expert consensus reduces the risk that respondents will view the critique as a partisan strategy and assume that it only includes members of the opposition party.

Finally, I present experts' alternative account of the military intervention to separate disagreement over the rationale for action from opposition to the intervention itself. For example, in the different but legitimate condition, respondents presented with humanitarian claims are told that experts believe that the president is concerned with national security rather than foreign civilians. They are not told whether experts approve or disapprove of the security-driven intervention. This approach helps distinguish the effects of the president's deception from the effects of expert opposition.

Capturing the costs of deception

If the public deters deception, it does so by imposing political costs on leaders who make misleading statements. These costs can come in the form of short-term changes in support for the intervention, as well as medium-term changes in the president's reputation and reelection prospects. Humanitarian advocates worry about a third, longer-term cost: reduced support for future humanitarian interventions. The survey's follow-up questions shed light on all three dimensions of political costs and on how an individual's willingness to impose these costs varies across foreign policy constituencies.

First, to investigate whether perceptions of deceit undermine the benefits of humanitarian justifications, I examine changes in support for the intervention. Second, I use two questions to evaluate the effect of perceived deception on different aspects of the president's reputation. I ask participants to rate their level of agreement with the statement, "I approve of the way the President handled the situation in Numar." To probe political costs of deceit more directly, I also asked "If the hypothetical President were running for reelection, how likely would you be to vote for him?"

Finally, I evaluate the risk that deceptive humanitarian claims pose to future humanitarian interventions by including information about a new crisis at the very end of the survey. By way of instruction, participants read that "Now we are going to describe another situation this hypothetical President faced about a year after taking military action in Numar." The scenario that followed included statements from the hypothetical president who now was making the case for intervention in response to an ongoing genocide. The text of this statement combines rhetoric used by multiple real presidents to condemn genocides in Rwanda, Bosnia, and Sudan, as well as more recent humanitarian crises in Libya and Syria. In his address to the nation about this humanitarian crisis, the hypothetical president said:

> My fellow Americans, tonight I have received gruesome evidence that genocide is taking place in Rundu. Innocent civilians, including women and children, are being massacred in their homes by neighbors who support Rundu's government. The United States cannot be the world's police force, but when we can stop children from being killed in their own homes, we have a responsibility to act. This is why, after careful deliberation, I have determined the United States must respond to this crisis with military action.

Following this statement, respondents reported their support or opposition to the proposed US military action. They were also asked whether they would trust the president to handle this situation and whether they believed the president described the situation in Rundu accurately. Comparing responses to these questions across different justifications and levels of deception is a first step towards understanding the consequences for the future of humanitarian intervention. If, as critics fear, leaders' abuse of humanitarian appeals creates skepticism towards future justifications and undercuts responses to mass atrocities, support for intervention and both measures of trust in the president will be lower for participants assigned to read a deceptive humanitarian statement in the earlier scenario. I expect this effect to be especially pronounced among doves, because their support turns on humanitarian considerations and because they are more likely to have been attentive to and remember the problems with the earlier humanitarian statement.

Notably, asking people to evaluate a current scenario and then think years into the future in a single survey is a heavy cognitive lift which limits the scope of the findings. For example, people are less likely to remember the details and critiques of a previous intervention when there are years instead of minutes between crises. Even significant differences between the experimental conditions could therefore be washed out in the time between real crises. Given this limitation, there are still two reasons why a cautious interpretation of these results is worthwhile. First, many high-profile cases of humanitarian inaction did develop simultaneously or on the heels of other international crises. The failure of US operations in Somalia is often cited as a contributing factor to inaction in Rwanda the following year, the horrors of the Rwandan genocide created additional pressure for action in Bosnia, and long-lasting military operations in Iraq and Afghanistan overlapped with evidence of genocide in Sudan in 2003 (Bellamy 2005; Western and Goldstein 2011). Past interventions thus influence public perceptions of current interventions in the real world and on a short timeline. Second, the experimental design offers insightful results as long as they are interpreted as the most likely case for observing negative effects on support for future humanitarian interventions. If evidence that the same president recently misused humanitarian claims does not undermine the support or trust of respondents—especially doves—in this controlled and condensed environment, then there is less reason to worry that insincere humanitarian appeals will weaken humanitarian intervention norms in the real world.

The staying power of presidential statements

Two additional follow-up questions gauged the sticking power of the president's statement, consistent with expectations that the White House has both the public's trust and significant information advantages in the context of international affairs. The first question captured the extent to which individuals continued to believe the president even when exposed to information that contradicted the official account of the intervention. It asked survey participants how much they agreed or disagreed that, "The President described the situation in Numar accurately." There is a baseline willingness to believe the president—74 percent of people in the true conditions thought his account was accurate. As expected, perceptions of accuracy declined significantly in the presence of expert disagreement. In the different but legitimate conditions, 57 percent of participants continued to believe that the president's claims were accurate. This proportion further drops to include only 50 percent of respondents when the intervention is illegitimate. This evidence that a narrow majority of people believed that the president was accurate, even in the face of strong expert disagreement, speaks to the magnitude of public trust in the executive when it comes to military action.

To better understand why some individuals continued to believe the president, an additional question captured assumptions about the president's motives. The question asked, "Which of the following do you think is the most important reason the President decided to take military action?" Participants could choose from a list that included protecting the people of Numar, protecting US security, demonstrating US strength, upholding international standards, and protecting the president's own political agenda. In Figure 5.1, I focus on the proportion of respondents who selected protecting the people of Numar, US security, or the president's political agenda because these motivations correspond most closely to the justifications offered in the survey and highlight the effectiveness of the manipulation.[2] The full results are included in the appendix.

Starting with the top row of Figure 5.1, when experts agreed with the president, the plurality of perceived motivations matched the White House statement. Moving from left to right, 58 percent in the true security conditions saw the president as primarily trying to protect US security, while 44 percent of respondents in the true humanitarian conditions thought the president was most concerned with protecting civilians. Notably, when the president combined true humanitarian and security justifications, 47 percent of

---

[2] The survey also concluded with two formal manipulation checks. The first asked, "To the best of your recollection, what points did the President use to explain the military action in Numar?" Across all conditions, at least 75 percent of survey participants correctly remembered the content of the president's statement. The second focused on the deceit manipulations, asking, "To the best of your recollection, did experts agree with the President?" 94 percent of respondents in the true conditions and 82 percent in the two deceit conditions correctly remembered whether experts agreed with the president.

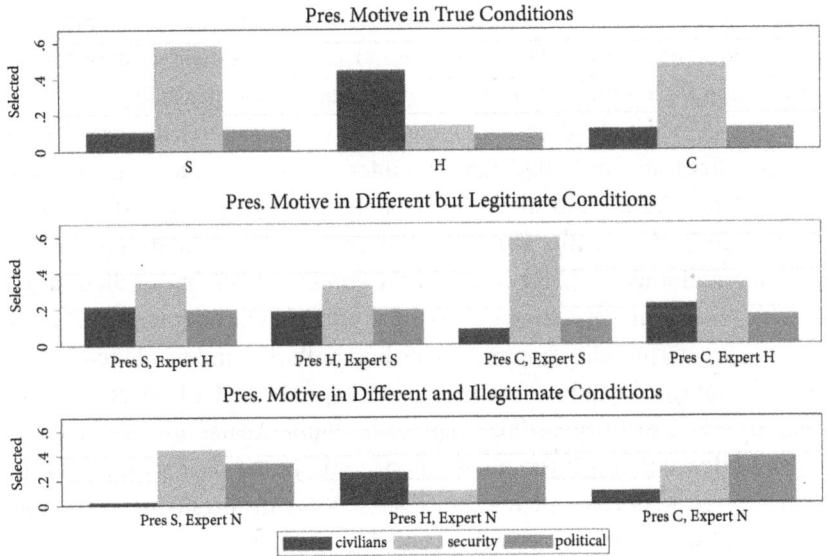

S: Security Rationale, H: Humanitarian Rationale, C: Combined Rationale, N: No legitimate rationale.

Figure 5.1 Assumptions about the president's motive for intervention

people thought the president's main motive was protecting national security compared to 12 percent who thought protecting civilians was the most
important reason for action. This pattern holds even among doves (45 percent protecting security, 12 percent protecting civilians). Leaders who add
humanitarian claims do not risk appearing weak on national security or distract attention from their security goals. Even the individuals who care most
about protecting civilians in their own evaluation of the intervention expect
the White House to prioritize security concerns.

Moving to the different but legitimate conditions in the second row of
Figure 5.1, when the president used humanitarian justifications but experts
said the intervention was really about protecting US security (second condition), 33 percent of participants thought security motives were the most
important. Similarly, moving right within the row, when the president
combined humanitarian and security claims but experts agreed with only
the security appeal, 59 percent thought security was the president's main
motive compared to 9 percent who thought humanitarian concerns were
predominant. While expert opinions influence perceptions of humanitarian
justifications, there is also evidence that security claims have more sticking
power in the face of expert disagreement. When the president used security

claims, or a combination of security and humanitarian claims, the plurality of respondents continued to view national security as the president's main motivation for action—even when experts suggested otherwise.

Turning to the third row of Figure 5.1, when experts disagreed with the president and indicated that the intervention was illegitimate, more respondents shifted into the political motive category. From left to right, 34 percent in the security conditions, 30 percent of people in the humanitarian conditions, and 38 percent in the combined conditions viewed the president as primarily acting on personal political considerations. Ulterior motives are the plurality response in the humanitarian and combined conditions. Notably, adding humanitarian claims does not offer leaders a helpful back-up when security justifications are in doubt. Again, however, there is some evidence that security justifications stick. In the security-only condition, 45 percent of respondents continued to think the president was mainly concerned with national security even when experts claimed there was no credible threat.

Examining public assumptions about the president's motives highlights the importance of official statements, even in the face of elite disagreement. People remember and assume that there is some sincerity behind how presidents make the case for intervention. People also assume that the president is prioritizing national security with very few exceptions—in all but four of the ten conditions, a plurality of respondents thought the president had national security in mind, even when experts suggested an alternative motive. The pattern of assumed motives is particularly interesting when compared with the analysis of individual motivations for support from Chapter 4. While protecting foreign civilians was an important reason for individual support, respondents expect the White House to think differently and prioritize national security.

The results in Figure 5.1 also provide initial evidence that security explanations are more robust to criticism than humanitarian appeals. In only three of the ten conditions did a plurality of respondents side with the experts' account over the president's statement,[3] all three of which included

---

[3] The effect of expert disagreement with the president could be further moderated by both the type of expert—including whether they are seen as a partisan or nonpartisan source—and overall public confidence in expert advice. There is an ongoing debate over the extent to which "expertise is dead" in contemporary politics (see Lupton and Webb (2022) for an overview of perspectives and evidence that the influence of experts varies across vocations). I would expect that further declines in public confidence would increase deference to the president's account across conditions—including reducing attention to experts in the humanitarian conditions where it is currently stronger—and

a humanitarian justification either alone or in combination with security concerns. This pattern is consistent with the expectation that humanitarian justifications create opportunities for accountability. Next, I examine responses to expert disagreement in more detail, evaluating (1) who reacts most strongly to the misuse of different justifications and (2) the long-term consequences for both presidents and the practice of humanitarian intervention.

Results: Are the effects of misuse the same for all justifications?

To understand what the domestic power of humanitarian justifications implies for their potential misuse, the first step is to determine whether individuals respond to evidence that presidents made insincere humanitarian statements. Using the aggregate sample, Figure 5.2 illustrates the

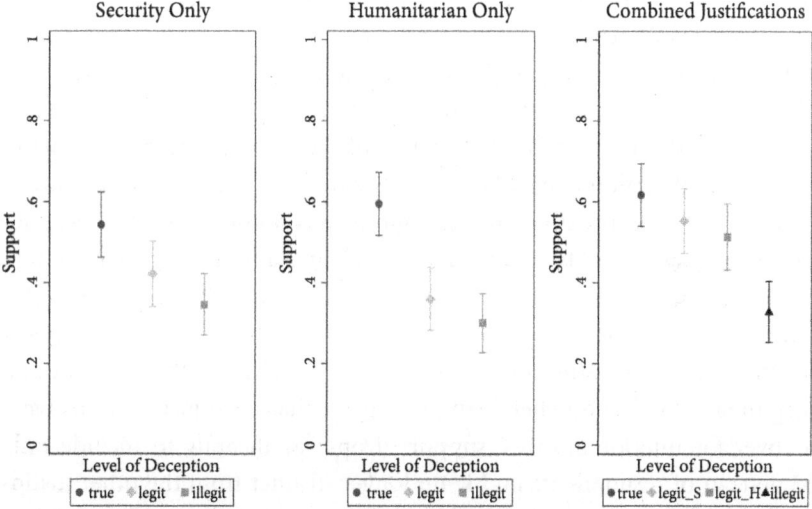

Figure 5.2 Effect of deception on support by justification

The legitimate combined justification condition varied expert disagreement with one claim at a time. In the legit_S condition, experts disagree with the humanitarian justification and think that the intervention is really about protecting US security. In the legit_H condition, experts disagree with the claim that intervention is about protecting civilians.

that nonpartisan experts would be generally seen as more credible than partisan experts. Among partisan experts, consistent with work on elite cues (Guisinger and Saunders 2017), the effect of new information is likely to depend on the polarization of the conflict.

effect of increasing deception on support for an intervention explained with each type of justification. Leaders face political costs for deception across justifications. In the security justification conditions, support drops from 54 percent in the true condition, to 42 percent in the different but legitimate condition, to 35 percent in the different and illegitimate condition.[4]

Support for humanitarian justifications also drops significantly when experts cast doubt on the president's statement. In the true condition, 59 percent of respondents supported the intervention. In the different but legitimate condition, support for humanitarian claims drops to 36 percent and further to 30 percent in the different and illegitimate condition. These changes are statistically significant relative to the true condition, but the legitimate and illegitimate conditions are not significantly different from each other. Presidents who misuse humanitarian claims as a cover for other motivations should expect to face political costs when this insincerity is exposed. Notably, humanitarian justifications are not unique in this regard—neither humanitarian nor security rationales alone insulate presidents from the costs of deception.

Leaders do, however, gain some insulation from these costs when they combine humanitarian and security concerns. The combined justifications, displayed in the right-hand panel of Figure 5.2, gain the support of 62 percent of respondents when experts agree with all parts of the president's account. In the different but legitimate conditions, support declines to 55 percent when the humanitarian claims appear insincere and to 51 percent when the security claim appears insincere.[5] Compared to different but legitimate conditions that used a single justification, support for the combined justifications is significantly higher. In the different and illegitimate condition, where experts suggest that both justifications were a cover for ulterior motives, support drops significantly to include only 33 percent of respondents and is no longer distinct from the other justification conditions. Using multiple justifications at once gives the president some room to diverge from the truth of either claim, but not from both at once.

---

[4] The decline in support for both the legitimate and illegitimate conditions is statistically significant relative to the true condition. These conditions are not, however, significantly different from each other.

[5] Comparing support in the true combined condition to the legitimate security condition does not reach conventional levels of statistical significance. The difference between the true condition and the legitimate humanitarian condition is statistically significant at the $p < 0.1$ level.

Who responds to misuse?

The results presented in Figure 5.2 demonstrate that the public generally holds presidents accountable for what they say—when experts cast
doubt on the president's explanation, the public imposes political costs by
withdrawing its support. These political costs only deter deception, however, if they are imposed by important members of the domestic coalition.
Figure 5.3 illustrates the effect of expert disagreement on support, dividing
respondents by foreign policy constituencies and their assigned justification
conditions.[6] This closer look reveals that different groups of individuals hold
leaders accountable for different types of statements. Democratic accountability for the use of force is strengthened when the domestic coalition has
diverse membership.

The top row of Figure 5.3 shows the effect of misusing each type of justification in the different but legitimate conditions, dividing respondents into
the same hawk, dove, and isolationist categories that were used in Chapter 4.
The bottom row highlights the disaggregated effect of deception on support
in the different and illegitimate conditions. Comparing the two rows sheds
light on how groups react to increasing perceptions of deception.

Turning first to the bottom row and moving from left to right, both
hawks and doves significantly reduce their support for intervention when
leaders appear motivated only by their own political agenda. Isolationists
do not offer significantly lower support in the different and illegitimate
conditions—in part because of their small numbers—but the magnitude of
their support drops to 12 percent in the security conditions, 7 percent in
the humanitarian conditions, and 18 percent in the combined conditions.
Neither security nor humanitarian justifications, nor their combination,
allow leaders to bolster support among any foreign policy constituency for
an intervention without a legitimate underlying cause.

Moving to the different but legitimate conditions in the top row of
Figure 5.3, the results reveal that different foreign policy constituencies
respond to the more moderate misuse of justifications in distinct ways. First,
consistent with hypothesis 4b, accountability for security justifications is
enforced by hawks. When experts disagreed with the president's security
rationale for action and suggested that the intervention was really motivated by a humanitarian crisis, hawks' support dropped from 82 percent

---

[6] Figure 5.3 uses a subset of the survey data reported in Maxey (2020).

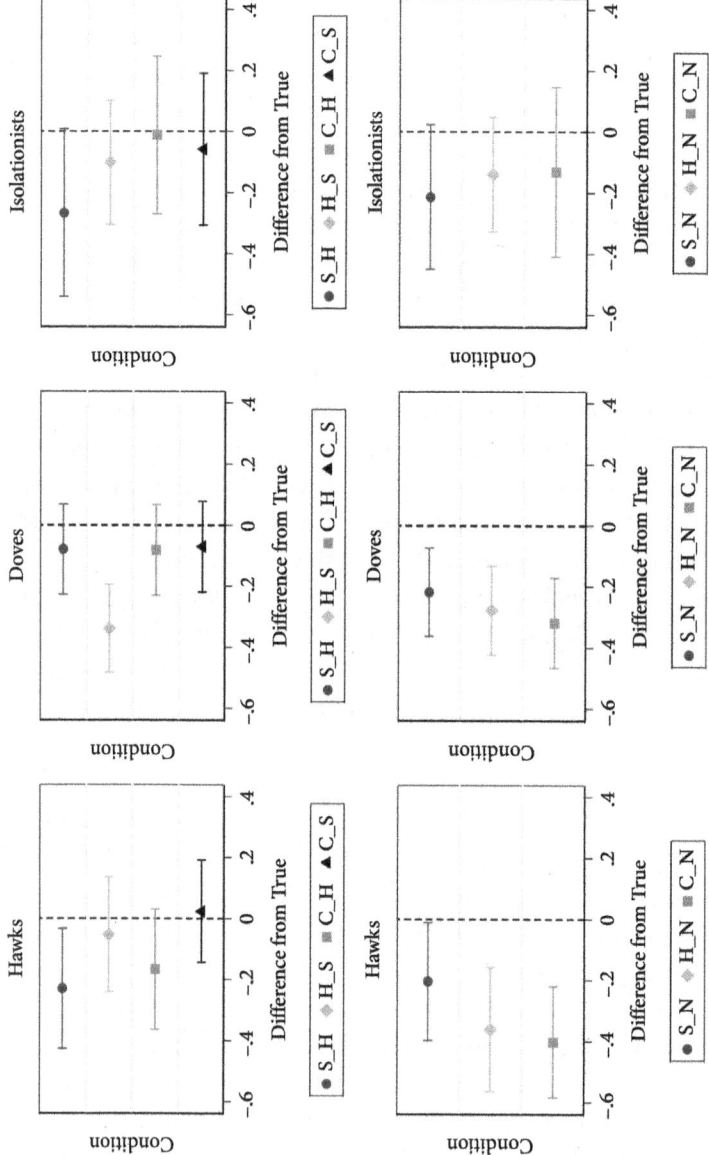

Figure 5.3 The effect of deception by justification and constituency

Figures report treatment effects for the deception condition relative to the true condition. Negative effects indicate reduced support for intervention. The first letter denotes the president's justification, second letter denotes experts' response. H: Humanitarian, S: Security, C: Combined, and N: No legitimate rationale.

to 59 percent in the security justification conditions and from 83 percent to 67 percent in the combined justification conditions. When statements about national security appear insincere, presidents stand to lose a substantial portion of support from the most reliable members of the domestic coalition. The same is not true for insincere humanitarian claims, which did not significantly influence hawks' support in the different but legitimate conditions. Consistent with hypothesis 4c, isolationists responded to evidence of deception in similar ways—reacting negatively to the misuse of security justifications and disregarding the misuse of humanitarian justifications. The substantive significance of this change is muted, however, because this group is a small and less reliable source of support than hawks.

Fortunately, hawks' relative lack of concern with insincere humanitarian claims does not mean that leaders have more leeway to misuse humanitarian justifications. Instead, consistent with hypothesis 4a, accountability for humanitarian rhetoric comes from doves. When the president offered humanitarian justifications but experts claimed that the intervention was really focused on security objectives, doves' support declined by 34 percentage points relative to the true humanitarian condition to include only 27 percent of respondents. The importance of keeping doves in the domestic coalition is a strong deterrent against humanitarian pretext. Leaders who present an intervention as primarily humanitarian and are accused of focusing on security goals risk a significant loss of support.

Presidents' hands are not, however, inevitably tied. While doves strongly rebuke presidents who stretch humanitarian claims too far—by casting national security operations as primarily humanitarian interventions—they are more forgiving of leaders who add humanitarian appeals alongside security justifications. In the combined justifications conditions, 60 percent of doves supported intervention if the president appeared to tell the truth. When experts cast doubt on the humanitarian claim, 53 percent of doves supported intervention, and when experts questioned the security claim, 52 percent maintained their support.[7] In these disagree but legitimate conditions, support for combined justifications remains significantly higher than support for either humanitarian or security justifications alone.

Doves' reactions to misused humanitarian justifications set boundaries around the power of these claims that would not exist if only hawks supported humanitarian appeals. Chapter 4 showed that offering

---

[7] Neither of these changes approaches conventional levels of statistical significance.

a humanitarian explanation for military action—even when US security is at stake—is key to broadening the domestic coalition of support. Leaders looking to bolster the support of an internationalist coalition are thus incentivized to include humanitarian statements in their speeches about intervention. The findings presented in Figure 5.3 show that leaders are also well-advised to use humanitarian claims carefully, consistent with the pattern of restraint uncovered in Chapter 2. Humanitarian appeals cannot provide the sole cover for interventions that primarily address security crises or that lack a legitimate motivation. Leaders who attempt to stretch humanitarian appeals too far in this regard will be punished by the same individuals the claims are intended to persuade. Leaders can, however, add humanitarian justifications to their stated security explanations with minimum risk, as long as at least one of the rationales maintains the appearance of sincerity. This moderate allowance for misuse falls short of an ideal form of democratic accountability, but assuages concerns about humanitarian pretext and identifies clear limits on how far leaders can stretch the truth without facing political punishment.

Do misleading leaders face political punishment?

Evidence of reduced public support alone carries significant political risks for leaders. As Chapter 3 outlines, without the public on their side, presidents will have a hard time pursuing other items on their political agenda and face increasing opposition from other political elites. In this section, I show that the consequences for leaders are even more direct. Negative public reactions to deception extend beyond the specific intervention to reflect a general loss of confidence in the president. These reactions are again different across foreign policy constituencies.

Survey two included two questions to capture the breadth of political punishment individuals inflict on leaders who misrepresent military action. The first asked participants whether they approved of how the president handled the situation in Numar, and the second asked how likely they would be to support the president's reelection. There are, of course, a number of factors that influence vote choice and the salience of foreign policy issues varies across elections (Aldrich, Sullivan, and Borgida 1989). In the experimental context, changes in the overall level of approval or support are informative for gauging the magnitude of political risk, even if they are only one of many factors that matter in actual elections.

Both approval of the president and reelection prospects suffer in the face of deceptive justifications. Where 64 percent of participants approved of the president in the true conditions, approval included only 50 percent of individuals in the different but legitimate conditions and 39 percent in the different and illegitimate conditions. Similarly, 61 percent of respondents were willing to support the president's reelection when he appeared to tell the truth but a minority of participants supported reelection when experts cast doubt on the president's statement (48 and 38 percent, respectively).[8]

Consistent with the pattern of support for military action, both hawks and doves view the president more negatively in the different and illegitimate conditions. Again, however, in the different but legitimate conditions, hawks primarily inflict punishment for misused security justifications while doves penalize the misuse of humanitarian justifications. Hawks approve of how the president handled the situation in significantly lower numbers when experts cast doubt on the sincerity of security claims (87 percent approval in the true condition, compared to 61 percent in the different but legitimate condition, $p < 0.01$). Their view of the president is not significantly affected by the perceived misuse of humanitarian appeals (82 percent true to 70 percent different but legitimate, $p = 0.18$). Doves, by contrast, significantly and negatively adjust their view of the president when humanitarian justifications are misused (63 percent in the true condition, 38 percent in the different but legitimate, $p < 0.01$). This same pattern also appears in hawks' and doves' willingness to reelect the president.

Presidents who misrepresent the impetus for military action risk not only support for the intervention itself, but also their own political futures. If the domestic coalition did not include both hawks and doves, leaders would have more leeway to misuse both security and humanitarian appeals—broad domestic coalitions also broaden democratic accountability for the use of force.

Partisanship and the limits of accountability

Partisanship has the potential to complicate these opportunities for accountability, tempering individuals' willingness to punish presidents from their

---

[8] These differences in approval and support all reach conventional levels of statistical significance.

own party. In related work (Maxey 2021b), I find that Republicans' support for copartisan presidents is robust to evidence that the White House stretched the truth about the reasons for military intervention, while Democrats punish even copartisans. Republican presidents thus have relatively more leeway to misuse justifications. Combining the partisan distributions of foreign policy constituencies from Chapter 4 with this chapter's finding that accountability comes from different sources adds depth to this dynamic.

When Republican presidents misuse humanitarian justifications, they may avoid punishment from the 38 percent of Republicans who are doves but they will still face backlash from the 69 percent of Democrats and 44 percent of independents with dovish priorities. Conditional on a marginal concern with independents or bipartisan support, doves still disincentivize Republican presidents from stretching humanitarian claims too far. Accountability for security justifications, on the other hand, stems primarily from hawks, who make up 49 percent of the Republican party. Again, though, Republican presidents concerned about winning over independents or building bipartisan support still risk backlash from roughly half of the hawks in the domestic audience. In an extreme case in which no Republicans are willing to punish a copartisan president, accountability for humanitarian justifications and especially security justifications is weakened, but not eliminated.

In work that uses a similar experimental design (Maxey 2021b), I found no evidence that Democrats held copartisan presidents to a different standard when they offered misleading rationales for military action. As polarization deepens the divides between parties (Iyengar et al. 2019; F. E. Lee 2015), however, Democrats could become less willing to punish copartisan presidents. This change is the context in which accountability for humanitarian justifications would be substantially eroded. Democratic presidents would both face strong incentives to use humanitarian claims to mobilize their base and be able to avoid punishment from the majority of doves.

Overall, partisanship complicates but does not erase the opportunities for accountability that stem from a broad domestic coalition. Its most substantial impacts are likely to be observed when Republican presidents misuse security justifications. Accountability for humanitarian justifications remains relatively robust barring dramatic—though plausible—changes in the domestic political environment.

Misused appeals and the future of humanitarian intervention

So far, the experimental evidence has assuaged concerns that humanitarian appeals could provide cover for otherwise illegitimate or unpopular military actions. Enabling unwarranted interventions is, however, only half of the worry raised by human rights advocates. Equally troubling is the risk that the misuse of humanitarian justifications—even as a supplement to legitimate security concerns—will create long-term skepticism and make it more difficult to mobilize public support to address grave human rights abuses in the future. Fortunately, the final step in survey two demonstrates that the public remains willing to address atrocities, even when the same president has recently misused humanitarian claims.

After reading about the intervention in Numar and answering follow-up questions, the survey presents participants with an additional humanitarian crisis in the hypothetical country of Rundu. Prior exposure to the misuse of humanitarian claims for the president's own political gain does not significantly affect future support for humanitarian intervention. As the first panel of Figure 5.4 illustrates, individuals assigned to the different and illegitimate conditions support the future intervention at levels that are not significantly different than individuals in the true conditions.[9] Only when humanitarian justifications were misused as a cover for security motivations—the different but legitimate condition—was support for the future intervention significantly reduced, and here, the substantive effect is muted. Among participants assigned to read about true humanitarian justifications in the first scenario, 65 percent supported the future intervention in Rundu, compared to 56 percent of people who read a humanitarian justification that experts saw as a cover for security motives. This difference in future support is statistically significant at the $p < 0.10$ level. The substantive implications are tempered, however, by the fact that support remains high and that the difference is not significant among any particular foreign policy constituency. Overall, while deception meaningfully changes support for the intervention which it targets, the long-term consequences of misused humanitarian claims fall short of the worst-case scenario.

The public's longer-term trust and confidence in the president also remains relatively high following misused justifications. Trust in the

---

[9] These results hold across all foreign policy constituencies. An analysis of each constituency's attitudes towards the future intervention is included in the appendix.

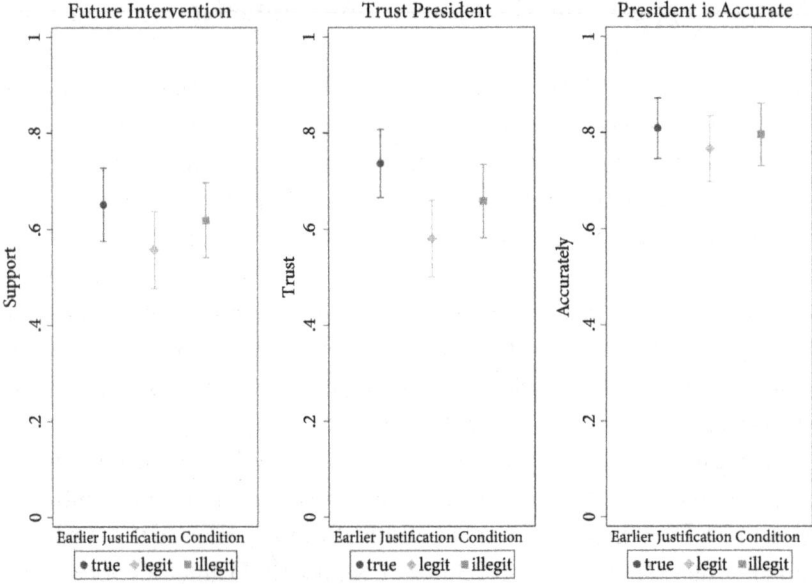

Figure 5.4 The effect of misused humanitarian claims on future humanitarian crises

president's ability to handle the future humanitarian crisis is most influenced by previous evidence of deception, with individuals reporting significantly lower trust in the president in the different but legitimate condition compared to the true condition. Despite this reduced trust in the president's capabilities, the accuracy of his statements about the crisis in Rundu was well-insulated from the effects of deception. Earlier misleading justifications did not influence beliefs that the president accurately described the atrocities. These results are illustrated in the second and third panels of Figure 5.4, respectively.

Earlier sections of this chapter acknowledge that simply telling participants that a crisis takes place in the future cannot capture the complexity surrounding consecutive crises in the real world. Instead, the survey results are more appropriately interpreted as a most likely case for deception to influence a hypothetical future. In the survey, participants read similar justifications from the same president over the course of a few minutes. They also answered questions highlighting expert disagreement before considering an intervention in Rundu. Given this unrealistically strong, direct, and time-condensed treatment, the absence of a clear connection between deception in the Numar intervention and support for the Rundu intervention is striking. If the misuse of humanitarian claims does not make people skeptical of a future humanitarian intervention—even when the two scenarios are presented back-to-back, with the same president and a reminder of deception—there is reason to be optimistic about the robustness of public support for responding to mass atrocities in the real world.

Conclusion

In the previous chapter, I identified the domestic political benefits that presidents can reap by offering humanitarian justifications for military action. The unique responsiveness of doves creates a strong incentive for leaders to use humanitarian justification whenever possible. The power of humanitarian appeals raises concerns for both democratic accountability and humanitarian pretext. If making a humanitarian appeal allows presidents to broaden public support at will, the resonance of these claims would make public consent easy to achieve and weaken the constraints democratic institutions are expected to place on the use of force. Similarly, if leaders misuse humanitarian justifications to gain political benefits, humanitarian appeals could become less effective at bolstering public support when it is most needed—in the face of mass atrocities and egregious human rights abuses.

In this chapter, I assuaged these concerns by highlighting how broad domestic coalitions also broaden opportunities for accountability. Critically, I show that doves not only create a demand for humanitarian justifications, they also explain why leaders exercise restraint to avoid overstating humanitarian appeals. The findings are good news for democracy and human rights norms. Hawks provide similar reasons for restraint regarding security justifications, which resonate more closely with their core values and preferences. Because different individuals hold leaders responsible for different statements, broad domestic coalitions that include both doves and hawks also increase opportunities to hold leaders accountable for the use of force.

To support this argument, the chapter introduced a survey experiment that varied both the type of justification the president used and the expert response. The results validated hypothesis four and each of its components. They did so in five steps.

First, I highlight the influence of presidential statements. Consistent with existing evidence that the public trusts the White House to handle foreign policy, participants generally believed the president meant what he said and had national security in mind. Second, I show that despite this general trust in official statements, the public does punish leaders for making misleading claims. The misuse of both humanitarian and security justifications causes individuals to lower their support for military action. Leaders have some leeway to diverge from the truth if they offer multiple justifications for action, as long as experts agree with one of the president's claims. When leaders attempt to justify an illegitimate intervention to further their own political agenda, no combination of justifications can bolster public support.

Evidence that the public dislikes deception in the aggregate bodes well for democratic accountability but is an insufficient test of the domestic coalition argument. In a third step, this chapter shows that foreign policy constituencies respond differently to the misuse of justifications. The differences between foreign policy constituencies are most evident in the conditions where experts disagree with the president's stated explanation but believe that the underlying reason for intervention is legitimate. When presidents stretch humanitarian justifications too far—using them as the primary justification for an intervention more closely tied to security concerns—doves inflict political punishment in the form of lower support for military action. Hawks and, to a lesser extent, isolationists do not react strongly to the misuse of humanitarian claims, but instead punish leaders who overstretch security justifications.

In a fourth step, the chapter considers how leaders are punished for making deceptive claims. In addition to reducing support for the intervention itself, deception also negatively influences presidential approval and the president's reelection prospects. Partisanship complicates these mechanisms of accountability—especially surrounding security justifications—but does not eliminate the risk of political backlash leaders face for misusing humanitarian claims.

Finally, I evaluate the long-term risks to humanitarian intervention more directly, showing that exposure to deceptive humanitarian claims does not dramatically undermine support for responses to future mass atrocities. Even when justified by the same president who misused humanitarian appeals in a previous intervention, a majority of both hawks and doves remained willing to support military action to stop a humanitarian crisis.

This evidence, combined with the ineffectiveness of deceptive humanitarian claims, alleviates the worst-case scenario concerns about humanitarian pretext.

The reasons for restraint outlined in this chapter combine with the benefits described in Chapter 4 to make up the public incentive structure that confronts White House communications teams. To simultaneously broaden public support for military action and minimize the risk of backlash, leaders should add humanitarian rationales to their speeches about military interventions. When the intervention is not primarily a response to a humanitarian crisis, however, communications teams should take care to avoid stretching humanitarian explanations too far. If humanitarian claims are used as the primary justification for an intervention the public perceives as a security crisis, backlash is more likely than support.

Focusing on public opinion, however, can only establish what strategic leaders *should* do. To capture the power humanitarian rhetoric exerts over contemporary foreign policy in practice, it is important to know whether leaders understand and respond to these public incentives in real cases of military intervention. The following chapter shows that the domestic coalition argument accounts for both public incentives and elite actions, moving the level of analysis to White House communication strategies in actual cases of military intervention. It demonstrates that White House communications teams recognized the importance of and intentionally used humanitarian justifications to build a broad domestic coalition of support for military actions in the Gulf War and Bosnia.

6

Building broad coalitions

White House communications in Iraq and Bosnia

By all accounts, the George H. W. Bush administration had an "overabundance of acceptable rationales for using force" in Operation Desert Shield and Operation Desert Storm (Teeter 1990b). When Iraq invaded Kuwait in August 1990, it committed an act of international aggression that violated international law while threatening US regional interests, allies, and access to oil. It exemplifies what Chapter 2 defines as a "security crisis" and is one of the first major military operations after the end of the Cold War. In this precedent-setting intervention which responded to a high-profile security crisis, the administration's talking points often included humanitarian justifications, highlighting Saddam Hussein's abuse of civilians in both Iraq and Kuwait. Who was the target audience of these claims and what, if any, benefits did the Bush administration expect to gain from its humanitarian appeals?

Answering these questions in the context of the 1991 Gulf War, this chapter establishes that the domestic coalition incentives exist in practice and are recognized by White House communications teams. It does so by tracing *how* the White House developed communication strategies for its foreign policy. I show that consistent with the domestic coalition expectations, the Bush administration chose between different viable justification strategies by focusing on the explanations that resonated with broad segments of the domestic audience. The communications team saw value in making humanitarian statements to persuade domestic groups who were skeptical of using military force. They also, however, emphasized humanitarian claims less than security explanations and explicitly recognized the risk of overstating human rights concerns. In line with the logic of Chapter 3 and individual-level evidence from Chapters 4 and 5, humanitarian justifications appeared in response to this security crisis because the White House believed that they were necessary and uniquely capable of maximizing support from an important constituency.

Doves into Hawks. Sarah Maxey, Oxford University Press. © Oxford University Press (2026).
DOI: 10.1093/9780197832738.003.0006

There are, however, other reasons presidents could decide to use humanitarian justifications. First, White House justifications could target an audience other than the domestic public. In the build-up to military action, both the international community and political elites within the United States have the power to enable or complicate the president's preferred policy. Rather than appealing to doves among the public, communications teams could instead use humanitarian justifications to appease advisors, members of Congress, or potential international allies. Second, if humanitarian claims are more dovish than expected, Republican administrations could use humanitarian justifications to send against-type signals and make their military interventions appear more moderate and credible. Democratic presidents, on the other hand, would have an incentive to emphasize security explanations in humanitarian crises for the same reason. From this perspective, the choice of justifications would reflect an attempt to bolster the leader's overall credibility rather than to mobilize a particular constituency. Third, humanitarian statements could be non-strategic. Contemporary interventions often combine military and humanitarian objectives, making it plausible that presidents simply mention humanitarian missions when they exist without expecting to receive any domestic political benefits. This chapter directly investigates the domestic coalition argument alongside these alternatives.

The Gulf War case illustrates the validity of the domestic coalition logic at the intervention level. It reveals that in actual cases of military action, the White House understands the importance of including doves and hawks in the domestic coalition and intentionally uses humanitarian justifications to achieve this goal. The Clinton administration's justifications for US involvement in Bosnia then establish the argument's scope, extending it to a case of humanitarian intervention. Humanitarian interventions also require a domestic coalition of support that includes both hawks and doves. In these cases, because the humanitarian dimensions of the crisis are front and center, doves are easier to persuade. Humanitarian justifications remain necessary, but presidents do not have to worry that these claims will appear insincere. As a result, I expect Clinton to use humanitarian appeals as the primary rationale for US involvement in Bosnia, emphasizing such claims without the concern for backlash that exists in the Gulf War case. Because they involve a Republican and a Democratic president addressing different types of crises, these cases also shed light on how partisanship influences the White House's view of the domestic audience and the benefits of different justifications.

In what follows, I first outline the domestic coalition argument's expectations for how the White House develops communication strategies around security and humanitarian crises. Given that presidents are not, for the most part, political scientists, conversations about internationalist coalitions are likely to take place using different terms and points of reference. With this in mind, I describe how the White House is likely to talk about persuadable doves in practice, highlighting known demographic correlates and signals of cooperative values.

Next, I apply standardized questions to each case, investigating the centrality of the domestic coalition and humanitarian justifications in White House communication strategies. Examining speech drafts, talking points, memorandum, polling reports, and other documents collected from archives at the George H. W. Bush and William J. Clinton Presidential Libraries sheds light on three important aspects of the relationship between the White House and the public. First, the domestic public is the target audience of presidents' national addresses. While communications teams consider both political elites and international audiences, justifications are chosen based on their public resonance and elite opposition is discussed in terms of its implications for public support. Second, leaders believe that they need broad domestic coalitions of support for their foreign policy decisions. Communications teams discuss building support across constituencies with distinct preferences and use polling reports to gauge what different groups will accept. Third, across security and humanitarian crises led by presidents from different political parties, doves are a critical part of the domestic coalition and humanitarian justifications are seen as the most effective way to maximize their support.

Theoretical expectations

The domestic coalition argument makes claims about how justifications for military action work at multiple levels of analysis. I began at the speech level, analyzing presidents' national addresses to reveal patterns of demand and restraint in humanitarian justifications (Chapter 2). Moving to the individual level, I examined public opinion to show that doves are important coalition members whose preferences account for both the power and limits of humanitarian appeals (Chapters 4 and 5). Here, I turn to the process through which the White House develops justifications for military interventions. I assert that the presence of humanitarian appeals reflects an intentional communication strategy designed to persuade and bring doves into the domestic coalition of support. Hypothesis five captured the theoretical expectations for this chapter:

> H5: When developing the communication strategy for a military interven-
> tion, leaders and their staffs primarily aim to persuade the domestic audience.
> They recognize that this audience is made up of different groups that must
> be brought into a coalition of support.

If the White House is in fact motivated by the need to build broad domestic coalitions of support for military action, I expect this concern to appear in discussions about speech drafts, talking points, and public opinion polls. Specifically, there are four pieces of evidence in archival documents that can provide support for the domestic coalition argument. First, I expect communications teams to focus primarily on persuading the domestic audience when they choose which justifications for military action to include in presidential addresses. Second, in White House discussions about the domestic audience, I expect members of the administration to express concern about persuading doves. Third, humanitarian justifications and an emphasis on human rights should appear as helpful tools for convincing doves who are skeptical of intervention. Fourth, savvy communications teams will express caution about the overuse of humanitarian claims in security crises to avoid the risk of backlash from doves.

The more consistently these four pieces of evidence are present, the more confidence in the domestic coalition explanation is warranted. The absence of evidence for any of the first three expectations would falsify the domestic coalition argument. A lack of evidence that administrations are cautious about the overuse of humanitarian claims would suggest that presidents know about and capitalize on the power of humanitarian appeals, but also risk political backlash—they are not using humanitarian justifications as effectively as they could.

Expectations beyond security crises

The domestic coalition argument primarily focuses on the role of humanitarian justifications in security crises because this is where the unique power of humanitarian claims is least expected and most overlooked. As a response to a clear security crisis, the Gulf War case is well-positioned to test the main theoretical expectations. Presidents' concerns with building domestic coalitions are not, however, limited to security crises. Public support also matters in responses to humanitarian crises.

Humanitarian interventions are still military interventions. As a result, public support in this context operates according to the same domestic coalition logic as security crises. Presidents broaden support when they convince both hawks and doves that humanitarian intervention is a good idea. Because hawks view military action as an effective tool of foreign policy, they have a high baseline willingness to support the use of force even for humanitarian purposes. Leaders may still use security justifications in an attempt to tie the humanitarian intervention to US national interests, but they will not have to work hard to get hawks on board. Doves remain skeptical of military action, but the more obvious and egregious the human rights abuses, the more likely they are to override this skepticism and support intervention.

The main difference I expect to find in communication strategies for humanitarian interventions is that communications teams are free to use unlimited humanitarian appeals. In these cases, humanitarian justifications reflect the primary impetus for action. Therefore, presidents do not need to worry that over-emphasizing humanitarian claims will make their statements appear insincere and spark public backlash. As a result, I do not expect discussions about justifying humanitarian interventions to caution against overstating humanitarian goals. Instead, the White House has an incentive to keep humanitarian concerns as front and center as possible.

Knowing a dove when you see one

Persuading doves is an important objective for communication strategies, but does the White House know this? Evidence of administrations' concern with building coalitions of hawks and doves is likely to appear as an acknowledgment that different groups hold distinct preferences for how the US should engage with the world. Before analyzing the archival documents, I set two standards for identifying references to hawks or doves within cases. First, I consider the issues a group raises in its expressions of support or opposition and map those issues onto the underlying priorities that distinguish doves and hawks. Groups that emphasize a preference for diplomatic strategies, draw attention to human rights, highlight the importance of using force only as a last resort and raise concerns about its effectiveness, evoke just war standards, or express hesitancy about the human costs of war are counted as likely doves. Alternatively, I consider constituencies that commend or lobby for overwhelming demonstrations of military force, emphasize military strength and the credibility of US threats, criticize the White House for being slow to take military action, or view diplomacy as an ineffective tool of foreign policy to be likely hawks. Because isolationism is a broader concept and source of political concern, it is more likely to be discussed by name. Beyond direct references, isolationism is also reflected in constituencies that express concern about the US trying to do too much in the world or that lobby for narrow definitions of the national interest.

Second, historical studies of foreign policy preferences, combined with information from the surveys presented in Chapters 4 and 5, highlight demographic factors that are correlated with doves and hawks. White House conversations that discuss the importance of demographic groups highly correlated with doves are consistent with the demands and incentives of the domestic coalition argument. In their analysis of public foreign policy attitudes, Mandelbaum and Schneiders' (1979, 43) liberal internationalists—defined by the cooperative priorities that overlap with this book's conceptualization of doves—are consistently younger, well-educated, and less likely to be Southerners than the population as a whole. This pattern is also reflected in the demographic information about doves collected and reported in Chapters 4 and 5. In the surveys, women, liberals, and college-educated individuals were disproportionately doves. I thus consider administrations' efforts to poll or target their justifications to students or young professionals, women, or liberals as appeals to constituencies of doves. In short, the White House's concern with doves is most likely to appear in archival materials as a concern with persuading these demographic or interest groups.

Alternative explanations

The domestic coalition argument expects White House communication strategies to focus primarily on the domestic audience, to be concerned with persuading doves, and to recognize the utility and limits of humanitarian justifications. Evidence from the Gulf War case that supports these expectations increases confidence that the pattern of humanitarian justifications described in Chapter 2 reflects an intentional White House effort to respond to the incentives set by public opinion identified in Chapters 4 and 5. There are, however, three alternative explanations for why presidents might turn to humanitarian appeals in their justifications for military action: attention to other audiences, against-type signaling, and humanitarian objectives.

Persuading other targets

First, instead of primarily appealing to the domestic public, humanitarian claims could be used to appease the international audience or domestic political elites. Turning first to the international audience, securing multilateral support from other countries has important consequences for the legitimacy of military operations and the potential for burden-sharing (Chapman 2011; Hurd 1999; Kreps 2010; 2011; Milner and Tingley 2013; Thompson 2006). Gaining approval from international organizations also carries a number of benefits, adding to the overall legitimacy of military action and serving as a second opinion that increases support among individuals who are skeptical of the president's motives (Grieco et al. 2011; Voeten 2005; Wallace 2013).

In the international context, humanitarian justifications evoke human rights norms and reinforce the "basic rules of the system about what action is permitted and where the boundaries of sovereign control lie" (Finnemore 2003, 2). Humanitarian claims both link action to these international standards for military intervention and reinforce norms of territorial integrity by communicating that conquest is not the goal of the operation (Zacher 2001). If the international—rather than the domestic—audience is the target of humanitarian justifications, the White House is expected to discuss humanitarian claims primarily in terms of their international benefits and emphasize these appeals more when international dissent is likely.

Alternatively, presidents could use humanitarian justifications to target the domestic audience but focus on appeasing political elites instead of the public. In this case, leaders are likely to highlight demands for humanitarian rationales from advisors, members of Congress, or other government officials. Such concerns are consistent with the well-established influence of elite cues on media coverage and public approval (Berinsky 2007; Guisinger and Saunders 2017; Saunders 2015). When political elites agree with the president, there is no clear counterargument for the media to cover and the White House narrative is broadcast relatively unopposed. When there is dissensus among elites, on the other hand, this disagreement acts as a fire alarm, alerting "rationally ignorant voters to problems with the leader's policies" and raising the political costs of action (Saunders 2015, 468). The political significance of elite cues means that leaders have strategic incentives "to bargain with and accommodate key elites, who can impose costs on leaders that may influence how democracies use force in ways unanticipated by voter-driven accounts" (Saunders 2015, 467).

If humanitarian justifications are part of White House efforts to appease elite demands, internal discussions will highlight advisors or other elites who insisted on attention to human rights concerns. These concerns are especially likely to appear in comments on speech drafts that have been circulated to top-level officials in different offices. Humanitarian justifications will be more likely to appear when elite opposition to the intervention is high. Here, the importance of maintaining public support is the end goal of avoiding negative elite cues, but the public is not the direct target of humanitarian appeals.

Partisan incentives for against-type signals

The second alternative explanation suggests that presidents could choose justifications to send against-type signals and increase the overall credibility of their policy decision (Kreps, Saunders, and Schultz 2018; Mattes and Weeks 2019; Trager and Vavreck 2011). Like the domestic coalition argument, the against-type alternative expects the White House to choose justifications based on their resonance with the domestic public. Three other factors set the against-type alternative apart: the relevance of different constituencies within the domestic audience, the lack of concern about overusing humanitarian appeals, and partisan differences in presidents' incentives to use humanitarian justifications.

The logic of against-type signals assumes that when leaders do or say something that deviates from their normal policy positions, the public interprets this divergence as a sign that the decision is especially prudent and credible. The classic example argues that it took a Nixon to go to China because of popular perceptions that a Republican hawk would only pursue rapprochement if it were truly a good idea (Kreps, Saunders, and Schultz 2018). The effectiveness of against-type signals stems from their deviation from expectations, not from an individual's underlying agreement with the president or policy. If justifications are chosen to send against-type signals, their effectiveness will primarily be discussed in terms of the domestic audience as a whole rather than particular constituencies of doves.

To the extent that Republican leaders are assumed to be hawkish and Democratic leaders are assumed to be dovish, this alternative also expects the domestic incentives for humanitarian justifications to vary by party. Scholarship on foreign policy attitudes casts doubt on whether the public makes assumptions about the hawkishness or dovishness of a leader based on their political party. For example, in their study of partisan types across a range of foreign policy and domestic issues, Kertzer, Brooks, and Brooks (2021, 1779) find that "political elites seeking to bolster support from the mass public by going against their partisan type are perhaps more limited in the range of foreign policy issues in which they can do so than many IR scholars realize." When it comes to the use of force to achieve humanitarian goals, individuals were neutral in their reported stereotypes about the partisan affiliation of the president behind this decision (Kertzer, Brooks, and Brooks 2021, 1772). Additionally, justifications do not change the underlying policy tool. As Friedman (2023, 132) highlights in the context of the Bosnian case, military interventions remain hawkish policy decisions that bolster perceptions of strong leadership, even when they are described in primarily humanitarian terms.

Taking the against-type logic on its own terms, despite these potential limitations, suggests that Republican presidents would stand to gain the most from humanitarian justifications and should use them as often as possible. Democratic presidents would benefit less from humanitarian justifications—because they match dovish expectations—but have an incentive to use security justifications as often as possible. The Gulf War and Bosnian interventions capture the scenarios where against-type expectations should be present and distinct between presidents. In the context of the Gulf War security crisis, Bush, as a Republican president, would reap the benefits of against-type signals by emphasizing humanitarian justifications. By contrast, in the humanitarian crisis in Bosnia, Clinton, a Democratic president, could most effectively send against-type signals by pointing to the security rationales behind his policy decisions while downplaying humanitarian justifications. Notably, following this against-type logic—and contrary to the domestic coalition argument's expectations of backlash—there is no clear reason for Republican presidents to worry about overstating humanitarian claims in security crises or for Democratic presidents to worry about overstating security claims in humanitarian crises.

Reporting humanitarian objectives

Finally, instead of strategically appealing to any audience, the presence of humanitarian claims in national addresses could simply report humanitarian objectives that are part of the "hearts and minds" approach to contemporary interventions. As a consequence of evolving human rights norms, attention to the treatment of civilians during war has increased since the end of World War II, arguably peaking in the post-Cold War period (Crawford 2002; 2013; Evangelista and Shue 2014; Finnemore 1996). These changes both legitimized humanitarian interventions and increased the salience of humanitarian objectives focused on saving strangers (Wheeler 2000). At the same time, US counterinsurgency strategy emphasized positive civilian outcomes as an important part of its hearts and minds approach to wars in Iraq and Afghanistan. The assumption, most clearly outlined in Field Manual 3–24, was that development aid and other forms of assistance would build trust in US forces and new governments instead of insurgencies (United States Army 2007).

Evidence for the effectiveness of hearts and minds strategies ranges from negative to mixed (Sexton 2016), though direct interactions with military personnel can improve views of the US (Allen et al. 2023). Given its prominent place in US counterinsurgency tactics during the period of interest, it is possible that humanitarian statements are simply non-strategic reflections of this policy. In this case, the public emphasis presidents place on humanitarian claims will be consistent with the prominence of humanitarian objectives in the military strategy. Discussions of humanitarian justifications will focus on facts rather than their ability to persuade any particular audience. Additionally, humanitarian statements should increase in the later stages of security interventions as the US turns its focus to reconstruction and the establishment of a lasting peace.

Assessing alternatives

The domestic coalition argument and the first two sets of alternative explanations are not mutually exclusive. Presidents can use humanitarian justifications to meet multiple domestic and international goals simultaneously. What would falsify the domestic coalition argument, however, is evidence that the White House exclusively or primarily targeted elites, the international audience, or the benefits of against-type signals without expecting humanitarian claims to have any unique effect on constituencies of doves among the domestic public. The humanitarian objective alternative does directly contradict the expectation that humanitarian justifications are a strategic part of the communication plan. With these alternatives in mind, the remainder of this chapter uses archival documents to trace the process through which the White House developed communication strategies for interventions in the Gulf War and Bosnia. Documents from both cases demonstrate that building a broad domestic coalition of public support for military action was the White House's primary reason for including humanitarian justifications in national addresses.

Case selection and methodology

The 1991 Gulf War case represents a security crisis that the US addressed with a month-long military intervention, including the deployment of ground troops. I use this intervention as the primary case and main test because it represents the context in which humanitarian justifications are most puzzling and the domestic coalition logic has the most to offer: a security crisis where credible security justifications were readily available. The conflict also involved multilateral support and approval from the United Nations, provoked significant political opposition in Congress, and concluded with a transition into humanitarian objectives with Operation Provide Comfort. The full range of alternative explanations is thus feasible in this case and it is possible to evaluate their strength relative to the domestic coalition logic. Additionally, as one of the first major military interventions of the post-Cold War period, the Gulf War set a precedent for how the US would conduct military operations for at least the next decade. It is a case in which both the White House and the world learned about the type of engagement the US public was willing to support (Gelpi, Feaver, and Reifler 2009, 5). The justifications used during the Gulf War are thus a most likely case for observing a communication strategy that is both intentional—rather than simply reusing phrases that were effective in previous interventions— and influential for future conflicts. Finally, because the Gulf War had fully concluded and the relevant archival documents were publicly available via the George H. W. Bush Presidential Library, testing the domestic coalition argument in this case reduces the risk of systematically missing information that could bias the interpretation of results.

I begin the analysis of the Gulf War case with Iraq's invasion of Kuwait on August 2, 1990. This moment constitutes the security crisis which entered Chapter 2's data as a potential case of intervention. I conclude the analysis following the withdrawal of Iraqi troops and the end of coalition attacks on February 28, 1991. The case includes both Operation Desert Shield, which deployed defensive US forces to Saudi Arabia, and Operation Desert Storm, in which the US engaged in combat operations against the Iraqi army. It does not include Operation Provide Comfort or Operations Southern and Northern Watch because these operations had distinct military objectives—addressing a developing humanitarian crisis as members of the Kurdish population attempted to flee Iraq and enforcing no-fly zones—and took place in the aftermath of combat operations. After the Gulf War case establishes the validity of the domestic coalition argument, I turn to the Bosnian case to evaluate the argument's scope, described in more detail below.

Structured questions for analysis

I structure the analysis by relying on five sets of standardized questions to evaluate my theoretical expectations across contexts (George and Bennett 2005; Saunders 2015, 47): (1) Is there an intentional communication strategy? To what extent does this strategy reflect a concern with domestic public opinion? (2) What is the content and pattern of justifications? Are humanitarian justifications emphasized in response to growing opposition or are they present throughout the crisis? (3) Does the White House recognize the importance of appealing broadly to groups with different values? (4) Are humanitarian justifications understood to appeal to some groups more than others? (5) Does the White House discuss any limits to the effectiveness of humanitarian claims?

I answer these questions by examining archival materials collected from the George H. W. Bush Presidential Library in College Station, Texas. My data collection efforts focused on files from: (1) White House communications staff, including drafts of national addresses, press guidance, and internal memos and meeting agendas, (2) domestic political advisors, including memos and meetings involving the Chief of Staff and election campaign staff, reports from and communications with polling firms, and communications with Congress, and (3) diplomatic and military advisors, including memos and meetings with the State Department, National Security Council, and Joint Chiefs of Staff. Documents from communications staff and domestic advisors examine whether humanitarian claims are part of an intentional strategy designed to maintain support among the domestic audience and specific groups. Where the dataset in Chapter 2 focused on national addresses to hold the audience constant, here I examine a wider range of speeches to investigate whether presidents adapted their justifications to match the relevant constituency. Following Druckman and Jacobs (2011, 2015), internal polling data sheds light on the groups the White House considers strategically important. Documents from diplomatic and military advisors are used to evaluate the international audience and humanitarian objective alternatives, as well as to track how US policy changed over time. Examining communications between the different actors allows me to investigate whether justifications are a product of internal elite debates.

In examining archival materials, I prioritized documents that shed light on the process through which communication strategies were developed, revised, and deployed. It is this process that the domestic coalition argument aims to explain. Specifically, the offices listed above include the communications teams responsible for drafting the speeches that make up the dataset in Chapter 2 and are thus an appropriate focus for understanding the logic behind the observed patterns of demand and restraint. Speech file drafts include responses and inputs from a broad range of different departments, including the National Security Council, as well as the Departments of State and Defense. They include public diplomacy efforts which capture concerns about how different statements would resonate with international actors, including polls of public opinion in relevant countries, statements to international audiences including Voice of America programing, and plans to counter an expected disinformation campaign from Iraq. In terms of understanding the drivers of the president's public statements—the goal of the book—these materials are comprehensive. However, this selection of materials cannot and is not intended to capture the full range of considerations that went into policy decisions.

The scope of the domestic coalition

After establishing that the domestic coalition explains why presidents use humanitarian justifications in security crises, I then use US involvement in Bosnia to show that the argument extends to humanitarian crises. The

US military involvement in Bosnia represents its foreign policy towards one of the worst humanitarian crises of the post-Cold War period. As in the Gulf War case, US participation in this conflict involved multilateral cooperation and drew significant dissent from members of Congress. The intervention was also complete and archival documents were widely available at the time the research took place. Additionally, because this crisis took place during the Clinton administration, it demonstrates that the domestic coalition logic is not limited to one president or one political party. I apply the same standardized questions outlined for the Gulf War to the Bosnian case, anticipating a different answer only to question five. I do not expect the White House to express concern about political backlash or the overuse of humanitarian justifications in the context of a humanitarian intervention.

I begin the analysis of the Bosnian case with Clinton's inauguration in 1993 and conclude with the announcement that the US would send troops to implement the Dayton Accords in December 1995. While the earliest stages of this conflict took place during the George H. W. Bush administration, the analysis focuses on the Clinton administration's communication strategy to hold constant both the president and the key decision-makers and speech-writers. Holding these factors constant accounts for differences in rhetorical style, as well as personal and personnel differences in the White House's approach to foreign policy—it would otherwise be difficult to tell if changes in language reflect changes in policy or people. Additionally, while the violence in Bosnia included conflicts between the Bosnian Serbs, Bosnian Muslims, and Bosnian Croats, I focus the analysis on the war between the Bosnian Serbs and Bosnian Muslims. This dimension of the conflict captures the most grievous and consistent violations of international humanitarian law, including ethnic cleansing, the siege of Sarajevo, and attacks on UN peacekeepers, and was the primary focus of the US response.

Justifying the Gulf War

The escalation of the Gulf War began on August 2, 1990, when Iraqi forces invaded and occupied Kuwait. In remarks to reporters that afternoon, President George H. W. Bush condemned the military invasion and called for "the immediate and unconditional withdrawal of all Iraqi forces" (G. H. W. Bush 1990d). The international community also reacted quickly. The United Nations Security Council (UNSC) passed Resolution 660 on the day of the initial invasion. The first of twelve eventual resolutions, 660 formally condemned Iraq's aggression and demanded that it withdraw its forces from Kuwait (UNSC 1990a).

The US role in the conflict intensified with the start of Operation Desert Shield on August 7. This operation encompassed a largely unilateral effort to protect allies and interests in Saudi Arabia with the deployment of US defensive forces (Kreps 2011, 49). At the same time, the UN increased its pressure on Iraq to withdraw, authorizing the enforcement of sanctions and the use of "all means necessary" to remove Iraqi troops from Kuwait if the government did not comply by January 15, 1991 (UNSC 1990b; 1990c).

Within the US, early opposition to the Gulf War appeared in the form of calls to give sanctions time to work and pursue diplomatic options before resorting to the use of military force. Public support for intervention increased gradually in the build-up to and over the course of the war. When Gallup polls asked the public in early November 1990 if it would "favor or oppose the United States going to war in order to drive the Iraqis out of Kuwait," only 37 percent of respondents favored military action (Gallup 2001). By the end of the month, after the UN authorized the use of "all means necessary" to remove Iraqi forces from Kuwait, support for war rose to include 53 percent of respondents (Gallup 2001). Support further increased to include 62 percent of the public by January 1991 and 80 percent of Americans approved of the decision to use force by the time the UN deadline expired (Gallup 2001).

In addition to UN approval, the Bush administration also sought and received authorization for the use of force from Congress. Four days before the US intervention began, both the House—in a vote of 250 to 183—and the Senate—in a vote of 52 to 47—authorized the use of force (Clymer 1991). Operation Desert Storm formally began with airstrikes on Iraqi targets on January 19, 1991, and the launch of a ground invasion on February 24. The US military quickly achieved its objectives and by February 27, Bush declared the liberation of Kuwait. Iraq formally accepted all UN resolutions the following day, February 28, marking the end of major US combat operations.

An intentional strategy for public persuasion

The argument that presidents use humanitarian justifications to build domestic coalitions assumes that the White House has an intentional communication strategy for military interventions which primarily targets domestic public opinion. The first set of standardized questions probes this assumption: Was there an intentional White House communication strategy in the Gulf War? To what extent did this strategy reflect the Bush administration's concern with domestic public opinion compared to other sources of opposition?

Archival documents from the Gulf War reveal a remarkably coordinated, consistent, and intentional communication strategy. Communications themes were planned and coordinated across time and spokespeople, even as the administration debated different options internally (National Security Council 1990b).[1] As early as October 1990, a National Security Council memorandum outlined the importance of a coordinated communication strategy, noting that statements about both military and diplomatic options "should be used consistently by spokesmen across the government" (National Security Council 1990a). The Office of the Public Liaison also emphasized consistent messaging, warning cabinet and agency contacts that, "Although we are not trying to mint hundreds of foreign policy spokespersons, it is important that those who do speak on behalf of the Administration are apprised of recent developments and are able, for example, to articulate clearly the four objectives the international community is pursuing in the Gulf" (Jackson 1990).

The administration also closely tied its messaging to domestic public opinion. In the initial outline of its communication plan, the Office of Public Affairs identified its primary objective as the need to "strengthen public support for Operation Desert Shield. Ultimately, our goal is *broad, grassroots support* for the President's initiative" (White House Office of Public Affairs 1990, emphasis added). Critically, the administration's own stated goal was to achieve broad public support, not the minimum necessary. Resulting efforts to standardize the administration's message and broaden public support included disseminating general and monthly themes that aligned with the president's speech schedule and press plan (Fitzwater 1991a; "Guidance, Gulf Policy Themes" 1990; "Guidance, Gulf Strategy January Themes and Messages" 1991). For example, a November 1990 memo

---

[1] For example, the phrases "the unconditional Iraqi withdrawal from Kuwait," "restoration of Kuwait's legitimate government," and "security and stability for the region" appear repeatedly across documents from as early as September 1990 through the beginning of the invasion in January 1991 ("Draft 1, Presidential Remarks: Address to Joint Session of Congress" 1990; Baker 1990b; "Draft, Christmas Eve Message to the Troops" 1990; "Guidance, Gulf Strategy January Themes and Messages" 1991).

outlined a communication plan for Operation Desert Shield that would correspond with the President's Thanksgiving trip to Saudi Arabia. The plan recommended op-eds, a CNN interview prior to the trip, and making sure "All speeches (Europe and Middle East) are clearly cross-linked with the themes of the new world order," as well as addressing the nation and briefing key constituent leaders after the trip (Demarest 1990d). The White House's public communications during the Gulf War were thus made up of intentional and carefully planned messages targeting the domestic public with the goal of building broad support.

Further evidence that White House's public rhetoric primarily focused on the domestic audience is found in the communications team's extensive collection and discussion of both external and internal polling data. Polls gauged public support over the course of the conflict, anticipated factors that would reduce public approval, and tested the relative salience of alternative justifications for military action, including a breakdown of responses into different demographic and regional groups ("Collection of Documents, Polls/Persian Gulf" 1991; Fabrizio 1990; "Folder, Poll Data— [Gulf War]" 1991; Teeter 1990a; 1991). The results of these polls gained significant attention from communications and public affairs staff who collected and summarized the main findings in memos. They also garnered a response from the President himself, who sent a handwritten note commanding Press Secretary Marlin Fitzwater to check a Time Magazine story that reported a "Most Precipitous Drop in polls??" (G. H. W. Bush 1991d, emphasis and punctuation from the original). In a news conference following the later release of a Wall Street Journal poll, Fitzwater assured reporters that the President was primarily guided by what was best for the country, but "the President is interested in public opinion. And he certainly was interested in that same distinguished network's finding that some 53 percent would support military action if that's the choice he has to make" (Fitzwater 1990a).

Most importantly for the domestic coalition argument, the Bush White House viewed presidential speeches as an effective way to influence public opinion and targeted its appeals accordingly. From the beginning of the crisis, the White House Communications Office crafted messages to "reassure the American people as to the objectives and purpose of our deployment" (Demarest 1990d). These messages targeted two stated goals. First, "Thematically, we need to tell people why we are there and what we mean to achieve. Specific information on details of our involvement, purpose, international and UN support, etc., should be updated regularly and as events dictate"

(Demarest 1990a). The second goal—consistent with the eventual declines in support outlined in Chapter 3—recognized that "As time passes, critics may become more vocal" (Demarest 1990a). The guidance continued to instruct staff that, "The message that the President has gone to historic lengths to avoid war (economic embargo and ten UN resolutions) and garnered unprecedented international support should be a fundamental component of all outreach activity" (Demarest 1990a).

In addition to communications teams, senior officials and the President also emphasized the importance of managing public perceptions of the war. In a letter explaining his foreign policy decisions to Former President Richard Nixon, Bush wrote:

> In any event, the combination of remarkably candid consultations and explanations [of military strategy] we have offered seems to have had a calming effect [on the public]. That said, we are under no illusions on this score; managing the congressional and domestic account will, as ever, prove one of our major challenges. I hope that the statement at my press conference of November 30, the Administration's testimony last week at Congressional hearings, and our stepped up public diplomacy efforts will shore up public support (G. H. W. Bush 1991c).

In sum, the Bush administration's communication plan for the Gulf War offers clear evidence that the White House had an intentional justification strategy with the goal of managing domestic public opinion. International support and congressional approval are also referenced—as in Bush's note to Nixon—but in the context of considering how these factors will affect public opinion. This focus on the domestic audience and view of presidential addresses as important tools for managing public opinion reflects the underlying logic of the domestic coalition argument.

The pattern of Gulf War justifications

As the White House attempted to broaden public support for the Gulf War via presidential statements, what justifications did it rely on to persuade the public? What role did humanitarian justifications play in the administration's public diplomacy efforts and when did they appear? If the Bush administration followed the incentives associated with the domestic coalition argument, White House speeches will include humanitarian appeals throughout the crisis but maintain a focus on security concerns as the main reason for action. Evidence from both the dataset of national addresses, first introduced in Chapter 2, and archival documents confirms this expectation.

From the earliest stages of the conflict, security justifications were the main rationale for military action and served as the core theme of the White House communication strategy ("Guidance, Gulf Policy Themes" 1990). In remarks to reporters on the day Iraq invaded Kuwait, Bush highlighted connections to US interests, asserting "Needless to say, we view the situation with the utmost gravity. We remain committed to take whatever steps are necessary to defend our longstanding, vital interests in the Gulf" (G. H. W. Bush 1990d). In his first address to the nation following the deployment of troops to Saudi Arabia, Bush reiterated this theme, explaining that the US "took action to assist the Saudi Arabian Government in the defense of its homeland" (G. H. W. Bush 1990b). The administration's early focus on protecting US interests in the region and rebuking Iraqi aggression remained the primary explanation for action throughout the conflict. These security justifications were in line with the military's objectives "to force Iraqi troops to leave Kuwait, to restore the legitimate government of Kuwait to its rightful place, and ensure Iraqi compliance with all relevant UNSC resolutions" (Gear, n.d.).

These quotes and hundreds of similar statements highlight the spectrum of security justifications available to the White House, among which standing up to naked aggression was deemed especially persuasive (Pinkerton 1990). Even with this multitude of security justifications, Bush's national addresses and White House communications guidance also offered humanitarian explanations for US action. When Bush appeared on television to announce the air strikes that began Operation Desert Storm, he mentioned the brutalization of Kuwait's people in his fifth sentence, before discussing UN resolutions or weapons of mass destruction. Similar humanitarian rationales emerge throughout this pivotal speech, helping to explain why the administration could not wait any longer for sanctions to work: "While the world waited, Saddam Hussein systematically raped, pillaged, and plundered a tiny nation, no threat to his own. He subjected the people of Kuwait to unspeakable atrocities—and among those maimed and murdered, innocent children" (G. H. W. Bush 1991a). Again, this concern with the treatment of foreign civilians came before claims that as the world waited "Saddam sought to add to the chemical weapons arsenal" and "more damage was being done to the fragile economies of Eastern Europe, to the entire world, including our own economy" (G. H. W. Bush 1991a).

The humanitarian dimension of the Gulf War narrative was neither buried nor an afterthought. Instead, it reflected an intentional strategy that centered around three alternative themes and appeared in speeches throughout the duration of the crisis. The first theme emphasized Iraq's abuse of civilians in Kuwait, asserting "The talks of rape and assassination, of cold-blooded murder and rampant looting are almost beyond belief. The whole civilized world must unite and say: This kind of treatment of people must end" (G. H. W. Bush 1990f). The second theme focused on Saddam Hussein's human rights record and Iraq's "history of aggression against its own citizens" (G. H. W. Bush 1990b). Related talking points noted that "We've seen him use chemical weapons on his own people" (G. H. W. Bush 1990f). A third and less common appeal evoked Hussein's treatment of for-eign hostages, drawing attention to "this cynical and brutal policy of forcing people to beg for their release, parceling out human lives to families and trav-eling emissaries like so much chattel" (G. H. W. Bush 1990f). Across all three themes, communications teams contrasted Hussein's record of human rights violations and use of human shields with assertions that the US was doing everything it could to minimize civilian casualties. To this point, Bush drew clear distinctions between the government of Iraq and its people, explain-ing that "We have no argument with the people of Iraq. Indeed, for the innocents caught in this conflict, I pray for their safety" (G. H. W. Bush 1991a).

The speech dataset introduced in Chapter 2 makes it possible to illus-trate how often the Bush administration used and emphasized humanitarian appeals in its speeches about the Gulf War. The left-hand side of Figure 6.1 uses this data to show when the White House used humanitarian claims—days with a non-zero data point—and what proportion of justifications in the given speech were humanitarian. The right-hand side of Figure 6.1 graphs the use and emphasis of security justifications for the sake of com-parison. The pattern of justifications surrounding the Gulf War reveals two points relevant to the domestic coalition argument. First, the examples and quotes presented earlier in this section were not rare. The Bush admin-istration used humanitarian claims from the beginning of the crisis until

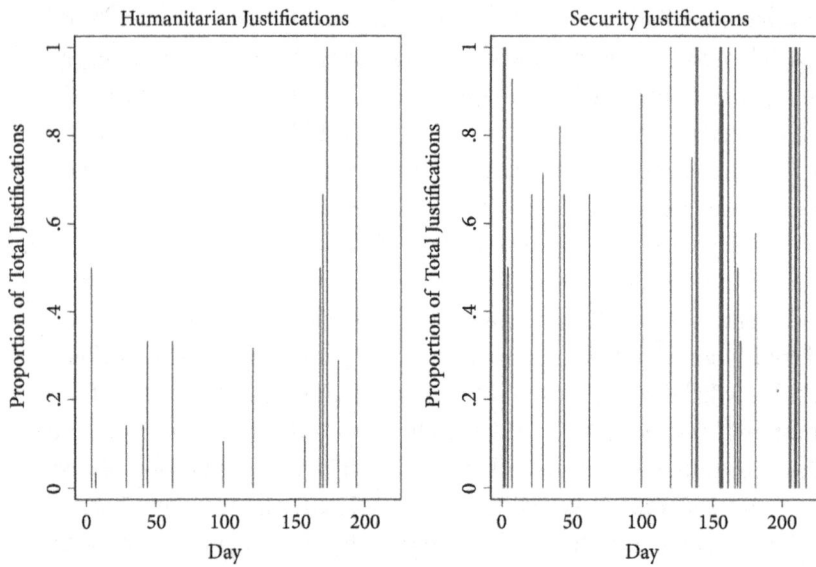

Figure 6.1   Emphasis of justifications for the Gulf War

Note: The presence of a bar indicates that there was a national address given on that day of the conflict.

its conclusion. The presence of humanitarian appeals in a case with obvious and accepted security implications indicates that the administration recognized the unique benefits of talking about protecting civilians. Second, security justifications were used more often and with greater emphasis than humanitarian appeals. This communication strategy made sure that the security rationale for military action had top billing, even in speeches that also used humanitarian claims. As a result, it avoided any perception of overstated or insincere humanitarian concerns. The Bush administration acted according to the expected domestic coalition incentives for humanitarian appeals.

Tracking potential coalitions

During the Gulf War, the Bush administration used and operated within the limits of humanitarian justifications, but did the White House know that it needed to build an internationalist coalition of doves and hawks? The archival evidence reveals that the answer is yes. Consistent with the need to build a broad domestic coalition, administration officials regularly disaggregated public opinion data and examined substantive shifts in the composition of public support for military action. Official polls broke down public reactions based on party identification, gender, region, age, race, and a hawk/dove scale (ABC News/Washingon Post 1991; CBS News Poll 1990; PA/Opinion Analysis 1991; 1990; Steeper 1990b; 1990a).

These polls informed the communication strategy and officials recognized that "the time available for the President to cultivate, thank, listen to, highlight, garner support from, and reach out to outside groups will be in short supply" (Demarest 1990b). As a result, the White House identified key domestic groups that "would be given the highest priority for time with POTUS" in the lead-up to the war (Demarest 1990b). Key groups included Bush's base, but also encompassed target constituencies that could broaden the coalition of support. The White House communications team recognized the importance of appealing to groups with distinct preferences. They developed a justification strategy that could mobilize and sustain the support of different constituencies rather than focusing on general appeals.

Based on its polling and evaluation of different views within the US public, the Bush administration's communications staff focused its attention on three key groups: religious leaders, college students, and veterans.[2] Of these three constituencies, religious leaders and college students are most likely to have dovish preferences, while veterans are more likely to hold hawkish preferences. The broadest possible coalition of support for the Gulf War would thus need to include all three groups.

The administration targeted religious leaders and communities because they were a part of Bush's broader political base and divided in their support for military action. For example, Roman Catholic Archbishop Roger Mahony "offered qualified support to U.S. action in the Gulf but urged the U.S. to consider the moral ramifications" of its actions ("White House News Summary" 1990). The Bishop of the Episcopal Church offered a similar assessment of the conflict, noting "Morally, we must respond to such an outrage, both as a member nation of the community of nations and as individuals who seek to respect and uphold the human rights of others"

---

[2] This list is not exhaustive. The official communication plans also referenced business leaders, Arab Americans, and minority groups, but these constituencies appear less frequently in the discussions surrounding presidential speeches. Examples focus on these three groups because each was the sole and explicitly identified target of at least one official communication.

(Browning 1991). Groups with pacifist traditions, on the other hand, were unlikely to be convinced to support military action and the administration hoped to, at best, limit their vocal dissent. A memorandum to speechwriters and researchers from the Office of Public Liaison instructed, "We can write off any support from left-of-center religious institutions such as Pax Christi USA and the National Council of Churches, but we really do need an ongoing and friendly dialogue with conservative and mainstream churches" (Fitch 1990).

Beyond the religious community, a concern with doves also shows up in the administration's focus on college students. With the anti-Vietnam movement still a salient memory for many members of the White House staff, college campuses were viewed as likely targets for opposition leaders and sites of antiwar mobilization. The Office of Public Liaison warned that "dissent among student bodies across the nation is growing and beginning to question the U.S.'s role in the Gulf" (Battaglia, n.d.). On average, doves are more likely to be young and have higher levels of education—they are thus likely to be overrepresented on college campuses. To persuade students to support the Gulf War, the administration briefed its interns about carrying the White House message back to their campuses and issued an open letter that aimed to "reach the students of our nation and directly communicate to them the President's views of the situation in the Gulf" ("Guidance, Presidential Letter to the College Students" 1991; Metzger 1990b). Consistent with perceptions of the religious community, the White House viewed students as skeptical of military action and concerned with humanitarian objectives such as the suffering of civilians—both preferences associated with doves.

At the other end of the internationalist spectrum, the White House also used its communication plan to activate and strengthen existing domestic support from veterans' groups. The assumption here is that veterans are more likely to have a security-focused understanding of the national interest and view military action as an effective way to resolve crises—they are more likely to be classified as hawks.[3] The Bush White House collected quotes and letters from current soldiers, sought the endorsement of veterans' organizations, and directly addressed the Veterans of Foreign Wars Convention.

---

[3] See Lupton (2017; 2022) for a discussion of how military experience influences the way individuals approach the use of military force.

Rather than convincing veterans that military action was necessary, this aspect of the communication plan aimed to solidify and "thank these leaders for their continuing support" (Metzger 1990a; 1991). This strategy for communicating with veterans is consistent with the expectation that hawks are a reliable source of support for interventions.

The White House also tracked growing isolationist sentiment, particularly among conservatives. Meeting notes include efforts to counter "those in the conservative camp who argue that we have no vital interests overseas and should retreat into isolationism" and caution against using quotes from isolationist thinkers in speech drafts (Metzger 1990c; Pinkerton, James 1990; Weyrich 1990). Notably, rather than persuading isolationists with the right justifications, the White House focused on preventing individuals from adopting an isolationist worldview in the first place. This approach is consistent with the expectation that isolationists are not reliable domestic coalition members.

Justifications for different constituencies

The Bush administration not only considered the preferences of different constituencies, it also identified humanitarian claims as particularly helpful for appealing to groups of doves. To maintain support from groups of doves—including mainstream churches and college students— communications guidance recommended focusing on the moral objectives and goals of action (Fitch 1990). Notably, humanitarian appeals were discussed in terms of targeting specific constituencies rather than strengthening the credibility of the intervention as a whole. The communications team targeted the religious community's concerns through personal letters, invitations to the White House, and an address to religious broadcasters that was designed to highlight the morality of US action and outline "principles which illustrate why it is indeed a 'just war'" (Demarest 1990c; Fitch 1991; Smith 1991). In this address, the President emphasized harm done to Kuwaiti civilians:

> Every war—every war—is fought for a reason. But a just war is fought for the right reasons, for moral not selfish reasons. Let me take a moment to tell you a story, a tragic story, about a family whose two sons, 18 and 19,

reportedly refused to lower the Kuwaiti flag in front of their home. For this crime, they were executed by the Iraqis. Then, unbelievably, their parents were asked to pay the price of the bullets used to kill them. Some ask whether it's moral to use force to stop the rape, the pillage, the plunder of Kuwait. And my answer: Extraordinary diplomatic efforts having been exhausted to resolve the matter peacefully, then the use of force is moral (G. H. W. Bush 1991f).[4]

Strikingly, when addressing a predominantly dovish audience, the White House delayed its primary communication theme—halting international aggression—to first emphasize moral concerns about preventing human rights abuses and protecting civilians.

Similar humanitarian appeals are also present in White House messages to college students, consistent with an understanding that doves were common among this group. To persuade college students, the President wrote an open letter that was distributed to college newspapers around the country. The letter began with a graphic and detailed description of Saddam Hussein's abuse of the people of Iraq and Kuwait:

> The terror Saddam Hussein has imposed upon Kuwait violates every principle of human decency. Listen to what Amnesty International has documented. "Widespread abuses of human rights have been perpetrated by Iraqi forces ... arbitrary arrest and detention without trial of thousands ... widespread torture ... imposition of the death penalty and the extrajudicial execution of hundreds of unarmed civilians, including children." [//] Including children. There's no horror that could make this a more obvious conflict of good vs. evil. The man who used chemical warfare on his own people—once again including children—now oversees public hangings of dissenters. And daily his troops commit atrocities against Kuwaiti citizens (G. H. W. Bush 1991e).

As in his appeal to religious groups, the humanitarian claims Bush used to target college students were both more prominent and graphic than the rhetoric used in national addresses. The centrality of humanitarian explanations in these speeches reflects an understanding by the White House that

---

[4] Earlier drafts were even more direct: "Some ask whether it is moral to use force to stop the rape, pillage, and plunder of Kuwait. My answer: It should be immoral not to use force" (Smith 1991).

specific, skeptical audiences could be persuaded by highlighting harm done to civilians.

White House communications also recognized that humanitarian rationales were less important when targeting audiences primarily made up of hawks. As the survey experiments in Chapter 4 detailed, hawks offer their maximum support even when security justifications are used by themselves. In the context of the Gulf War, veterans' groups represented the target audience most likely to be hawks. The President addressed the Veterans of Foreign Wars (VFW) Annual Conference on August 20, 1990, to solidify support from this constituency. Humanitarian claims are notably absent from this speech. Instead, the communications team crafted the remarks to highlight Bush's "commitment to a strong national defense" and "the importance of a national defense policy that responds to the security demands of a complex and still precarious world" (Smith 1990).

The speech also included references to the morality of US action, with the President asserting "I acted knowing that our cause would not be easy but that our cause is right" (G. H. W. Bush 1990e). In contrast to addresses for religious leaders or college students, however, in this speech, Bush made the case that action was just by using exclusively security explanations. He explained that "while one should not underestimate those who endanger peace, an even greater mistake would be to underestimate America's commitment to our friends when our friends are imperiled or our commitment to international order when that, too, is imperiled" (G. H. W. Bush 1990e). Alliances and stability, not protecting civilians, made military action moral in this context. When the VFW speech did mention civilians, it was to discuss foreign civilians trapped in Kuwait.

Together, these official statements highlight how the White House adjusted its communication strategy to target different foreign policy constituencies. Even if the Bush communications team did not always refer to groups as doves or hawks, they understood how to target and win over each constituency. Speeches to audiences with more dovish members placed human suffering front and center, while audiences with hawkish values heard about US alliances and strategic interests. Supplementing these targeted speeches with national addresses that combined security and humanitarian rationales, the Bush administration had an intentional communication plan to build a broad domestic coalition. Notably, while consistent with the domestic coalition expectations, the variation in justifications across audiences stands in contrast to the against-type argument—if unexpected justifications increase the general credibility of a president's statements, humanitarian claims would remain important even when addressing audiences of hawks.

Reasons for restraint in humanitarian appeals

Internal discussions also provide evidence that the Bush administration confronted and was constrained by the political risk of overusing humanitarian explanations. In his letter to the President following a personal meeting, the Bishop of the Episcopal Church explicitly outlined the limits of humanitarian claims among doves: "While I share your outrage over the atrocities reported from Kuwait, such atrocities should not be used as the necessary or sufficient basis for our actions against Iraq when we have not acted in a similar fashion towards other nations commiting [sic] abuses of human rights" (Browning 1991).

The White House also recognized and operated within these limits. Drafts of the open letter to college students provide the clearest example of the White House intentionally restraining its emphasis of humanitarian appeals to avoid backlash. An early draft of the letter exclusively emphasized humanitarian concerns, focusing on Saddam Hussein's long and documented history of abusing his own citizens, as well as the targeting of children in Kuwait (Jackson 1991). In their review of this version, however, officials cautioned against making an exclusively humanitarian argument. Special Assistant to the President and Executive Secretary for Cabinet Liaison Michael Jackson (1991) responded to an Office of Speech Writing memo that the draft "is too emotional or sappy. College kids are a hard sell. They will be very skeptical. Our arguments should in some way respond to or anticipate criticism of our policy. College students should get a very blunt, not very rhetorical enumeration of our objectives and arguments. I like very much using the Amnesty International report." National Security Council staff raised similar concerns, noting that "The almost exclusive focus on human rights arguments is not an accurate reflection of what lies behind our involvement. The letter does not adequately treat our goals, why we feel a sense of urgency, and why the United States is assuming so much of the responsibility of the international response" (Sittmann 1990). Ultimately, the letter was revised to include security rationales for action, referencing Iraq's international aggression, attempts at nuclear proliferation, and connections to terrorism (G. H. W. Bush 1991e).

Other examples of caution surrounding humanitarian claims appear in the second draft of a speech given at Hickam Airfield on October 28, 1990. Official comments on this draft capture a debate over whether to mention that Iraq "gassed its own people" (McNally and Simon 1990). Critics of the line warned that "The use of CW [chemical weapons] was years ago. It has nothing to do with this crisis and we were mum about it at the time" (McNally and Simon 1990). Presenting past and unaddressed human rights abuses as the impetus for contemporary action was thus seen as stretching humanitarian claims too far—something the White House should avoid if it wanted to persuade doves and broaden public support.

Conclusions from the Gulf War

Humanitarian justifications played a common but secondary role in the Bush administration's communication strategy for the 1991 Gulf War. In line with the expectations of the domestic coalition argument, archival materials demonstrate that the administration was concerned about and made a concerted effort to build broad domestic support for the use of force. These efforts included disaggregating the public into key target groups and using humanitarian claims to appeal to skeptics and block potential channels of dissent. In this case, the religious community and college students acted as critical constituencies for the Bush coalition. Both groups espoused concerns and values consistent with dovish priorities and were the target audiences for many of the administration's humanitarian appeals. Additionally, the evidence suggests that the White House recognized both the utility and limits of humanitarian claims and cautioned against their overuse. Taken as a whole, the Bush administration's communication strategy establishes that the President and his team both knew about the diversity of the domestic audience and developed justifications with a broad coalition in mind. The Gulf War case thus demonstrates that the logic of the domestic coalition argument is plausible in post-Cold War security crises.

Alternative explanations

The Bush administration was concerned with domestic public opinion, viewed White House communications as an effective way to manage public perceptions, and recognized both the benefits and limits of humanitarian claims, especially when addressing audiences with dovish preferences. This evidence from the archival materials is consistent with the domestic coalition argument, but I also rule out alternative explanations more directly by looking at how the administration's concern with the domestic public compared to other audiences and objectives. This section considers the role of different audiences, against-type signals, and humanitarian goals.

The international audience

Maintaining the support of allies and managing relationships with both the former Soviet Union and China received significant attention from policymakers, especially in the immediate aftermath of Iraq's invasion of Kuwait (Dyke 1990a). In line with these efforts, the Gulf War communications team paid attention to the international audience and designed unique public diplomacy efforts to shape international opinion. These efforts, however, followed distinct talking points and were developed separately from the domestic communication strategy—the former did not create pressure to include humanitarian claims in the latter. A National Security Council memo, for example, noted "It has been suggested that we put out a set of public diplomacy themes specifically aimed at countering overseas expectations of a short war and criticisms that it seems to be turning into a longer war" (Dyke 1991c). Similarly, the "Public Diplomacy Themes to Target on Iraqis," outlined ways to break apart coalitions of support within Iraq, developing different talking points for all Iraqis, military leadership, Iraqi military in Kuwait, and the Iraqi public (Dyke 1990c). The themes identified twenty-two different points to make in communications with Iraq, none of which mirror the humanitarian justifications that appear in US national addresses. The closest humanitarian themes accused Hussein of plundering Kuwait and its people and warned Iraq's military leadership that they would "bear legal responsibility, including criminal prosecution, for the war crimes of Iraqi soldiers against civilians or for the first use of chemical weapons" (Dyke 1990c).

When international communication themes did appear in national addresses, they took the form of appeals to the world order and giving credit to allies rather than humanitarian rationales. Messaging for the international audience emphasized the creation of a new world order that included cooperation between the United States and the former Soviet Union, the formation of a multilateral coalition endowed with international legitimacy by the UN, and the support of Arab States. Drafts of Bush's September 11, 1990 Address to the Joint Session of Congress highlighted the creation of a new world order by asking listeners to "Just imagine how different this crisis would be if, as in decades past, a dictator like Saddam has [sic] been able to count upon the Soviet Union and East-West confrontation to inhibit an international response to his aggression" ("Draft 1, Presidential Remarks: Address to Joint Session of Congress" 1990). Official comments in the margins of this same draft encouraged speechwriters to use this section of the address to "Dramatize signal to Hussein/Give Gorb [Gorbachev] some credit" ("Draft 1, Presidential Remarks: Address to Joint Session of Congress" 1990). Similarly, comments on speech drafts from advisor Ed Rogers highlighted the broader international theme, of which Soviet cooperation was only one dimension, instructing, "In every set of remarks re Persian Gulf we should include ref. to the Rule of law and/or Iraq violations of International law. This is important" (Rogers 1990, emphasis and formatting from original).

The emphasis on international cooperation and the rule of law was reinforced by the multilateral nature of the operation and the involvement of the United Nations. By its end, the intervention had support from a coalition of twenty-eight states and was enabled by twelve UN resolutions. US officials worked to build and maintain this international coalition, but primarily relied on "a quiet diplomatic effort to develop support for the use of force" rather than official statements (National Security Council 1990a). The visible outreach that did exist included a "Video Address to the Community of Nations United Against Iraqi Aggression," which highlighted the importance of the January 15 deadline for Iraq's withdrawal (Mcgroarty 1991).

Bush also gave an address to the United Nations General Assembly, which intended to:

> [...] reflect on the efficacy of UN action on Iraq, the importance of firm support for the UN Charter and the Security Council, and the emergence on the world stage of the United Nations as effective [sic] instrument for peace. In particular, this speech to the UN also offers a good opportunity to stress the importance of pushing harder to prevent nuclear, chemical, biological, and missile proliferation. The Gulf crisis brings into sharper focus the danger of such proliferation. (Roy 1990)

With these goals in mind, the major Gulf War theme for the address was "United UN Action Against Aggression." The related talking points highlighted the collective strength of the world community, evidence that "The UN is now correcting its course," and that "The UN Security Council's response to the crisis in the Gulf has been nothing less than historic" (Roy 1990). The administration placed particular emphasis on the UN's ability to "stand between small states and more powerful neighbors," using responses to Iraq's invasion of Kuwait as an example (Roy 1990). While the speech itself drew attention to the plight of innocent civilians in Kuwait, the communication strategy presented this concern in the context of lifting the burden on allies in the region, noting "The effect of Iraqi aggression on developing nations is particularly evident in the plight of scores of thousands of innocent civilian foreigners trapped in the desert trying to flee Iraq. Their situation is desperate. The Jordanians and Turks are are [sic] doing the best they can to care for them, but the numbers involved are overwhelming. We and the rest of the world community are helping through the UN" (Roy 1990).

The logic and themes behind Bush's UN speech capture the administration's concern with international audiences and efforts to build international support. The process through which this speech was developed, however, shows that international outreach efforts had distinct goals, few of which centered on humanitarian rationales. This concern with the international audience does not account for the pattern or the content of humanitarian appeals in the White House's national addresses or domestic communication plan.

As a result of continued diplomatic efforts, the international coalition remained stable and there is no evidence that the justifications used in the White House's domestic communication strategy were driven by concern about maintaining international support. An exception to the overall stability of the international coalition was the administration's concern with anti-American sentiment in Arab states. Diplomatic communications from the day after Iraq's invasion of Kuwait found that the leaders of Jordan, Egypt, Yemen, and Saudi Arabia "felt this was an Arab matter, and that they asked for time to resolve the issue themselves" (Fitzwater 1990b). In January 1990, as the diplomatic efforts of Arab states and the international community increasingly appeared unsuccessful, Secretary of State James Baker warned the President that Iraq's foreign minister "wants to make it Iraq vs. U.S" (Fitzwater 1991b). The following day, Bush spoke with UN Secretary General De Cuéllar, emphasizing the multilateral nature of the intervention and opportunities to demonstrate that military action was driven by the UN rather than the US alone (Fitzwater 1991c). From this point forward, the assertion that "This is not, as Saddam Hussein would have it, the

United States against Iraq. It is Iraq against the world" became a common feature in presidential speeches and official statements (G. H. W. Bush 1990a; 1990c; "Draft Comments, McGroarty/Dooley, Presidential Remarks: Video Address to the Iraqi People" 1990).

Managing international opinion in Arab states became even more important after the war began and Hussein launched a disinformation campaign. This propaganda accused the United States of targeting religious sites, while Iraq's use of human shields drew attention to civilian casualties (Rugh 1991a). When polls indicated that these accusations were shifting international opinion, the US's public diplomacy campaign coordinated an effort to contradict disinformation as it arose (Rugh 1991b). The guidelines for this response were to avoid praising Saddam's military sagacity, emphasize coalition unity, and publicize officials from high profile but non-White House agencies such as the Department of Defense ("Memorandum, Summary of Iraq Public Diplomacy Meeting" 1991; Rugh 1991b).

As part of this plan, humanitarian justifications were used to juxtapose Hussein's history of brutality in the region with US concern about protecting civilians: "We deeply regret any loss of life, military and civilian, on all sides, and will do everything possible to minimize civilian casualties. For much of his career, Saddam Hussein has brutalized his own people" ("Cable, Gulf Public Diplomacy During Hostilities," n.d.). These humanitarian concerns primarily focused on the coalition's attempts to avoid hitting civilians and holy sites and were designed to lay the groundwork for post-war stability (Dyke 1991c; 1991a). Additionally, while US officials noted that a drawn-out war could spark anti-American resentment in allied Arab countries, they ultimately concluded that "whether even a relatively long war will or will not generate sufficient public pressure to overturn the basic policies or political control of friendly Arab governments remains uncertain at this point" (Helman 1991). Given the expeditious end of the Gulf War, these concerns did not come to fruition and the coalition remained stable throughout the combat operation. Together, these factors indicate that humanitarian claims were helpful to, but not primarily an outgrowth of, international public diplomacy campaigns.

Finally, the administration also used international support to bolster domestic public opinion.[5] For example, even the communication plan for international public diplomacy aimed to "Look for spinoffs that positively

---

[5] This evidence is consistent with the finding that international support and the approval of international organizations increase public support through a variety of mechanisms (Grieco et al. 2011; Thompson 2006; Wallace 2013).

affect American public opinion; do not negatively affect American opinion" (Dyke 1990b). In this regard, the multilateral coalition was particularly help-ful in addressing domestic concerns about the cost of the war, where internal polling indicated, "The public does believe that the U.S. is carrying more than its fair share of the financial costs of the war. This could be a prob-lem for the Administration in the aftermath of the War" (Steeper 1991a). As long as the international coalition remained stable—as was the case for the duration of Operation Desert Storm—White House national addresses prioritized domestic politics.

Managing political elites

The administration's use of humanitarian appeals in its domestic com-munication strategy could also, however, reflect concern with domestic political elites rather than public opinion. White House efforts to manage elite dissent primarily centered on securing a congressional resolution in support of military action. To garner support from the House and Senate, the President spoke at congressional meetings, sent letters to congressional leadership, and sent officials to testify before the House Foreign Affairs Committee and Senate Foreign Relations Committee (Baker 1990b; 1990a; G. H. W. Bush 1991b; McClure 1991; "Meeting with Bipartisan Congres-sional Leadership" 1991; "Speech Cards, Republican Congressional Lead-ership" 1990). Talking points for communicating with Congress empha-sized the US national interest and the need to send a strong signal in response to Iraq's aggression. In his letter to congressional leadership, Bush explained:

> The current situation in the Persian Gulf brought about by Iraq's unpro-voked invasion and subsequent brutal occupation of Kuwait, threatens vital U.S. interests. The situation also threatens the peace. It would, however, greatly enhance the chances for peace if Congress were now to go on record supporting the position adopted by the UN Security Council on twelve separate occasions. Such an action would underline that the United States stands with the international community and on the side of law and decency; it also would help dispel any belief that may exist in the minds of Iraq's leaders that the United States lacks the necessary unity to act deci-sively in response to Iraq's continued aggression against Kuwait. (G. H. W. Bush 1991b)

Bush did use humanitarian claims in his meetings with congressional leadership after Operation Desert Storm began. For example, White House talking points for meetings with Republican Congressional Leadership on January 24, 1991 included, "I will say though that I am outraged by what Saddam is doing and by targeting innocents with scuds and by his exploitation of prisoners of war [POWs]. He will be held accountable for any and all war crimes committed" ("Talking Points, Points to Be Made for Meeting with Republican Congressional Leadership" 1991). Humanitarian appeals are notably absent, however, from communications prior to the passage of House and Senate resolutions. The White House's efforts to appease political elites—both within the administration and in Congress—cannot alone account for the consistency of humanitarian claims in official statements throughout the conflict.

Additionally, the administration's efforts to gain congressional approval were driven by concern about what support or opposition from Congress would mean for public opinion. White House officials were divided over whether to seek a congressional vote authorizing the President to enforce UN resolutions. Bush recognized that his "opposition to the war powers resolution is well known" (G. H. W. Bush 1991c) and White House Counsel advised that "there are few legal advantages to a declaration of war," informing the President that he could proceed "without any formal congressional approval at all" (Gray 1990). In particular, opponents of a resolution argued that "It would be a mistake to ask for a Cong. Vote if they won't give overwhelming support" and the President believed that there would be "Nothing worse than a hung jury or negative vote" (Fitzwater 1991d).

Despite these risks, the White House ultimately pursued and received congressional approval. Internal discussions in the lead-up to this decision outlined the benefits of congressional approval for domestic public opinion:

> We believe it is legally sufficient to proceed with no formal congressional authorization at all. However, if U.S. forces will be involved in hostilities or situations where involvement in hostilities is imminent and you wish to avoid a dispute over the War Powers Resolution, or if a congressional endorsement would useful [sic] in gaining public support for your action, you should consider seeking a joint resolution approving your action. (Gray 1990)

Internal polls confirmed that a majority of the public thought the President should get approval from Congress before taking military action in

Iraq (Morin 1991; Office of Communications 1991). Combined, these discussions reveal that while the White House actively sought congressional approval, elite pressure did not primarily drive either the broader communication strategy or the use of humanitarian justifications. Instead, concern about the public's reaction contributed to the President's decision to pursue a congressional resolution of support.

Credibility from against-type signals

The against-type alternative is consistent with evidence that the White House cared about domestic public opinion. It is challenged, however, by the way the Bush administration talked about perceptions of his foreign policy leadership, by variation across constituencies, and by concern about the overuse of humanitarian appeals. Instead of being concerned about appearing too hawkish, internal polling reports and campaign materials cast Bush's decisive action in the Gulf War as one of his main strengths. National surveys conducted by the Republican National Committee (RNC) in the lead up to the November 1990 mid-term elections found that "The President is positively perceived on foreign affairs, Iraq, and education" and noted that "Basic support for U.S. policy in the Persian Gulf has not eroded in October" while support for hawkish policy options was increasing (Teeter 1990c). Bush's assertive approach to foreign policy remained a strength after the war and during his 1992 presidential campaign. Reports from exit polls and focus groups during the 1992 primary elections concluded that "Our focus groups said he is a strong leader once he decides to put his mind to it. They even went on to say that his foreign policy expertise could be put to our economic advantage by opening new markets to American-made products" (Steeper 1992).

Consistent with Friedman's (2023) account of the "commander-in-chief-test," the campaign attempted to capitalize on Bush's perceived foreign policy strength. Campaign talking points emphasized that "The President's decisive actions stood in sharp contrast to the doubt-ridden Democrat [sic] leadership in Congress. His decisive action in the Middle East saved the world from the threat of nuclear terrorism and guaranteed the safety of the Persian Gulf oil supplies" (Snow 1992b). The same speech cards contrasted Bush's strong and decisive action against Saddam Hussein with points that "Clinton waffled on the most important national security issue in years—whether to kick Saddam Hussein's Iraqi army out of Kuwait" (Snow 1992a). To the extent that the Bush administration and campaign considered perceptions of the president's foreign policy type, his hawk-like focus on national security and experience with assertive action were presented as strengths and contrasted with Clinton's more dovish preferences. Neither before nor after Desert Storm did the administration appear concerned with making Bush's policies seem less hawkish.

Additionally, from the against-type perspective, if the Bush administration used humanitarian appeals to make intervention appear more moderate and credible, these benefits should exist across foreign policy constituencies—it is the unexpected aspect of the statement rather individual agreement that makes against-type signals effective. The administration did use humanitarian justifications to argue that the Gulf War was a war of last resort, but these claims targeted specific constituencies and their presence varied across different audiences. The communications team designed humanitarian rationales in part to appeal to younger generations and religious groups. The evidence from the speech drafts and memos outlined above shows that the goal of these references was to appeal to groups' core values and policy priorities. In the collected speech files, there are no clear references to humanitarian appeals being powerful because they made Bush appear more dovish than normal. Instead, consistent with the domestic coalition logic, the goal was to mobilize groups of doves by referencing the issues they cared about. This nuanced distinction helps explain why Bush included humanitarian appeals in speeches to the nation as a whole and when targeting religious groups and college students but left them out when addressing audiences of hawks like the VFW.

Finally, the against-type logic also implies that if humanitarian appeals are helpful, presidents should use them widely—the more humanitarian the Gulf War appeared, the stronger the against-type signal. From this perspective, there is no clear reason for the White House's concern about overstating humanitarian appeals or for its restrained emphasis of humanitarian rationales. Instead, this aspect of the communication strategy is better explained by the domestic coalition expectation that the same individuals who humanitarian appeals persuade also pose a risk of backlash if leaders stretch these claims too far.

Reporting humanitarian objectives

The Bush administration's use of humanitarian claims could also simply reflect a military strategy focused on humanitarian objectives. Instead, discussions of strategy and humanitarian conditions reveal that humanitarian objectives did not become a significant part of US operations until the post-war period. Throughout the conflict, US officials monitored reports of Saddam Hussein's past human rights abuses, atrocities and potential war crimes committed in Iraq and Kuwait, the status of refugees in neighboring states, and the effect of sanctions on Iraq's food and medical supplies (Alexander et al. 1991; Crowder 1990; "Guidance, Iraq and War Crimes" 1991; "Report, Iraq: Impact of the Sanctions" 1990; Rosenblast 1991). Despite widespread evidence of Iraq's human rights violations, military strategy did not focus on preventing the suffering of Kuwaiti civilians. Discussions of US military options reveal that the White House considered making the case for military action by arguing that giving sanctions more time to work "comes into potential conflict with the need to act to stop Iraq atrocities and the destruction of Kuwait" (National Security Council 1990b). However, officials' concern with the stability of Kuwait was connected to its status as a "vital country" rather than a response to human rights violations. Additionally, throughout the intervention, the stated military objectives remained consistent and did not mention the welfare of Kuwaiti civilians.[6] Humanitarian objectives were thus not an explicit part of US military strategy during Operation Desert Storm.

Instead, tactical discussions of humanitarian objectives focused on how the US would promote stability and avoid anti-American sentiment in the post-war environment. A memorandum from the National Security Council in the final weeks of war noted that, "It is very much in our interest now and after the war to demonstrate our humanitarian principles, which have guided us in the past. We are on a good track now, which should be continued, in cooperating with international humanitarian organizations and in our public sentiments" (Dyke 1991b). In line with this approach, when the end of the war became imminent, focus shifted to preparing to work

---

[6] Throughout the war, these goals included: "First, the immediate, complete and unconditional withdrawal of Iraq from Kuwait. Second, restoration of Kuwait's legitimate government. Third, release of all hostages. Fourth, a commitment to the security and stability of the Persian Gulf" ("Guidance, Gulf Policy Themes" 1990). Notably, freeing hostages focused on protecting American citizens rather than foreign civilians.

with international organizations to achieve humanitarian objectives and staff noted that, "We really need to push on UN and ICRC [International Committee of the Red Cross] so they are in a position to take this problem [humanitarian assistance in Safwan and Southern Iraq] on when we pull out" (Wolfowitz 1991).

In short, the administration did integrate humanitarian objectives into its military strategy at the end of the conflict and humanitarian efforts intensified further during Operation Provide Comfort. Humanitarian goals were not, however, an initial focus of US operations. The reality of US military objectives cannot, therefore, account for the presence of humanitarian claims in official speeches and statements prior to and in the early stages of the war.

The scope of the domestic coalition: Humanitarian intervention in Bosnia

The Gulf War case provides evidence for the domestic coalition argument, focusing on a security crisis where humanitarian claims are conventionally seen as unnecessary. US military action in Bosnia, by contrast, responded primarily to a humanitarian crisis. As an instance of humanitarian intervention, the Bosnian case captures the context in which humanitarian justifications are most often studied and expected to influence public opinion. Its purpose here is to establish the scope of the domestic coalition argument, showing that the White House continues to use justifications strategically when addressing humanitarian crises. The Bosnian case also helps rule out the against-type alternative by shedding light on whether Democratic presidents face stronger incentives to use security justifications than humanitarian claims. I use the same five standardized questions from the Gulf War case to evaluate the domestic coalition logic in the Bosnian case. The only exception is that I do not expect the Clinton administration to be worried about overusing humanitarian claims in the context of a humanitarian intervention.

The crisis in Bosnia has its origins in the dissolution of Yugoslavia in the early 1990s. Against this backdrop, Bosnia held its own independence referendum in March 1992. The US and European Community recognized Bosnia-Herzegovina as a sovereign independent state in April of the same year. Following the independence vote, war broke out as Bosnian

Serbs, opposed to the separation and aided by Yugoslav national forces under the direction of Serbian President Slobodan Milosevic, began a campaign of ethnic cleansing that drove Bosnian Muslims and Croats from their homes (Christopher 2001, 253).

US involvement in the crisis began in July 1992 when troops conducted airlifts of humanitarian aid to Sarajevo to assist the UN mission (United Nations High Commissioner for Refugees 1996). By the time the Clinton administration entered the White House in January 1993, NATO had agreed to enforce a no-fly zone and peace efforts were stalled. In the face of perceived international and domestic constraints, the Clinton White House first pursued a policy of non-intervention, focused on achieving a negotiated solution to the conflict, from 1993 through 1994. This approach changed in 1995 as Serbian forces shelled Sarajevo and attacked UN-declared safe areas in Zepa and Srebrenica. In a July meeting with allies in London, the US and NATO committed to using airstrikes to respond to future attacks on safe areas. When Bosnian Serbs again shelled a Sarajevo marketplace on August 28, NATO and the US upheld their London agreement, launching intensive airstrikes on Serbian targets that continued until September 14 (Christopher 2001, 257). The duration of these airstrikes represents the period in which US policy changed from a potential to an actual humanitarian intervention. I examine documents in the build-up to the 1995 airstrikes—beginning with the Clinton administration's involvement in 1993—to evaluate how the White House approaches domestic coalitions of support for humanitarian interventions.

The military conflict ended on November 21, 1995, when Bosnian and Serbian leaders signed the Dayton Accords. In support of the Dayton Accords, Clinton promised to deploy 20,000 US troops as part of the NATO Implementation Force (IFOR) (Power 2002, 440). IFOR completed its one-year mandate in 1996 and handed over responsibilities to the Stabilization Force in Bosnia and Herzegovina, which remained in place until 2004.

Intentional communications

During its first few months in the White House, the Clinton administration referenced Bosnia rarely and inconsistently. By 1994, with the prospect of military action increasing, the White House realized that its silence came with political costs and developed an intentional communication strategy designed to build support among the US public. A memo from the National Security Council marked this change, outlining the need for a careful and coherent communication plan:

> With the exception of a few soundbites from the President, the Administration has offered little in the way of public explanation or defense of our position. A strategy which appears defensive, or even worse, a strategy of silence will not quell public uproar; it will make it worse. We need to lay out our policy but with care not to promise more or less than we many intend to do in the long-run. (Sonenshine, n.d.)

The administration's increased focus on controlling the Bosnian narrative came amid statements of opposition from Congress ("Bosnia Hill Strategy" 1994; Dole and Lieberman 1994; Molinari 1993) and media coverage of elite debates. This growing domestic pressure informed the White House's public affairs strategy for 1994, which acknowledged that coverage of attacks on civilians and the resulting calls for escalation could not be avoided: "This story is not going to fade away although the initial press hysteria will subside," in part because "Media interest is great and the number of outlets is equally great" (Ross/Sonenshine 1994). Despite this pressure, the White House remained optimistic that it could influence public opinion with official statements, noting "it is possible to alter the tone and tenor of the press coverage of Bosnia, and to contribute to public understanding of our interests in the Bosnian conflict" (Ross/Sonenshine 1994). In the context of humanitarian crises, the presence of an intentional White House communication strategy focused on the domestic public remains consistent. The Clinton administration's early (mis-)handling of communications about the crisis also highlights the political risks the White House incurs when it does not address the public in an intentional, coordinated way.

Justifications for humanitarian crises

Given the political importance of public communications in the Bosnian case, the next question considers which justifications the White House used to build support for its foreign policy and how much emphasis it placed on humanitarian appeals. The pattern of presidential speeches referencing Bosnia—illustrated in Figure 6.2—shows that humanitarian justifications were a consistent and central part of the administration's communication strategy. Humanitarian explanations for US policy were present from the beginning of the conflict and were emphasized as the primary reason for action in the majority of speeches. As the right-hand panel of Figure 6.2 details, Clinton also offered security justifications for US policy towards Bosnia—often referencing allies and noting during periods of non-intervention that the conflict did not concern US national interests. These security justifications appeared less often than humanitarian claims and were not the primary rationale for US policy. Notably, Clinton's limited use of security justifications in this context runs counter to the expectations of the against-type alternative. Rather than trying to make policy decisions appear more hawkish, the administration showed restraint in its references to US national security. Consistent with the domestic coalition argument, Clinton increased his use of security justifications when policy shifted towards military action and mobilizing hawks became a benefit rather than a risk. Even in these latter stages, however, humanitarian justifications remained the primary explanation for US involvement. In the context of

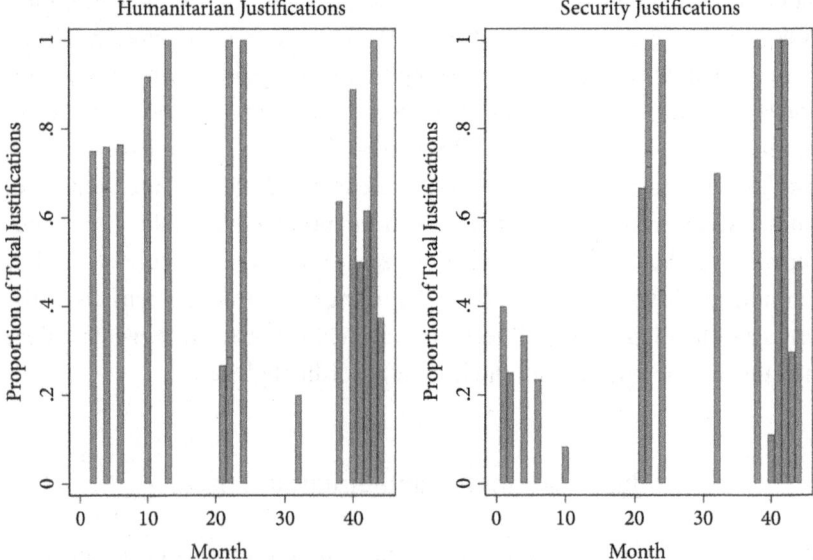

Figure 6.2 Emphasis of justifications for the Bosnian conflict

Note: The presence of a bar indicates that there was a national address during that month of the conflict.

a humanitarian crisis, the administration used humanitarian justifications without any obvious concern that such appeals would appear insincere or overstated.

Different crisis, same coalition

Even in the presence of humanitarian justifications, assessing the scope of the domestic coalition argument hinges on whether the Clinton administration tried to build a coalition of support across different foreign policy constituencies. Internal discussions of White House policy and communications reveal that the Clinton administration actively worked to counter domestic pressure, acknowledged that the public held a range of foreign policy preferences, and identified doves as the target audience for its appeals. As early as 1993, press strategy advised that:

> The best explanation is the truth. We have chosen not to pursue either of the extremist positions: the do-nothing approach nor the massive use of force approach. We strive to find a middle ground between full-fledged isolationism, and full scale war. The middle ground is a mixture of minimal force and maximum diplomacy. It satisfied neither those who want us to stay out of internal conflicts, altogether, nor those who want us to bomb everything in sight. We will accept the fact that both ends of the spectrum are dissatisfied. (Sonenshine, n.d.)

The administration's understanding that the domestic audience held a spectrum of beliefs informed its communication plan. This logic reappeared in a 1994 memo explaining, "There are those who are trying to portray the US position as either totally passive/inactive. On the other end of the spectrum are those who are trying to portray this position as one of over-activity. They are both WRONG" (Sonenshine 1994). Concern with internationalist and isolationist sentiments also appeared in discussions of public opinion. Using the same Chicago Council on Global Affairs measures as in Chapter 3, memos tracking foreign policy preferences concluded that despite media coverage of isolationism, internationalist sentiment was "holding steady" and "About 60 percent of Americans now favor a generally active, cooperative U.S. role in world affairs, compared to about a fourth who oppose active involvement abroad" (Richman 1993).

Across these sources, while "full-fledged isolationists" were unhappy that the White House was engaged in the Bosnian conflict at all, the other, "bomb everything" end of the spectrum was consistent with a hawkish view. By the White House's own logic, doves represented a middle ground that would reliably support diplomatic solutions, as well as humanitarian intervention.[7]

The domestic groups expressing dovish preferences for US policy towards Bosnia are comparable to the constituencies expected to hold these values in the Gulf War. As before, religious constituencies both espoused dovish preferences and were electorally important to the White House. For example, criticisms from the American Jewish Congress—a non-pacifist religious group with dovish preferences—garnered White House attention and a response. The group condemned the White House's early lack of engagement, asserting "The cold indifference to the massive human catastrophe in Bosnia expressed by your Administration's policy constitutes a betrayal of fundamental American values no less than of America's national interest" (Lifton and Siegman 1993). Critiques like this led the administration to develop a more robust communication plan justifying its policy.

Disapproval from doves, however, stopped short of calling for full-scale military action. Instead, the American Jewish Congress urged Clinton to "take immediate steps to assert U.S. leadership in mobilizing international action to stop the carnage in Bosnia" (Lifton and Siegman 1993). Similarly, when religious and civic groups organized "A Day for Bosnia" in Dallas, Texas, the group coordinated the signing of the "world's largest postcard" to communicate its concerns to the White House but advocated for US leadership short of intervention. The postcard's text urged Clinton to "Please utilize our country's global leadership and give voice to our great nation's moral force. If we do not act now, how shall we one day tell our children that we did nothing." Organizers, however, emphasized that "the inscription is in no way critical of the President's efforts, and calls only for increased exertion

---

[7] This understanding of doves' preferences also helps make sense of why the claim "humanitarian justifications are necessary to maximize doves' support for military intervention" is distinct from the claim "doves demand military intervention when presented with humanitarian concerns." While doves become willing to consider military action when there is a humanitarian rationale, they maintain their preference for diplomatic solutions. If the White House can demonstrate that it is paying attention to human rights abuses and asks doves for time to allow diplomacy to work—instead of galvanizing support for military action—doves are likely to comply. It is for this reason that doves do not create domestic pressure for humanitarian intervention in all cases of humanitarian crises.

on present White House policy. Neither United States military intervention nor a repeal of the arms embargo are included among the demands" (Saperstein 1993). Doves pressure the White House to pay attention to humanitarian crises, but they do not demand that attention take the form of military action.

These examples from the Bosnian case establish both that the Clinton White House knew it faced distinct foreign policy constituencies and that doves were politically relevant. Consistent with their other-regarding concerns, groups with dovish priorities pressured the White House to do something about the humanitarian crisis in Bosnia. Unlike hawks, however, doves did not explicitly push for military intervention and could be convinced to support a range of active diplomatic policies.

Mobilizing support for a humanitarian intervention

When US policy did shift to active military involvement in 1995, the White House needed support from both hawks and doves. The Clinton administration recognized the importance of building this broad domestic coalition, using press guidance to outline a plan "to have *broadest possible based* [sic] of public support—*in both parties*—for U.S. role in implementation of settlement if we achieve one" (Bremner 1995; Feeley 1995, emphasis added). The main difference between the Gulf War and military action in Bosnia is that the latter represents a case of primarily humanitarian intervention. In the context of the domestic coalition argument, this difference means that the White House could reap the benefits of humanitarian claims without worrying about their limits—in the face of ethnic cleansing, humanitarian concerns were not at risk of being overstated. As expected, speeches during this period place a primary emphasis on humanitarian issues, which maximize support among doves, and give relatively less attention to US security and national interests.

With the prospect of direct military action looming in the summer of 1995, White House staff prepared for a change in their communication strategy. In contrast to earlier appeals for patience, they recognized, "It is likely that U.S. military will soon be in harm's way, either as part of UNPROFOR withdrawal or retaliatory strikes. It is not too soon to establish justifications for further U.S. intervention" (Lorin 1995). The content of Clinton's speeches shifted accordingly. Where he previously presented the use of force as a limited tool that could not resolve the underlying conflict, his later statements asserted that force was critical to policy success (Clinton 1995b).

The administration's use of humanitarian justifications supported this new narrative. Clinton explained airstrikes in response to the shelling of Sarajevo in late August 1995 by saying, "The massacre of civilians in Sara- jevo on Monday, caused by a Bosnian Serb shell, was an outrageous act in a terrible war and a challenge to the commitments which NATO had made to oppose such actions by force if necessary. The United States took the lead in gaining those commitments by NATO, and we must help NATO keep them" (Clinton 1995c). He went on to note that a military campaign was necessary to "make clear to the Bosnian Serbs that they have nothing to gain and everything to lose by continuing to attack Sarajevo and other safe areas and by continuing to slaughter innocent civilians" (Clinton 1995c).

Humanitarian justifications not only highlighted the suffering of civilians, they presented the US as the actor with the power to prevent a return to vio- lence and bloodshed. In his announcement of the peace agreement, Clinton summarized this logic, stating, "Our leadership made this peace agreement possible and helped to bring an end to the senseless slaughter of so many innocent people that our fellow citizens had to watch night after night after night for 4 long years on their television screens. Now American leadership, together with our allies, is needed to make this peace real and enduring" (Clinton 1995b). Without the continued involvement of the US military, civilians would not be safe because "If we're not there, NATO will not be there; the peace will collapse; the war will reignite; the slaughter of innocents will begin again" (Clinton 1995a).

As the administration argued that military action was now the only way to end the humanitarian crisis and protect civilians—a persuasive com- munication strategy for targeting doves—it also abandoned its efforts to beg patience from hawks by claiming that the crisis was beyond vital US national interests. Clinton instead characterized the crisis as one in which, "Our values, our interests, and our leadership all over the world are at stake" (Clinton 1995b). Instead of being a mainly European problem, Bosnia now represented "a region of the world that is vital to our national inter- ests" and warranted protection from US troops (Clinton 1995a). Both shifts in rhetoric are consistent with White House incentives to build a broad internationalist coalition of support for military action.

Examining the Clinton administration's communication strategy in Bosnia illustrates how the domestic coalition logic can translate to cases of humanitarian intervention. In this context, presidents can place a primary emphasis on humanitarian justifications without worrying about stretching these claims too far. Doves remain politically relevant and are an important target audience for White House messaging. Although humanitarian explanations for military action appeal to both doves and hawks, Clinton's changing characterization of US national interests in Bosnia is also consistent with White House efforts to mobilize hawks who are dissatisfied with diplomacy. When military action is on the table, in response to security or humanitarian crises, internationalist coalitions are at the forefront of White House communication strategies and domestic politics.

Conclusion

Even when US security is on the line, post-Cold War presidents have consistently evoked humanitarian appeals in their addresses to the nation (Chapter 2). The pattern of demand and restraint in official justifications is consistent with the incentives set by public opinion (Chapters 4 and 5). Shifting the focus to White House decision-making, this chapter showed that presidents rely on humanitarian appeals for the reasons the domestic coalition logic anticipates—to broaden public support among a domestic audience made up of distinct foreign policy constituencies. White House communication strategies from the Gulf War and Bosnian crises established the plausibility and scope of the domestic coalition argument in three steps.

First, the Bush administration's communication strategy during the Gulf War revealed that the White House knows about and takes seriously the incentives set by domestic public opinion. In the build-up to US military action, the Bush White House explicitly considered the spectrum of justifications available and developed an intentional, cohesive communication plan to persuade the broadest possible segment of the domestic audience. This plan and Bush's resulting speeches made strategic use of humanitarian justifications while also directly acknowledging the importance of restraint. The administration understood the benefits of humanitarian appeals in terms of their ability to persuade important constituencies of doves that were otherwise skeptical of military force.

Second, the Gulf War case rules out the most likely alternative explanations for leaders' reliance on humanitarian justifications in their national addresses. Beyond domestic public opinion, the White House was also attentive to the support of the international community and political elites. Neither of these alternative audiences, however, was the primary target of presidential addresses. While the White House worked to manage political elites and international perceptions through other channels, the communication strategy reflected in national addresses—where the puzzling pattern of humanitarian claims appears—was designed to sway domestic public opinion. In fact, references to international and congressional support were often discussed in terms of their ability to strengthen domestic public support. Additionally, instead of using humanitarian appeals to send against-type signals and bolster the intervention's overall credibility, the administration varied its use of humanitarian justifications across constituencies, highlighting other-regarding concerns when the goal was to mobilize doves. Evidence from campaign materials also demonstrates that the administration viewed its assertive, security-focused policy as a strength rather than a weakness. Similarly, conversations about humanitarian appeals do not track changes in military strategy—these justifications do more than factually report the magnitude of humanitarian objectives on the ground.

Third, where the Gulf War case established the plausibility of the domestic coalition argument in its original context—security crises—the Bosnian case clarified its scope. In humanitarian crises, building an internationalist coalition of support remains central. To appeal to doves and hawks, Clinton's humanitarian statements asserted that only the US could end and prevent the return of ethnic cleansing. When security justifications appeared in this case, their goal was to reverse earlier claims that the crisis was not a vital national interest. The key difference in communication strategies for the Gulf War and military action in Bosnia is that Clinton did not worry about overstating humanitarian appeals. Instead, his speeches offered these claims as the primary reason for action without concern about political backlash or perceptions of insincerity.

Taken as a whole, evidence from the Bush and Clinton administrations shows that presidents: (1) understand the preferences of different foreign policy constituencies, (2) intentionally craft speeches to appeal across these preferences, and (3) understand both the benefits and limits of using justifications to achieve this goal. The real-world communication strategies of multiple presidential administrations are in line with the domestic coalition argument. Moreover, the domestic coalition logic helps makes sense of why humanitarian claims appear in security crises and of what it takes to sell foreign policies to the public in a broad range of situations.

7

What powerful humanitarian claims mean for democracy

Less than a month after the 2022 Russian invasion, President Biden introduced plans for sending US assistance to Ukraine by telling the public, "Now, I want to be honest with you: This could be a long and difficult battle. But the American people will be steadfast in our support of the people of Ukraine in the face of Putin's immoral, unethical attacks on civilian populations" (Biden 2022c). In the months that followed, Biden continued to offer detailed references to civilian harm, especially when justifying costs to Americans. After outlining "horrifying evidence" of Russian "atrocities and war crimes against the Ukrainian people," he announced that "we have to accelerate that assistance package to help prepare Ukraine for Russia's offensive that's going to be more limited in terms of geography, but not in terms of brutality" (Biden 2022b). Even rising prices at the pump were worthwhile, he argued, because "We could have turned a blind eye to Putin's murderous ways, and the price of gas wouldn't have spiked the way it has. I believe that would have been wrong" (Biden 2022a).

Biden was not alone in this rationale for supporting Ukraine. Despite greater proximity to the conflict and its costs, European leaders also repeatedly emphasized Putin's barbarity. Hours after Russia's initial invasion, then UK Prime Minister Boris Johnson (2022) warned that "If the worst happens, then a European nation of 44 million men, women and children would become the target of a full-scale war of aggression." His successor, Rishi Sunak (2023), echoed these concerns 500 days into the war, noting "we have witnessed the most terrible crimes and human tragedies in Ukraine." In Germany, facing an uphill battle within his own party, Federal Chancellor Olaf Scholz (2022; 2024) emphasized that Putin's actions endangered "the lives of countless innocent people in Ukraine," later noting that, "It's absolutely our duty to support the innocent Ukrainian people in defending themselves."

Doves into Hawks. Sarah Maxey, Oxford University Press. © Oxford University Press (2026).
DOI: 10.1093/9780197832738.003.0007

The domestic coalition argument makes sense of leaders' decisions to regularly talk about innocent Ukrainians in a crisis where nuclear escalation, territorial integrity, and the protection of NATO allies are also at stake. It also highlights the consequences of humanitarian language, which appeared in the Ukraine case as political backlash against the US decision to send military aid that included cluster munitions (DeYoung, Horton, and Ryan 2023). By making humanitarian concerns salient, Biden mobilized the support of doves. At the same time that he reaped this political benefit, he also created an opportunity for this constituency to hold the administration to its word. When an administration couches its foreign policy decision in terms of protecting civilians but then engages in actions that put civilians at risk,[1] doves notice, care, and are likely to voice their opposition. In this regard, their support raises the political costs of hypocrisy and can bolster accountability. In the Ukraine case, the decision to send cluster munitions while offering humanitarian justifications was normatively problematic for doves and thus politically problematic for the Biden administration.[2]

The consistent presence of humanitarian justifications in cases like Ukraine—across time, presidents, and different types of crises—revealed that our conventional picture of what it takes to sell war to the public is incomplete. In this book, I offered a new and more comprehensive picture of the relationship between the public, the White House, and war, based on the political incentives set by a broad domestic coalition. This domestic coalition framework calls for two fundamental changes to how we think about persuading democratic publics to bear the burden of war. First, national security is not sufficient for mobilizing broad, sustainable domestic support. Leaders who fail to offer a humanitarian justification for military action leave support on the table and incur unnecessary political risks. Second, the persuasiveness of humanitarian appeals is inherently threatening to neither human rights norms nor democracy. Instead, broad coalitions of support create opportunities for accountability. It is up to individuals and civil society to seize these opportunities.

---

[1] In the case of cluster munitions, such condemnation and concern about the risk to civilians can be found among human rights groups (Convention 2022), but also from high-level officials within the Biden administration who previously claimed this weapon has "no place on the battlefield" (Kelly 2022) and said Russia's use of it could "potentially be a war crime" (Psaki 2022). The Convention on Cluster Munitions—an international treaty with over 100 signatories, not including the US or Ukraine—bans these weapons based on the "unacceptable harm to civilians" caused by unexploded munitions that remain after conflicts are over, can be picked up by anyone, and are indiscriminate in the damage they cause (Convention 2022).

[2] The political costs of this decision are evident in the outpouring of criticism from "liberals" and "progressives" who are associated with doves (Boot 2023; Leahy and Merkley 2023; Meer 2023).

In this concluding chapter, I expand on the theoretical, practical, and normative implications of the domestic coalition argument. I begin by summarizing the book's main findings and then explore their relevance to past and future interventions beyond the scope of the initial analysis. Next, I consider what these findings mean for policymakers and civil society, highlighting areas for action that could strengthen processes of democratic accountability for military interventions. I end by identifying a path forward, applying the domestic coalition logic to additional contexts and outlining its limitations.

Summary of findings

In the first chapter of the book, I identified a puzzling pattern in contemporary military interventions: presidents consistently offer humanitarian rationales for military action, even when threats to US security are salient and credible. In Chapter 2, I introduced an original dataset of US presidents' justifications for potential interventions and systematically outlined the use and emphasis of humanitarian appeals in forty-six crises across four presidential administrations. The speeches reveal evidence of demand and restraint that is out of sync with multiple strands of conventional wisdom about public attitudes towards the use of force. Presidents from both parties used humanitarian justifications in the majority of their speeches about both security and humanitarian crises, challenging rational public accounts that expect security concerns to be sufficient for mobilizing public support. The speeches also, however, show that White House communications are strategically cautious in the emphasis they place on humanitarian appeals. In security crises, presidents emphasize humanitarian issues as secondary rationales rather than presenting them as the primary or equal motive for action. This restraint challenges emotional public accounts, which expect the domestic audience to respond impulsively to humanitarian appeals and leaders to thus have an incentive to use them as often as possible.

In Chapter 3, I present a domestic coalition argument that accounts for the patterns of both demand and restraint that appear in presidential speeches. I argued that presidents' routine use of humanitarian justifications—even when US security is at stake—reveals something important and overlooked about the underlying nature of public support for military action. The White House gains wide-ranging political benefits from building broad coalitions of public support for military intervention. Broadening the domestic coalition means winning over both hawks and doves. Hawks are reliable supporters of military action, but persuading doves takes more work. Doves are skeptical of military force and prefer to see conflicts resolved with diplomacy and cooperation. They are also, however, committed to solving global problems and sensitive to other-regarding concerns. Humanitarian explanations give these individuals a reason to temporarily override their skepticism about the use of force in service of protecting and promoting the wellbeing of foreign civilians. In other words, humanitarian justifications give traditional doves a reason to become temporary hawks. Because doves are key members of the domestic coalition, presidents have a political incentive to use humanitarian rationales and maximize support from this group.

Next, I tested the validity and implications of this domestic coalition argument on two distinct pieces of the relationship between the public and war: individual attitudes and White House communication strategies in cases of intervention. Drawing on multiple methods and levels of analysis, the empirical findings offer reasons for both caution and optimism. In Chapter 4, I showed that doves are uniquely responsive to humanitarian justifications for military action, even when the intervention would also protect US security. Humanitarian justifications maximized support from doves for the reasons the domestic coalition argument expected—they caused these individuals to think more about how intervention could help foreign civilians.

Chapter 5 tackled the concern that humanitarian justifications are the "magic words" that allow presidents to pursue military action without political consequences. I show that adding humanitarian justifications to security explanations does grant the White House more leeway at the beginning of the intervention, but this leeway comes at a cost. Presidents risk significant political backlash from doves if they stretch humanitarian claims too far and appear insincere. The same individuals who incentivize the use of humanitarian appeals also limit their effectiveness. Hawks' reactions provide similar accountability for the use of security justifications, making broad coalitions especially well-equipped to hold leaders to their words.

Chapter 5 also investigated the concerns raised by human rights advocates that presidents' strategic use of humanitarian appeals could undermine efforts to prevent atrocities in the future. Fortunately, I find no evidence to support this worst-case scenario. The abuse of humanitarian rationales did not substantially undermine support for future humanitarian interventions to stop genocide, even in the short timeframe captured by the survey experiment.

Together, Chapters 4 and 5 identify the political incentives that encourage the White House to offer humanitarian justifications for security crises and to exercise restraint to avoid appearing insincere. Chapter 6 then used archival materials from the Bush administration's communication strategy during the 1991 Gulf War to confirm that the White House understands and follows these incentives. During this crisis, the White House communications team recognized that it needed to persuade a domestic audience with diverse preferences, that important constituencies were skeptical of military force but could be convinced by humanitarian appeals, and that humanitarian rationales would only be helpful if they were not overstated. Archival evidence from the Clinton administration's response to ethnic cleansing in Bosnia years later reveals that this understanding of the domestic audience is not limited to one president, one party, or security crises. It also explains why doves are willing to support but do not create pressure for humanitarian interventions—when the White House wants to stick with diplomacy, doves are understanding.

The past and future of humanitarian justifications

The book's main analysis considered potential military interventions in the post-Cold War period and the justification dataset examines national addresses given between 1990 and 2013. I focused on this time period because it holds constant potentially confounding factors: the global balance of power, the international legitimacy of humanitarian interventions, and the presence of human rights norms, including norms of civilian protection. This narrow focus avoided tipping the scales in favor of the domestic coalition argument, ensuring that if it were false, the lack of supporting evidence would be conclusive. During this period, for example, the absence of humanitarian justifications could not be attributed to the illegitimacy of humanitarian intervention as a practice.

Now, having found widespread support for the domestic coalition perspective, a key implication is that the power of humanitarian justifications is not directly tied to international humanitarian intervention norms. Presidents use these claims in their national addresses primarily because they match the incentives set by domestic public opinion, not because of their international acceptance. This distinction means that the power of humanitarian justifications in security crises likely predates the rise and international recognition of humanitarian intervention norms. Evidence from the longitudinal Chicago Council surveys in Chapter 3, for example, indicates that a substantial portion of the US population has held dovish priorities since at least the early 1970s.

A closer look reveals that humanitarian rationales appear in presidential speeches across the major military interventions of the twentieth century. In World War II, Roosevelt (1942) unsurprisingly referenced "the women and children whom Hitler is starving" and asserted that "Many thousands of civilians all over the world have been and are being killed or maimed by enemy action." Decades later, Johnson (1965) justified the "tragedy, disappointment, and progress" of military operations in Vietnam by directly calling on the public to set aside its skepticism of military action and think of the welfare of foreign civilians:

> I understand the feelings of those who regret that we must undertake air attacks. I share those feelings, but the compassion of this country and the world must go out to the men and women and children who are killed and crippled by the Viet Cong every day in South Viet-Nam. The outrage of this country and the world must be visited on those who explode their bombs in cities and villages, ripping the bodies of the helpless. The indignation of this country and the world must extend to all who seek dominion over others with a violent and ruthless disregard for life, happiness, or security.

The use of humanitarian claims while US security is at stake is therefore not an exclusively post-Cold War phenomenon. The domestic political incentives identified in Chapters 4 and 5 help make sense of this long history. By studying humanitarian justifications primarily in the context of humanitarian intervention norms, political science has underestimated their breadth and power.

The book's domestic coalition argument also has important implications for how justifications are—and are not—likely to shift in the future. The landscape of America's international and domestic politics is rapidly changing. The past decade witnessed contested changes in leadership, a global pandemic, and uncertainty about the future of the liberal world order. Any one of these changes could be enough to destabilize domestic coalitions and further alter the relationship between the public and war. Particularly threatening, however, is the fact that these changes have occurred in the context of growing political polarization (Abramowitz 2010; Iyengar et al. 2019; F. E. Lee 2015; Mason 2018; Myrick 2022). One consequence of political polarization is that presidents increasingly campaign by appealing directly to a narrow base within their own party (Panagopoulos 2016). Over time, domestic coalitions could become less politically relevant as presidents focus on deepening support among their base rather than broadening public approval. However, given the distribution of doves and hawks across parties—discussed in Chapters 3 and 4—even presidents focused on their base can still benefit from appealing to both doves and hawks.

To date, despite the Trump administration's aim to upend the practice of post-Cold War US foreign policy, White House communication strategies have not fully abandoned the goal of targeting a broad domestic coalition. Instead, the consistent presence of humanitarian appeals in the security crises facing the first Trump administration—which otherwise diverged dramatically from the conventional rhetoric and policy of international affairs—suggest that the domestic coalition logic has significant staying power. In his first address to a joint session of Congress, Trump explained that his administration would develop a new plan to "demolish and destroy ISIS, a network of lawless savages that have slaughtered Muslims and Christians, and men and women and children of all faiths and all beliefs" (Trump 2017a). The following year, his State of the Union address called out the threat posed by North Korea, noting that "no regime has oppressed its own citizens more totally or brutally than the cruel dictatorship in North Korea" and telling the story of Mr. Ji Sung-ho, a defector who endured torture and starvation, who was also an invited guest in the audience (Trump 2018). Similarly, Trump justified US airstrikes against Syria as a response to the regime's "horrible chemical weapons attack on innocent civilians. Using a deadly nerve agent, Assad choked out the lives of helpless men, women, and children. It was a slow and brutal death for so many" (Trump 2017b). These justifications were surprisingly similar to Obama's call to action when Syria used chemical weapons in 2013, saying, "Assad's government gassed to death over a thousand people, including hundreds of children. The images from this massacre are sickening: Men, women, children lying in rows, killed by poison gas. Others foaming at the mouth, gasping for breath" (Obama 2013). Despite the myriad ways in which his rhetoric broke with norms and convention, the first Trump administration relied on humanitarian rationales as consistently as other recent presidents. Less surprisingly, humanitarian explanations also played a role in the Biden administration's public statements on potential interventions, especially in the response to Russia's invasion of Ukraine outlined at the beginning of this chapter.

In a changing global and domestic environment, the rhetoric of recent administrations indicates that humanitarian justifications remain powerful political tools. This book's domestic coalition argument highlights how this power influenced past interventions and offers clearer predictions about the future resonance of humanitarian appeals. It does so by building on a critical insight: the political incentives that drive presidents' strategic use of humanitarian rationales are domestic. When presidents frame interventions in terms of helping foreign civilians, these justifications match the values of and sway a key domestic constituency. The preferences that define foreign policy constituencies do not change easily or often, even in tumultuous times. Because the incentives for their use are resistant to change, humanitarian justifications can persist as necessary and effective domestic tools, even if international consensus and the practice of humanitarian intervention fades. Persistence is not permanence, however. If democratic backsliding in the US continues, eventually weakening the importance of elections and access to credible information about human rights abuses, then the importance of public support, prospects for accountability, and relevance of the domestic coalition will also suffer.

Additionally, growing isolationism among Republicans (Smeltz et al. 2023) could also influence the character of future domestic coalitions. On the one hand, if Republican presidents primarily focus on maintaining favorability with their base, growing isolationism could disincentivize their use of humanitarian claims. The experimental evidence in Chapter 4 revealed that humanitarian justifications decrease support among isolationists. Normally, this decrease carries few political costs because isolationists are both a small segment of the population and unreliable supporters of military action in the first place. Rising numbers of isolationists—combined with an increased focus on base supporters as a result of polarization—could mean that the costs of humanitarian claims eventually outweigh the benefits for Republican presidents.

On the other hand, because isolationists' support for military action is harder to mobilize and sustain, Republican presidents interested in reliable support for interventions could instead face an increased incentive to appeal to doves across the aisle. To compensate for the loss of reliable supporters within their own party, Republican leaders would benefit from adding humanitarian claims to their security rationales to appeal to as many remaining internationalists as possible. This latter alternative is consistent with elite efforts in the House and Senate to maintain aid for Ukraine in the face of pushback from the more isolationist, "America First" segments of the Republican Party (Caldwell and Sotomayor 2024; Perry et al. 2024). It is also consistent with evidence that a combination of cross- and bipartisanship defined debates about military force during the Obama and Trump administrations (Tama 2024). It is too soon to tell how these dynamics will play out, but the domestic coalition logic offers a helpful lens for understanding the implications of future changes in the distribution of foreign policy constituencies. Where broad coalitions facilitate accountability, the narrowing of desired coalitions creates loopholes for leaders to avoid responsibility.

Implications for theory

The domestic coalition argument and findings provide a more coherent picture of public accountability for military action. This updated picture advances two main areas of international relations theory: the domestic politics of international security and the effects of international norms.

The domestic politics of international security

By using a multi-method approach that captures both public incentives and White House reactions, I find clear evidence that public opinion and domestic politics matter for foreign policy decisions. The White House takes public opinion seriously. Presidents have meaningful power over the magnitude of support for military action, but only when they operate within the limits set by public preferences. Across presidents, administrations anticipate these limits and act accordingly.

The link between democracies' domestic and international politics is well-established (Baum and Potter 2015; Brutger 2021; Milner and Tingley 2015; Reiter and Stam 2002; Tomz and Weeks 2013). What the domestic coalition argument adds is an understanding that public morality matters for foreign policy—and that the influence of other-regarding moral concerns can be helpful, rather than dangerous for democratic institutions. Existing scholarship has focused on how leaders discuss security threats to bolster public support (Gadarian 2010; Krebs and Lobasz 2007), implicitly capturing appeals that resonate with the moral foundations of hawks (Kertzer et al. 2014). By turning its focus to the political importance of doves, this book uncovers an additional, influential instrument in the White House toolkit: the appearance of helping foreign civilians. Humanitarian appeals to the protection of foreign civilians are effective because they target the underlying moral values of doves, who otherwise view the costs of military action as outweighing the benefits. By accounting for different moral views in their speeches, presidents can mobilize a broader range of the public. This aspect of the domestic coalition argument contributes to a growing recognition that morality is not a monolith (Haidt and Graham 2007; Rathbun and Stein 2020). It shows that not only does the public hold diverse views about when going to war is the right thing to do, leaders also recognize this variation and strategically appeal across groups to reap political benefits.

On its surface, the finding that humanitarian appeals are key to mobilizing broad public support—even when national security interests are at stake—evokes the worst fears of early realists (Kennan 1985; 1993; Lippmann 1922; Mandelbaum 1996) and would seem to undermine more recent accounts of a rational, prudent mass public (Jentleson and Britton 1998; Shapiro and Page 1988). A counterintuitive implication of the domestic coalition argument is that such concerns are unwarranted. Appeals to public morality engage the broadest possible segment of the prudent public and create opportunities for accountability. People pay attention to the aspects of a crisis that they care about the most. By using humanitarian justifications in security crises, presidents win the temporary support of doves and broaden their domestic coalition, but there are strings attached to this support. In the process of mobilizing support, leaders also broaden engagement and attention to the issues they raise. The side effect of activating doves' support is that they pay attention to the humanitarian dimensions of the conflict and it becomes more important for the White House to keep its promise to protect civilians. Whether the public acts on this opportunity for increased accountability depends on its access to credible information about human rights abuses and the consequences of war. Civil society and advocacy organizations play a critical role in providing this information, discussed in greater detail below.

Taken as a whole, this book's investigation of how humanitarian appeals influence the public, the president, and war shines a spotlight on the dynamic nature of democratic institutions that constrain the use of force. The war-making powers of the White House are neither absolute nor consistently constrained. Instead, the leeway that presidents have in their foreign policy depends on the success of their strategy for building domestic coalitions. At its furthest reaches, the domestic coalition argument adds an additional, reinforcing mechanism to drivers of the democratic peace (Baum and Potter 2015; Reiter and Stam 2002; Russett 1993; Tomz and Weeks 2013; Valentino, Huth, and Croco 2010). Popular interventions demand credible humanitarian justifications. In addition to evidence that democracies perpetrate fewer human rights abuses, on average (Bueno de Mesquita et al. 2005; Davenport and Armstrong 2004), convincing doves that military action would improve the wellbeing of civilians in a foreign democracy is a steep hill to climb—no combination of justifications will be able to easily build a broad domestic coalition in this context.

Humanitarian intervention norms

By changing how we think about the domestic politics of military action, the book also has implications for the study of humanitarian rhetoric and humanitarian intervention norms (Bellamy 2006; Booth Walling 2013; Crawford 2002; Finnemore 1996; 2003; Holzgrefe and Keohane 2003; Pattison 2010). It shows that the power of humanitarian explanations is not limited to the context of humanitarian interventions or responses to mass atrocities. Instead, humanitarian claims have significant influence over contemporary US interventions, even those that responded to security crises as direct as the 9/11 terrorist attacks. This decoupling of humanitarian language from humanitarian interventions highlights its strategic utility and suggests that the former will continue to play an important role in foreign policy, despite any changes in the acceptance of the latter. The practice of humanitarian intervention may fade, but humanitarian justifications are here to stay.

The strategic benefits of humanitarian appeals also shine light on the potential for their misuse, but the domestic coalition argument reveals that humanitarian claims are both more influential and less dangerous than conventionally expected. Scholars and humanitarian advocates have warned that leaders could misuse humanitarian justifications to create a false pretext for interventions, undermining efforts like the Responsibility to Protect (Bellamy 2004; 2005; Evans 2004). Moyn (2021) goes a step further, arguing that an increasing concern with preventing civilian casualties—and the turn towards the forms of war that make this possible—led the public and elites to sidestep questions about when, where, and whether wars can be justly conducted in the first place.

The domestic coalition argument adds nuance to these concerns and indicates that the worst-case scenarios are unlikely. It is true that leaders have political incentives to raise humanitarian issues, even when they are not the primary focus or motive for the intervention. What leads the domestic coalition argument to more optimistic conclusions, however, is its evidence that presidents can only stretch humanitarian—or security—claims so far before they risk political backlash from the same individuals such claims are intended to persuade. By using humanitarian rationales to mobilize the domestic coalition, leaders also give civil society the tools with which to tie their hands and hold them accountable in the future.

Policy implications: Making the most of opportunities for accountability

Building broad domestic coalitions of support also broadens opportunities for accountability. By raising humanitarian concerns that engage doves, leaders link their ability to sustain this constituency's support to the sincerity of humanitarian efforts. Because the support of doves is politically relevant and built on concerns about protecting the wellbeing of foreign civilians, the importance of maintaining it creates an opportunity for civil society to pressure leaders to keep their promises and protect civilians.

Capitalizing on this opportunity, however, requires a concerted effort. Democratically elected leaders are deterred from lying and held accountable for their actions by the risk of public backlash (Reiter 2012), which has the power to both threaten their reelection prospects and jeopardize their political agendas (Gelpi and Grieco 2015; Tomz and Weeks 2013; Tomz, Weeks, and Yarhi-Milo 2020). The experimental results in Chapters 4 and 5 show that to undermine public support and create the credible risk of political backlash, doves need access to accurate information about whether the record of human rights abuses matches presidential rhetoric. It is up to transnational advocacy networks and civil society to provide this information.

The book's argument implies that a straightforward way to undermine support for war is to break doves away from the domestic coalition. The same task can be accomplished by undermining the support of hawks, but because doves begin with skepticism towards military force, they are the easier target for opposition. In turn, the best way to create opposition among doves is to draw attention to negative humanitarian consequences. Showing that military action hurts foreign civilians more than it helps invalidates the logic that persuaded doves become temporary hawks in the first place. By publicizing how military action negatively impacts the lives of civilians and highlighting gaps between the urgency of presidential rhetoric and the pattern of human rights abuses, civil society organizations can make the domestic coalition of support difficult to sustain. The influence of information from human rights groups is evident in the Ukraine case outlined at the beginning of the chapter, with critics of the Biden administration citing reports from Human Rights Watch and the Convention on Cluster Munitions to show that this form of military aid harms rather than helps civilians (Convention 2022; Human Rights Watch 2023; Leahy and Merkley 2023; Sampson, Bisset, and Ledur 2023). The domestic coalition argument suggests that these groups could have even more of an impact by directly linking the civilian consequences of cluster munitions to Biden's earlier humanitarian appeals, which opened the door for this type of political pressure.

The argument also highlights which groups and individuals are the most effective targets for civil society outreach and information. Beyond addressing doves in general, the Gulf War and Bosnian cases analyzed in Chapter 6 suggest that religious organizations are particularly well-positioned to pressure presidents to pursue intervention only as a last resort. Both White Houses—despite being led by different parties—referenced mainstream religious groups as critical constituencies, designated time to talk with religious leaders, and adapted communication plans to address their concerns.

There is also an active role for the media to play in publicizing information from human rights groups that contradicts official justifications and could change doves' minds. Granting media access to diverse voices is a cornerstone of democratic institutions (Baum and Potter 2015). What the domestic coalition argument adds is the reason that covering the president's humanitarian promises—and any conflicting evidence—is worthwhile. Even when the primary narrative of a potential intervention focuses on US national security, there is a sizeable segment of the viewing audience who cares about and will tune in to coverage of the conflict's humanitarian dimensions. When civil society and media coverage work together to vet and publicize any discrepancies in the president's humanitarian appeals, the payoff is a broadly engaged public with the tools it needs to hold leaders accountable.

In addition to identifying ways to prevent war, the domestic coalition argument also changes how we think about mobilizing the political will to stop and prevent mass atrocities. Samantha Power (2002, XVIII) famously claimed that "It is in the realm of domestic politics that the battle to stop genocide is lost. American political leaders interpret society-wide silence as an indicator of political indifference." In pointing the finger at a disinterested American public, she reiterated the conventional wisdom—outlined at the beginning of this book—that domestic concern is activated when security rather than humanitarian interests are at stake. The domestic coalition argument shows that this view is incorrect and that public opinion is not the obstacle to stopping genocide. Given credible and clearly communicated humanitarian rationales for military action, the public responds with high levels of support. Doves do not, however, independently pressure leaders to pursue military interventions over diplomatic options because of their preference for cooperative solutions. As a result, what is required for humanitarian interventions is for leaders to make a compelling case that the humanitarian crisis is urgent and can only be solved with US military action. To the extent that the US has a track record of standing by while genocides take place, it is a failure of leadership not of public will.

Paths forward

In making the domestic coalition argument, I focused on what it takes to sell war to the US public. The book examines the US because, at least for the post-Cold War period, the US had the most powerful military in the world with the unique capability to project its power globally. As such, it represents the country most consistently capable of starting or becoming involved in military operations. Considered the "first citizen" in the liberal world order (Ikenberry 2009), US actions also set important precedents for what counts as a legitimate use of force in contemporary politics. When and why the American public supports the use of military force thus has implications for international security that extend well beyond the country's borders.

A necessary extension of this book's findings and implications, however, and an important avenue for future research is to investigate the content and role of domestic coalitions in other countries. As Chapter 1 explained, compared to other advanced industrialized democracies, the relative distribution of foreign policy constituencies within the US makes it a hard case for the argument—humanitarian justifications should be less important for mobilizing the US public than for mobilizing European publics, for example. Evidence that humanitarian justifications are a powerful political tool in security crises in the US makes it more plausible that domestic coalitions inform how leaders justify military interventions across established democracies.[3] In countries where doves make up a non-negligible segment of the domestic population, democratic leaders will have an incentive to use humanitarian appeals, even when their national security is at stake—the book's findings should generalize most easily to these cases. In countries with higher proportions of doves than the US, leaders' political fates may be even more closely tied to the perceived sincerity and success of their humanitarian efforts. Where hawks or isolationists appear in higher proportions, leaders will have distinct political incentives and likely choose different justification strategies.

Two additional factors that could influence how well this argument travels to other countries are the type of democratic institutions and great power status. First, differences in executive power between presidential and parliamentary systems could increase the influence of political elites relative to the public. Second, middle or small powers may be more concerned with using justifications to build their reputation, making the international community a primary target audience for their justification strategies. Additional research into these areas is necessary, but the evidence from the US case provides strong reasons to expect that domestic audiences will remain important across democracies and that humanitarian justifications will be one of leaders' most powerful tools for broadening domestic support.

Taken as a whole, the book highlights the overlooked power of humanitarian justifications in security crises. This power stems from the fact that

---

[3] Rathbun's (2004) account of the partisan cleavages and coalitions that shape debates over humanitarian intervention in European states is consistent with this expectation.

doves in the domestic audience can be persuaded to support military action when humanitarian rationales are present. Leaders who combine security and humanitarian justifications to mobilize a broad domestic coalition reap multiple political benefits, while also expanding opportunities for public accountability. The findings change assumptions about the most effective way to sell military action to the public, the role of public morality in foreign policy, and the limits of executive power. It is my hope that future work will build on these findings to examine the full power of humanitarian justifications across contexts and uncover new ways to create pressure for protecting civilians in war.

Chapter 4 Appendix

Survey one instrument

This section details the survey instrument used for the main experiment in Chapter 4. I fielded this survey via Dynata in July 2017. All participants first completed the consent prompt and then answered a series of standard demographic questions. The measure of foreign policy constituencies was included in the middle of these demographic questions. After completing the demographic questions, all participants received the same set of instructions. They were then randomly assigned to one of the three treatment conditions: humanitarian, security (foreign policy restraint), or combined justifications. I followed each treatment vignette with a bullet point summary that reiterated: (1) that the president had announced an intended military action, (2) the reasons given for military action, (3) expert agreement with the president, and (4) experts' stated reasons for the military action.

Foreign policy constituency

Which of the following best reflects the role you think the United States should play in the world?

1. It is essential for the United States to work with other nations to solve problems such as overpopulation, hunger, and pollution. *(Doves)*
2. It is important for the United States to maintain a strong military to ensure world peace. *(Hawks)*
3. It is best for the future of the United States if we stay out of world affairs. *(Isolationist)*

Instructions

Now you are going to read about a situation the US has faced many times in the past and will likely face again in the future. The situation reflects actions taken by presidents from both political parties. It is NOT about the current president and it is NOT about any specific country in the news today.

Humanitarian justification treatment

Over the last few months, a violent conflict has developed in the country of Numar. In his address to the nation about this conflict, the US President said:

"My fellow Americans, tonight I want to talk to you about the situation in Numar—why it matters, and where we go from here. The regime in Numar poses a grave threat to its own civilians, including innocent women and children. It has killed thousands of its own people and directly targeted civilians. // This is not a world we should accept. The safety of Numar's civilians is at stake and we must act. This is why, after careful deliberation, I have determined that the United States must respond to this crisis with military action."

After the President's address, most experts publicly agreed with the President's reasons for intervention. They, too, thought the US action would protect Numar's civilians.

Security justification treatment (foreign policy restraint)

Over the last few months, a violent conflict has developed in the country of Numar. In his address to the nation about this conflict, the US President said:

"My fellow Americans, tonight I want to talk to you about the situation in Numar—why it matters, and where we go from here. The regime in Numar poses a grave threat to the security of the United States, including the American people. It has invaded its neighboring state and is a threat to the United States. // This is not a world we should accept. The safety of the United States is at stake and we must act. This is why, after careful deliberation, I have determined that the United States must respond to this crisis with military action."

After the President's address, most experts publicly agreed with the President's reasons for intervention. They, too, thought the US action would protect US security.

Combined justification treatment

Over the last few months, a violent conflict has developed in the country of Numar. In his address to the nation about this conflict, the US President said:

"My fellow Americans, tonight I want to talk to you about the situation in Numar—why it matters, and where we go from here. The regime in Numar poses a grave threat to its own civilians and to the security of the United States. It has invaded its neighboring state and killed thousands of its own people. // This is not a world we should accept. The safety of Numar's civilians and the United States is at stake and we must act. This is why, after careful deliberation, I have determined that the United States must respond to this crisis with military action."

After the President's address, most experts publicly agreed with the President's reasons for intervention. They, too, thought the US action would protect Numar's civilians and US security.

Dependent variable

Would you oppose or favor US military action in this situation? [*oppose strongly/oppose somewhat/favor somewhat/favor strongly*]

Follow-up questions

Political Action: Which of the following actions would you be willing to take to show your support or opposition to this military action? Check all that apply. (*Response order randomized*)

1. Use social media to express my opinion about the military action.
2. Sign a petition about the military action.
3. Write a letter to the editor of a newspaper expressing my opinion about the military action.
4. Contact my Member of Congress to express my opinion about the military action.
5. Participate in a rally about the military action.
6. None of the above.

Military Assertiveness: Some people believe the United States should mainly solve international problems by using diplomacy and other forms of international pressure. They think the US should use military force only if absolutely necessary. Suppose we put such people at #1 on this scale. Others believe diplomacy and pressure often fail and the US should mainly be ready to use military force. Suppose we put them at #7. And, of course, others fall at positions in between. What about you, where would you place yourself on this scale? Do you think the US should:

1. Mainly solve problems with diplomacy and international pressure.
2. Always be willing to solve problems with diplomacy and international pressure.
3. Not rule out solving problems with diplomacy and international pressure.
4. Equally consider diplomacy and military force.
5. Not rule out the use of military force.
6. Always be willing to consider military force.
7. Mainly be ready to use military force.

Vote: Did you vote in the 2016 general election? [*No/I usually vote, but did not in 2016/I am not sure/Yes. I definitely voted.*]
   Yes coded as 1, all other responses as 0.

Manipulation Check: To the best of your recollection, in the previous section, what reasons did the hypothetical president give for taking military action in Numar?

1. Only humanitarian goals. The president talked about protecting the civilians of Numar.
2. Only security goals. The president talked about the safety of the United States.
3. Both humanitarian and security goals. The president talked about protecting the civilians of Numar and the safety of the United States.
4. Neither humanitarian nor security goals. The president didn't mention protecting the civilians of Numar or the safety of the US.

Manipulation check results

For the survey experiment to work, participants must notice the justifications that the hypothetical president offered for the intervention. In survey one, 66 percent of participants correctly remembered the justifications the president used. The fact that participants answered this question correctly at a higher-than-chance rate, even after responding to a number of different survey items, indicates that a majority of people paid attention to the justifications in the hypothetical statement. Moreover, the most common mistake was to remember humanitarian justifications where none existed—if failure to understand or internalize the treatment affects the results, it would work against the theoretical expectations, making it more difficult to observe differences in support between the security and combined conditions.

Survey two instrument

To help validate the results from the main experiment, Chapter 4 also includes results from part of the expert agreement experiment designed for Chapter 5. I fielded this survey via Amazon's Mechanical Turk (MTurk) in July 2016. In Chapter 4, I use the conditions in which experts agreed with the president's account of the intervention to show that the main results (a) replicate across samples and (b) extend to terrorist threats. Chapter 4 also uses follow-up questions from this survey to analyze the reasons participants supported military action. The expert disagreement conditions from this survey are included in the appendix for Chapter 5.

As in the main experiment, participants in this expert agreement experiment first completed a standard demographic battery that included the measure of foreign policy constituencies and the survey instructions. They were then randomly assigned to one of the ten treatment conditions—crossing three justifications with three levels of expert responses. The first three of these conditions—humanitarian justifications, security (terrorism) justifications, or combined justifications, all holding expert agreement constant—are reported in Chapter 4. The humanitarian justification treatment wording is identical to that outlined in the main experiment above. As before, all treatments concluded with bullet points that summarized the main points of the vignette.

Security treatment (terrorism)

Over the last few months, a violent conflict has developed in the country of Numar. In his address to the nation about this conflict, the US President said:

> "My fellow Americans, tonight I want to talk to you about the situation in Numar— why it matters, and where we go from here. The regime in Numar poses a grave threat to the security of the United States, including the American people. It has created a safe haven for terrorists and threatened the United States. // This is not a world we should accept. The safety of the United States is at stake and we must act. This is why, after careful deliberation, I have determined that the United States must respond to this crisis with military action."

After the President's address, most experts publicly agreed with the President's reasons for intervention. They, too, thought the US actions would protect US security.

Combined justification treatment

Over the last few months, a violent conflict has developed in the country of Numar. In his address to the nation about this conflict, the US President said:

> "My fellow Americans, tonight I want to talk to you about the situation in Numar— why it matters, and where we go from here. The regime in Numar poses a grave threat to its own civilians and to the security of the United States. It has created a safe haven for terrorists and killed thousands of its own people. // This is not a world we should accept. The safety of Numar's civilians and the United States is at stake and we must act. This is why, after careful deliberation, I have determined that the United States must respond to this crisis with military action."

After the President's address, most experts publicly agreed with the President's reasons for intervention. They, too, thought the US action would protect Numar's civilians and US security.

Dependent variable

Would you oppose or favor US military action in this situation? [*oppose strongly/oppose somewhat/neither oppose nor favor/favor somewhat/favor strongly*]

If "neither oppose nor favor" was selected, the participant was then asked:

If you had to choose, would you lean towards opposing or favoring military action in this situation? [*lean towards opposing/lean towards favoring*]

Note that the expert agreement experiment measured support using a five-point scale and asked respondents at the midpoint the direction in which they leaned. Analysis of leaners across all treatment conditions showed an even 50/50 split between those who leaned towards support or opposition. The implication of these findings is that omitting the neutral category and forcing respondents to report the direction in which they lean is unlikely to systematically skew the reported support or opposition to intervention. Building on this finding, respondents in the main experiment were given only four response options, omitting the neutral category.

Reason for support

Which of the following did you think about most in your decision to support or oppose the military action? (*Response order randomized*)

1. Whether or not the action would protect civilians in Numar.
2. Whether or not there was a threat to US national security.
3. Whether or not failing to act would make the US appear weak.
4. Whether or not action would help uphold international standards.

Replication of main results with survey two sample

The foundational piece of evidence for the domestic coalition theory is the finding from survey one that doves respond to humanitarian claims strongly and uniquely. Because doves are the only group whose support significantly increases when humanitarian appeals are present, they set the incentive for presidents to include such claims, even when talking about security crises. Survey one, however, only captures attitudes towards one type of security crisis. Specifically, the scenario evokes a crisis similar to the 1991 Gulf War in which the target state invades its neighboring country and intervention is intended to push the target back from this territory. The details of this crisis reflect what Jentleson (1992; 1998) classifies as "foreign policy restraint" and finds to be among the most popular principle policy objectives for military action. It is because of this popularity that I use a foreign policy restraint scenario as the primary test of my theory—popular forms of intervention should be a hard case, making it difficult for humanitarian claims to further increase already high support. If humanitarian appeals influence doves in this context, it is reasonable to expect them to also have an effect in cases where there is more room for support to grow.

In the post-9/11 world, however, many US interventions—from operations in Afghanistan and Iraq to strikes against the Islamic State—are linked to the war on terror. This link reflects a major rhetorical shift in the dominant national security narrative (Krebs 2015) and is an extremely effective way to build public support (Gadarian 2010; 2014; Gershkoff and Kushner 2005). References to terror may therefore have a unique

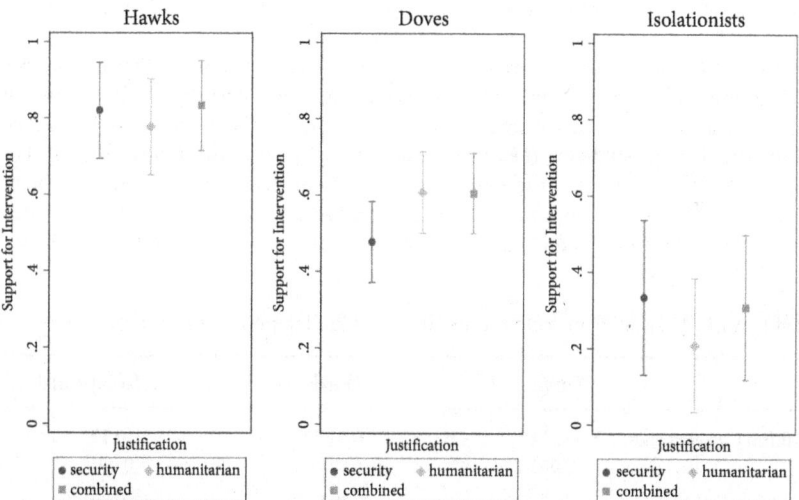

Figure A4.1   Replication of Figure 4.2 with MTurk data (Support by foreign policy constituency)

Each panel shows support divided by respondents' foreign policy constituency. The first panel shows results for hawks, the second for doves, and the third for isolationists. Within each panel is the average level of support for security, humanitarian, and combined justifications, moving from left to right.

effect on support for intervention that limits how much the results from survey one can tell us about non-foreign policy restraint operations.

Survey two used a terrorism scenario to confirm that humanitarian claims are necessary to maximize the support of doves, even when military action involves a terrorist threat. To demonstrate that the main results from Chapter 4 can be replicated across samples and are robust to the type of security threat used, I conducted the same analysis on the data from the expert agreement experiment. The results are displayed in Figure A4.1 and the findings are robust. As in the main experiment, doves are the only group whose support is significantly increased when leaders combine humanitarian and security justifications.

Alternative measures as predictors of foreign policy constituencies

Chapter 4 used a single-question measure of foreign policy constituencies. This measure was theoretically informed and intended to force a trade-off between the different perspectives—it captures which constituency individuals identify with most when forced to choose. There are, however, alternative ways of placing individuals on a hawk/dove scale and capturing their foreign policy preferences. The main experiment in Chapter 4 included a post-treatment measure of military assertiveness—high assertiveness is associated with hawks, low with doves—and I also conducted an additional survey that measured foreign policy constituencies with the single-item measure used in the text and foreign policy orientations using the full battery of questions used by Kertzer et al. (2014). I fielded the follow-up survey via MTurk to a sample of 251 US adults in June 2018.

Table A4.1 below reports results from logistic regression models that capture the relationship between the single-question measure and the alternatives. The dependent variables in these models are binary indicators of whether the individual fell into each foreign policy constituency (i.e., dove yes/no, hawk yes/no, isolationist yes/no). For the independent variables, the models in the first row use responses to the military assertiveness question from survey one. The remaining models use an index created from the full battery of foreign policy orientation questions from the follow-up survey,

Table A4.1 Alternative measures as predictors of foreign policy constituency

	Dove	Hawk	Isolationist
Military assertiveness	−0.39***	0.51***	−0.12
	(0.06)	(0.07)	(0.09)
CI factor index	1.31***	−0.97***	−0.86***
	(0.23)	(0.24)	(0.25)
MI factor index	−0.91***	1.55***	−0.18
	(0.22)	(0.29)	(0.24)
ISO factor index	−0.30*	−0.55***	1.42***
	(0.18)	(0.20)	(0.29)

Note: Table reports the coefficients from logistic regression models with standard errors in parentheses and ***p < 0.01; **p < 0.05; *p < 0.10. The dependent variables for each model are binary measures of whether the individual was classified as a dove, hawk, or isolationist by the single-question item used in the main text.

based on principle factor scores for each foreign policy orientation. The results of the index models are robust to the use of principle component factor scores and an additive index, with some variation in the statistical significance of the isolationist factor index.

Across all indices, the results demonstrate that responses to the military assertiveness measure and full battery of orientation questions are significant predictors of an individual's response to the single-statement measure. These relationships are also consistently in the expected direction. The likelihood that the single-statement measure classified an individual as a dove is consistently positively and significantly influenced by their score on the cooperative internationalist indices, negatively and significantly influenced by scores on the militant internationalist indices, and negatively associated with scores of the isolationist indices. Similarly, individuals were significantly more likely to be classified as hawks by the single-statement measure as their scores on the militant internationalist indices increased. Isolationists were negatively associated with both internationalist indices (though only cooperative internationalism is significant) and positively associated with the index measure of isolationism.

Predicted probabilities

The results in Table A4.1 highlight the significant relationships between an individual's foreign policy constituency and their level of military assertiveness as well as their foreign policy orientation score. Figures A4.2 and A4.3, respectively, plot the predicted probability that an individual is a member of the given foreign policy constituency at each level of the military assertiveness measure and for each quartile of the foreign policy orientation index score.

Consistent with the results in Table A4.1, Figure A4.2 shows that military assertiveness is a negative predictor of being a dove, a positive predictor of being a hawk, and has no clear relationship with isolationism. Moving from the lowest level of military assertiveness (1) to the highest level (7) reduced the predicted probability that an individual was a dove from 0.68 to 0.24. Similarly, moving from the lowest to the highest value increased the predicted probability that an individual was a hawk from 0.13 to 0.65. For isolationism, there is little change in predicted probabilities across the military assertiveness scale (0.19 to 0.12).

Also consistent with the results in Table A4.1, Figure A4.3 illustrates the predicted probability that an individual falls into each foreign policy constituency based on their score on the principle factor index for the related foreign policy orientation. I collapse responses into quartiles for each foreign policy orientation for the ease of interpretation (because the factor score index is continuous).

Moving from the bottom to the top quartile of cooperative internationalism scores increases the predicted probability that an individual is a dove from 0.31 to 0.85. While not included in the figure, the relationship between doves and militant internationalism parallels these results and is also as expected. Moving from the bottom to top quartile of militant internationalism decreases the predicted probability that an individual is a dove from 0.70 to 0.37.

In terms of hawks, Figure A4.3 shows that moving from the bottom to the top quartile for militant internationalism scores increased the predicted probability that an individual was a hawk from 0.06 to 0.47. Similar to the negative relationship between doves and militant internationalism, increasing cooperative internationalism makes

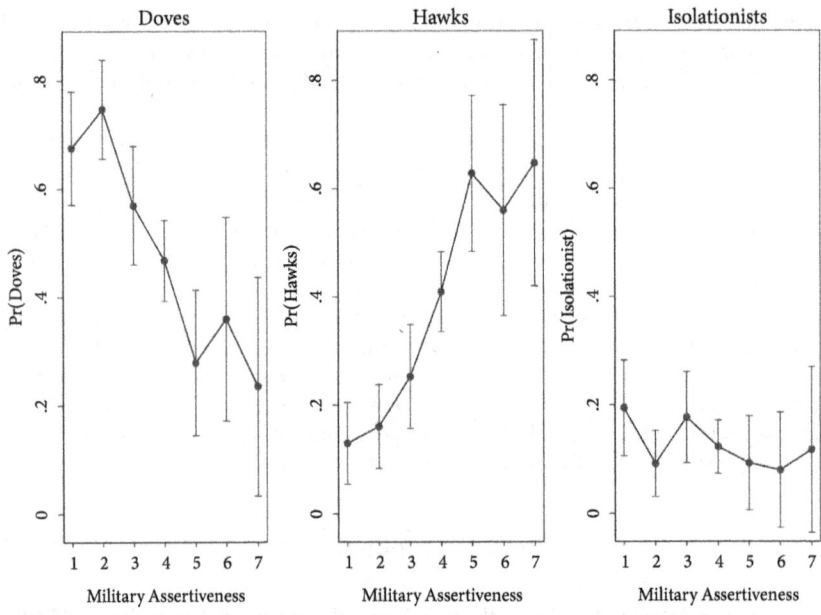

Figure A4.2 Predicted probabilities of constituency membership by military assertiveness

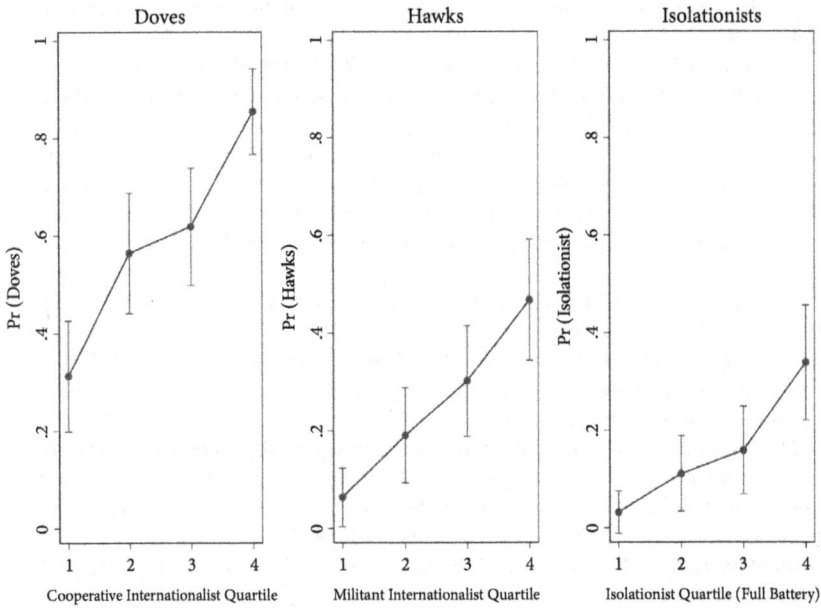

Figure A4.3 Predicted probability of constituency membership by foreign policy orientation score (quartiles)

an individual less likely to be a hawk, decreasing the predicted probability from 0.41 (lowest CI) to 0.10 (highest CI).

For isolationists, the full battery of foreign policy orientation questions is positively associated with the single-question measure. Moving from the bottom to top quartile of isolationism factor score changed the predicted probability that an individual selected the isolationist statement in the single-question measure from 0.03 to 0.34. Also, as expected and in line with previous research, isolationism has a less clear but negative connection to militant and cooperative internationalism. At the bottom quartile of cooperative internationalism scores, the predicted probability that an individual was an isolationist was 0.28, dropping to 0.05 for individuals in the top quartile of CI. At the bottom quartile of militant internationalist scores, the predicted probability that an individual was an isolationist was 0.24, changing to 0.16 in the top quartile of MI.

Political engagement across foreign policy constituencies

The main survey in Chapter 4 asked respondents about their participation in elections and their willingness to take political action to express their support or opposition to military action. Table A4.2 below reports the mean for each form of political action, disaggregated by respondents' foreign policy constituencies.

Table A4.2 Political action items by constituency

	Dove	Hawk	Isolationist
Voted	0.74 (0.03)	0.75 (0.03)	0.61 (0.06)
Political action index score	1.42 (0.08)	1.16 (0.09)	1.18 (0.15)
Social media	0.41 (0.03)	0.40 (0.04)	0.36 (0.06)
Sign petition	0.46 (0.03)	0.36 (0.04)	0.38 (0.06)
Letter to the editor	0.10 (0.02)	0.08 (0.02)	0.06 (0.03)
Contact member of Congress	0.33 (0.03)	0.26 (0.03)	0.30 (0.06)
Participate in rally	0.13 (0.02)	0.05 (0.03)	0.08 (0.03)
No action	0.27 (0.03)	0.32 (0.04)	0.36 (0.06)

Note: Table reports the proportion of respondents in each foreign policy constituency who were willing to take the relevant action. Standard errors are in parentheses. All results are mean proportions of respondents, with the exception of the political action index score, which records the average number of actions individuals were willing to take.

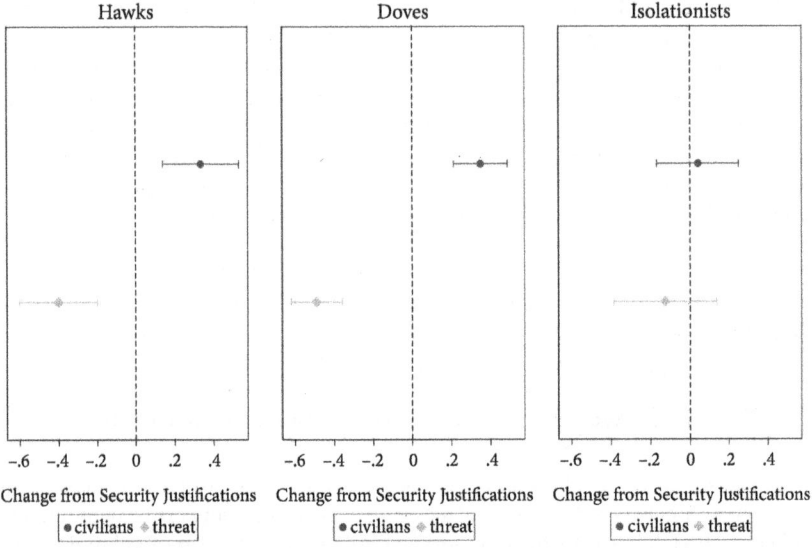

Figure A4.4 Reasons for support: Humanitarian-only compared to security-only

The figure reports the effect of the humanitarian treatment compared to the security treatment on respondents' concern with civilians and security threats by foreign policy constituencies.

Reasons for support in humanitarian-only conditions

Figure 4.3 in Chapter 4 illustrates how the combined treatment condition—relative to the security treatment condition—caused respondents to think more or less about protecting foreign civilians. Figure A4.4 reports the results of the same analysis comparing the humanitarian-only condition to the security-only condition. Unsurprisingly, when the president references humanitarian concerns without offering a security rationale, respondents across constituencies think more about protecting civilians and less about security threats—it is the combination of security and humanitarian justifications that separates hawks and doves.

Additional reasons for support

In addition to thinking about foreign civilians or security threats, the main experiment in Chapter 4 offered respondents two other reasons for support: not making the US look weak and upholding international standards. Figures A4.5 and A4.6 illustrate changes in reported concerns for the humanitarian-only and combined conditions (relative to the security-only condition). The treatment conditions have no significant effect on concerns about whether the US looks strong or weak for any foreign policy constituency. The humanitarian-only condition does make doves significantly more concerned about upholding international standards, which is consistent with their preference for pursuing global goods and commitment to human rights norms.

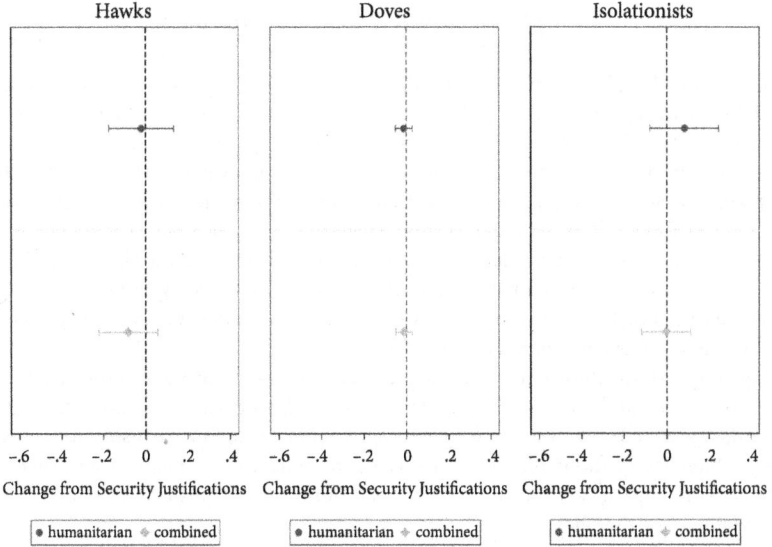

Figure A4.5 Treatment effect on alternative reasons for support: US strength

The figure reports the effect of the humanitarian or combined treatment relative to the security treatment on respondents' concern with whether failing to act would make the US appear weak.

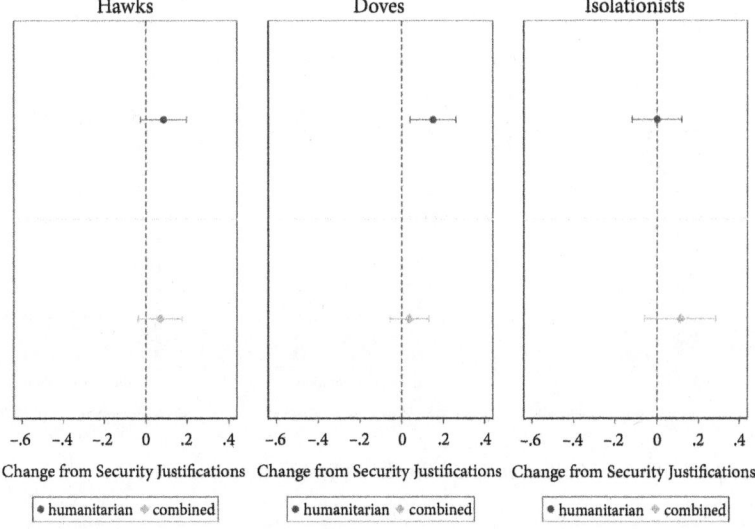

Figure A4.6 Treatment effect on alternative reasons for support: International standards

The figure reports the effect of the humanitarian or combined treatment relative to the security treatment on respondents' concern with whether action would help uphold international standards.

Perceptions of intervention difficulty

To more directly rule out operational difficulty as a confounder, survey two also asked participants to report the level of success, the number of military casualties, and the financial burden they assumed the intervention would require.

The specific questions were "Based on your best guess and what you've read about the situation in Numar, to what extent do you disagree or agree with each of the following statements: If the US takes military action, the operation will be successful./If the US takes military action, the US will suffer many military casualties./If the US takes military action, the operation will cost the US a lot of money." Response options were a four-point scale ranging from disagree strongly to agree strongly and have been collapsed into a binary measure of agreement or disagreement.

Figure A4.7 shows the average level of agreement with each statement across the different justification conditions. There is no indicator of difficulty that is significantly higher when the hypothetical president used both security and humanitarian justifications. Ruling out changes in the perceived difficulty of the intervention helps ensure that the differences in support are linked to the content of presidents' justifications and cannot be explained by other factors.

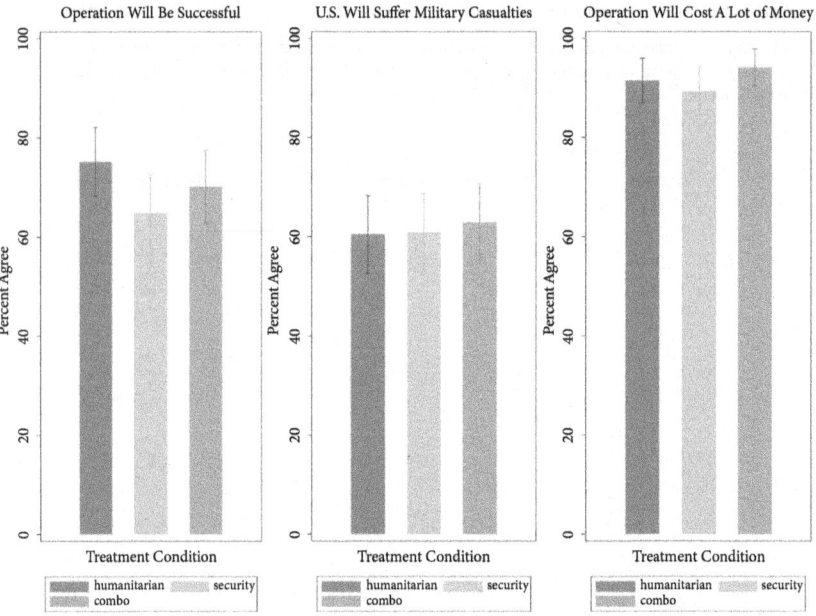

Figure A4.7 Perceived intervention difficulty by justification condition

Chapter 5 Appendix

Survey two expert agreement instrument

Chapter 5 makes use of the full expert agreement experiment introduced in Chapter 4.[1] After answering standard demographic questions, including the foreign policy constituency measure, and reading short instructions, participants were randomly assigned to one of the ten conditions: humanitarian, security, or combined justifications fully crossed with expert agreement, a different but legitimate reason for intervention, and a different and illegitimate reason for intervention. The combined justification/different but legitimate conditions were split to cast doubt on one aspect of the justification at a time—humanitarian or security—creating the tenth condition. The wordings of the expert agreement conditions, the president's humanitarian, security, and combined justifications, and the dependent variable are included in the appendix for Chapter 4.[2]

Different but legitimate

After the President's address, most experts publicly disputed the President's reasons for intervention. They thought that ...

Humanitarian: . . . instead of concern for civilians, the real motivation for the US action was to protect US security.

Security: . . . instead of concern for US security, the real motivation for the US action was to protect Numar's civilians.

Combined, Sincere Security: . . . instead of concern for civilians, the only motivation for the US action was to protect US national security.

Combined, Sincere Humanitarian: . . . instead of concern for US security, the only motivation for the US action was to protect Numar's civilians.

Different and illegitimate

After the President's address, most experts publicly disputed the President's reasons for intervention. They thought that protecting . . .

[1] Chapter 4 Appendix
[2] Chapter 4 Appendix

Humanitarian: . . . Numar's civilians was a story to cover up the President's own political agenda.

Security: . . . US security was a story to cover up the President's own political agenda.

Combined: . . . Numar's civilians and US security was a story to cover up the President's own political agenda.

Follow-up questions

To what extent do you disagree or agree with each of the following statements:

I approve of the way the President handled the situation in Numar. [*Disagree strongly/Disagree somewhat/Agree somewhat/Agree strongly*]

The President described the situation in Numar accurately. [*Disagree strongly/ Disagree somewhat/Agree somewhat/Agree strongly*]

If the hypothetical President were running for reelection, how likely would you be to vote for him? [*Very unlikely/Somewhat unlikely/Somewhat likely/Very likely*]

Which of the following do you think is the most important reason the President decided to take military action? [*Response order randomized*]

1. To protect the people of Numar.
2. To protect the security of the United States.
3. To demonstrate the United States is a strong country.
4. To demonstrate the United States upholds international standards.
5. To protect his own political agenda.

Based on your best guess and what you've read about the situation in Numar, to what extent do you disagree or agree with the following statements:

If the US takes military action, the operation will be successful. [*Disagree strongly/ Disagree somewhat/Agree somewhat/Agree strongly*]

If the US takes military action, the US will suffer many military casualties. [*Disagree strongly/Disagree somewhat/Agree somewhat/Agree strongly*]

If the US takes military action, the operation will cost the US a lot of money. [*Disagree strongly/Disagree somewhat/Agree somewhat/Agree strongly*]

If the US takes military action in this case, how likely do you think each of the following outcomes will be:

Civilians in Numar will be safe. [*Very unlikely/Somewhat unlikely/Somewhat likely/ Very likely*]

The US will be more secure. [*Very unlikely/Somewhat unlikely/Somewhat likely/Very likely*]

Manipulation checks

Just a few more questions about the situation in Numar.

To the best of your recollection, what points did the President use to explain the military action in Numar?

1. Only humanitarian: the quotes talked about protecting the civilians of Numar.
2. Only security: the quotes talked about the safety of the United States.
3. Both humanitarian and security: the quotes talked about protecting the civilians of Numar and the safety of the United States.
4. Neither humanitarian nor security: the quotes didn't mention protecting the civilians of Numar or the safety of the US.

To the best of your recollection, did the experts agree with the President?

1. Yes, they agreed with the President's reasons for military action.
2. No, they disputed the President's reasons for military action.

Future humanitarian intervention scenario

Instructions: Now we are going to describe another situation this hypothetical President faced about a year after taking military action in Numar. As before, the scenario reflects a situation the US has faced many times in the past and will likely face again in the future, but it is not about any country in the news today.

Scenario: In an address to the nation, the President said:

"My fellow Americans, tonight I have received gruesome evidence that genocide is taking place in Rundu. Innocent civilians, including women and children, are being massacred in their homes by neighbors who support Rundu's government. The United States cannot be the world's police force, but when we can stop children from being killed in their own homes, we have a responsibility to act. This is why after careful deliberation, I have determined the United States must respond to this crisis with military action."

Future intervention dependent variable

Would you oppose or favor US military action in this situation? [*Oppose strongly/Oppose somewhat/Favor somewhat/Favor strongly*]

Follow-up questions

Based on your best guess and what you've read about the situation in Rundu, to what extent do you agree with the following statements:

I trust the President to handle the situation in Rundu. [*Disagree strongly/Disagree somewhat/Agree somewhat/Agree strongly*]

The President described the situation in Rundu accurately. [*Disagree strongly/ Disagree somewhat/Agree somewhat/Agree strongly*]

Full results of presidential motives analysis

Figure 5.1 of Chapter 5 reports the percentage of respondents who assumed protecting the people of Numar, the security of the United States, or his own political agenda was the president's main motive for taking military action. In addition to these three choices, the motivation question presented participants with two alternative motivations: to demonstrate that the United States is a strong country or to demonstrate that the United States upholds international standards. Figure A5.1 reports the percentage of respondents who assumed strength or standards were the main motivation for action. The percentage of respondents who assumed the president acted out of concern for US strength or international standards is lower than the concerns reported in the main text across all conditions.

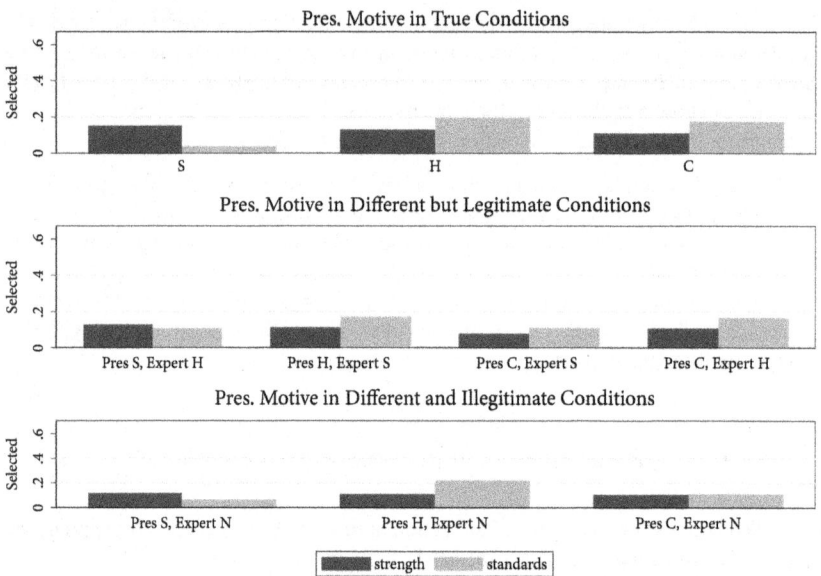

S: Security Rationale, H: Humanitarian Rationale, C: Combined Rationale, N: No legitimate rationale.

Figure A5.1 Alternative assumptions about the president's motive for intervention

Attitudes towards future interventions by foreign policy constituencies

Figure 5.4 in Chapter 5 reports the effect of the expert agreement treatments on support for a future humanitarian intervention using the aggregate sample. Figure A5.2 reports the results of the same analysis for each foreign policy constituency.

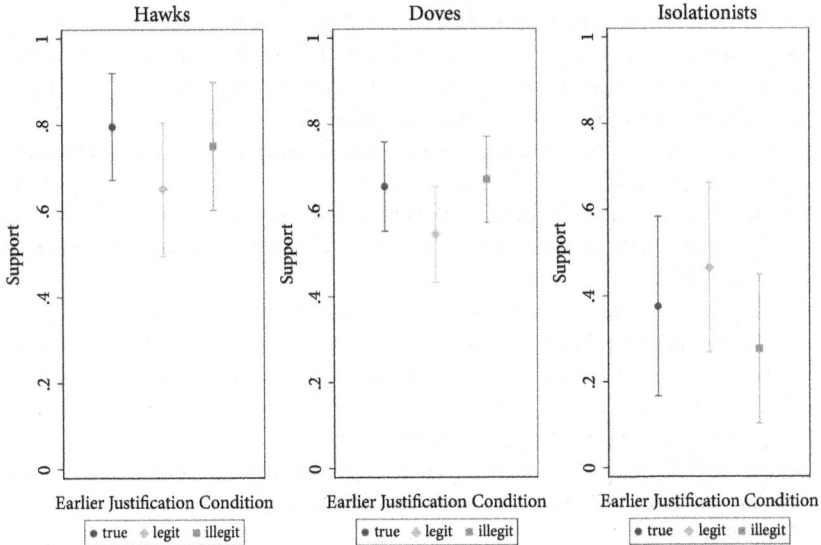

Figure A5.2 Effect of misused humanitarian claims on future intervention, by constituency

The figure reports the proportion of respondents who supported the future intervention in each treatment condition, divided by their foreign policy constituencies.

References

ABC News/Washington Post. 1991. "Halfway Through Term, Bush Popularity Peaks but Economic Concerns Lurk Behind War Support." Box 93, White House Press Office, Marlin Fitzwater Files, Guidance Files, folder "Wednesday, January 30, 1991 [2]" OA/ID: 12994–010. George H.W. Bush Presidential Library.

Abramowitz, Alan I. 2010. *The Disappearing Center: Engaged Citizens, Polarization, and American Democracy.* Yale University Press.

Aldrich, John H., John L. Sullivan, and Eugene Borgida. 1989. "Foreign Affairs and Issue Voting: Do Presidential Candidates 'Waltz Before a Blind Audience?'" *American Political Science Review* 83 (1): 123–41.

Alexander, Ernest, Maria Mirales, Paul R. V. Pawlowski, and Jerry Willis. 1991. "Transcript, Testimony of the Former American Hostages to House Foreign Affairs Committee, Human Rights Abuses in Iraq and Kuwait." FOIA 1998-0099-F, White House Office of Public Affairs, Kristen Gear Files, folder "Iraq-Pos-Comments" OA/ID 03418-013. George H.W. Bush Presidential Library.

Allen, Michael A., Michael E. Flynn, Carla Martinez Machain, and Andrew Stravers. 2023. *Beyond the Wire: US Military Deployments and Host Country Public Opinion.* Oxford University Press.

Almond, Gabriel. 1950. *The American People and Foreign Policy.* Praeger.

Asmus, Ronald. 2004. "Power, War, and Public Opinion: Looking behind the Transatlantic Divide." Hoover Institution. February 1, 2004. https://www.hoover.org/res earch/power-war-and-public-opinion.

Baker, James. 1990a. "Excerpts from Secretary Baker's Statement Before the House Foreign Affairs Committee." Box 6, White House Office of Speechwriting, Carol Aarhus Files, Alpha File 1990-1992, folder "Persian Gulf [1]" OA/ID 13864-006. George H.W. Bush Presidential Library.

Baker, James. 1990b. "Transcript, Statement by the Honorable James A. Baker, III Secretary of State before the Senate Foreign Relations Committee." Box 6, White House Office of Speechwriting, Carol Aarhus Files, Alpha File 1990–1992, folder "Persian Gulf [1]" OA/ID 13864-006. George H.W. Bush Presidential Library.

Battaglia, Lisa. n.d. "Memorandum, Lisa Battaglia, Student Activism Against U.S. Involvement in the Gulf." FOIA 2003-0257-f, White House Office of Public Liaison, James Schaefer Files, folder "Students Against Saddam Hussein" OA/ID: 07541-007. George H.W. Bush Presidential Library.

Baum, Matthew. 2002. "The Constituent Foundations of the Rally-Round-the-Flag Phenomenon." *International Studies Quarterly* 46 (2): 263–98.

Baum, Matthew, and Tim Groeling. 2010. "Reality Asserts Itself: Public Opinion on Iraq and the Elasticity of Reality." *International Organization* 64: 443–79.

Baum, Matthew A., and Philip B. K. Potter. 2008. "The Relationships Between Mass Media, Public Opinion, and Foreign Policy: Toward a Theoretical Synthesis." *Annual Review of Political Science* 11 (1): 39–65.

Baum, Matthew A., and Philip B. K. Potter. 2015. *War and Democratic Constraint: How the Public Influences Foreign Policy.* Princeton University Press.

Bellamy, Alex J. 2004. "Ethics and Intervention: The 'Humanitarian Exception' and the Problem of Abuse in the Case of Iraq." *Journal of Peace Research* 41 (2): 131–47.

Bellamy, Alex J. 2005. "Responsibility to Protect or Trojan Horse? The Crisis in Darfur and Humanitarian Intervention After Iraq." *Ethics & International Affairs* 19 (2): 31–53.

Bellamy, Alex J. 2006. "Whither the Responsibility to Protect? Humanitarian Intervention and the 2005 World Summit." *Ethics & International Affairs* 20 (2): 143–69.

Berg, Stephanie van den. 2023. "Russia Using Genocide 'Lie' as Pretext to Destroy, Ukraine Tells World Court." *Reuters*, September 19, 2023, sec. Europe. https://www.reuters.com/world/europe/ukraine-tells-world-court-russia-uses-genocide-pretext-destroy-2023-09-19/.

Berinsky, Adam. 2007. "Assuming the Costs of War: Events, Elites, and American Public Support for Military Conflict." *Journal of Politics* 69 (4): 975–97.

Berinsky, Adam. 2009. *In Time of War.* University of Chicago Press.

Berinsky, Adam, and Donald R. Kinder. 2006. "Making Sense of Issues Through Media Frames: Understanding the Kosovo Crisis." *The Journal of Politics* 68 (3): 640–56.

Berinsky, Adam, Gregory A. Huber, and Gabriel S. Lenz. 2012. "Evaluating Online Labor Markets for Experimental Research: Amazon.Com's Mechanical Turk." *Political Analysis* 20 (3): 351–68.

Berinsky, Adam, Michele F. Margolis, and Michael W. Sances. 2014. "Separating the Shirkers from the Workers? Making Sure Respondents Pay Attention on Self-Administered Surveys." *American Journal of Political Science* 58 (3): 739–53.

Biden, Joseph. 2022a. "Remarks on Efforts To Reduce Gasoline Prices." The American Presidency Project. June 22, 2022. https://www.presidency.ucsb.edu/documents/remarks-efforts-reduce-gasoline-prices.

Biden, Joseph. 2022b. "Remarks on Ukraine and Russia and an Exchange with Reporters." The American Presidency Project. April 21, 2022. https://www.presidency.ucsb.edu/documents/remarks-ukraine-and-russia-and-exchange-with-reporters.

Biden, Joseph. 2022c. "Remarks on United States Assistance to Ukraine and an Exchange With Reporters." The American Presidency Project. March 16, 2022. https://www.presidency.ucsb.edu/documents/remarks-united-states-assistance-ukraine-and-exchange-with-reporters.

Blair, Tony. 2001. "Full Text of Tony Blair's Speech to Parliament." *The Guardian*, October 4, 2001, sec. US news. https://www.theguardian.com/world/2001/oct/04/september11.usa3.

Boot, Max. 2023. "Opinion | Why Liberals Protesting Cluster Munitions for Ukraine Are Wrong." *Washington Post*, July 12, 2023. https://www.washingtonpost.com/opinions/2023/07/11/cluster-munitions-ukraine-war-russia/.

Booth Walling, Carrie. 2013. *All Necessary Measures: The United Nations and Humanitarian Intervention.* University of Pennsylvania Press.

"Bosnia Hill Strategy." 1994. Box 22, National Security Council, European Affairs-Kerrick, Donald, folder "Bosnia Principals Committee/Deputies Committee 1994 Meetings [1]" OA/ID: 367.

Braumoeller, Bear F. 2010. "The Myth of American Isolationism." *Foreign Policy Analysis* 6: 349–71.

Bremner, Sue L. 1995. "Email, Sue L. Bremner, [UNCLASSIFIED], Attachment: Foreign Affairs Guidance." Box 6, NSC Emails, MSMail-Record (Sept 94–Sept 97) [Srebrenica and Ethnic Cleanse . . .], folder "08/18/1995-01/30/1997" OA/ID: 590000. William J. Clinton Presidential Library.

Brenan, Megan. 2021. "Americans Split on Whether Afghanistan War Was a Mistake." *Gallup.* July 26, 2021. https://news.gallup.com/poll/352793/americans-split-whether-afghanistan-war-mistake.aspx.

Brody, Richard. 1991. *Assessing the President: The Media, Elite Opinion, and Public Support.* Stanford University Press.

Browning, Edmond L. 1991. "Letter, Edmond L. Browning to The President." FOIA 1998-0099-F, White House Office of Public Liaison, Leigh Ann Metzger Files, folder "Operation Desert Shield-Religious Leaders, Negative" OA/ID: 04380-030. George H.W. Bush Presidential Library.

Brutger, Ryan. 2021. "The Power of Compromise: Proposal Power, Partisanship, and Public Support in International Bargaining." *World Politics* 72 (1): 128–66.

Brutger, Ryan, Joshua D. Kertzer, Jonathan Renshon, Dustin Tingley, and Chagai M. Weiss. 2023. "Abstraction and Detail in Experimental Design." *American Journal of Political Science* 67 (4): 979–95. https://doi.org/10.1111/ajps.12710.

Bueno de Mesquita, Bruce, George W. Downs, Alastair Smith, and Feryal Marie Cherif. 2005. "Thinking Inside the Box: A Closer Look at Democracy and Human Rights." *International Studies Quarterly* 49 (3): 439–57.

Bush, George H. W. 1990a. "Address Before a Joint Session of the Congress on the Persian Gulf Crisis and the Federal Budget Deficit." Public Papers of the Presidents.

Bush, George H. W. 1990b. "Address to the Nation Announcing the Deployment of United States Armed Forces to Saudi Arabia." Public Papers of the Presidents.

Bush, George H. W. 1990c. "President's News Conference on the Persian Gulf Crisis." Public Papers of the Presidents.

Bush, George H. W. 1990d. "Remarks and an Exchange with Reporters on the Iraqi Invasion of Kuwait." Public Papers of the Presidents.

Bush, George H. W. 1990e. "Remarks at the Annual Conference of the Veterans of Foreign Wars in Baltimore, Maryland." The American Presidency Project. http://www.presidency.ucsb.edu/ws/index.php?pid=18774&st=VFW&st1=.

Bush, George H. W. 1990f. "The President's News Conference." Public Papers of the Presidents.

Bush, George H. W. 1990g. "The President's News Conference in Orlando, Florida." Public Papers of the Presidents.

Bush, George H. W. 1991a. "Address to the Nation Announcing Allied Military Action in the Persian Gulf." Public Papers of the Presidents.

Bush, George H. W. 1991b. "Letter, George H.W. Bush to Representative Robert Michel, Text of Letter to Congressional Leadership." Box 6, White House Office of Speech-writing, Carol Aarhus Files, Alpha File 1990-1992, folder "Persian Gulf [1]" OA/ID 13864-006. George H.W. Bush Presidential Library.

Bush, George H. W. 1991c. "Letter, George H.W. Bush to Richard Nixon." Box 81, White House Office of Chief of Staff, John Sununu Files, Issues Files, folder "Persian Gulf War 1991 [6]" OA/ID: 29166-008. George H.W. Bush Presidential Library.

Bush, George H. W. 1991d. "Note, George Bush to Marlin Fitzwater." Box 91, White House Press Office, Marlin Fitzwater Files, Guidance Files, folder "Wednesday, January 2, 1991" OA/ID: 12992-015. George H.W. Bush Presidential Library.

Bush, George H. W. 1991e. "Press Release, Text of the President's Open Letter to College Students." Box 17, White House Press Office, Marlin Fitzwater Files, Alphabetical Subject Files, folder "Iraq [1991]" OA/ID: 12918. George H.W. Bush Presidential Library.

Bush, George H. W. 1991f. "Remarks at the Annual Convention of the National Religious Broadcasters." The American Presidency Project. http://www.presidency.ucsb.edu/ws/?pid=19250.

Bush, George H. W. 1992. "Address to the Nation on the Situation in Somalia." The American Presidency Project. December 4, 1992. http://www.presidency.ucsb.edu/ws/index.php?pid=21758&st=somalia&st1=.

Bush, George W. 2001a. "Address Before a Joint Session of the Congress on the United States Response to the Terrorist Attacks of September 11." Public Papers of the Presidents.

Bush, George W. 2001b. "Address to the Nation on Homeland Security From Atlanta." Public Papers of the Presidents.

Bush, George W. 2001c. "The President's News Conference." Public Papers of the Presidents.

Bush, George W. 2002a. "Address Before a Joint Session of the Congress on the State of the Union." Public Papers of the Presidents.

Bush, George W. 2002b. "Remarks in Aurora, Missouri." Public Papers of the Presidents.

Bush, George W. 2002c. "The President's Radio Address." The American Presidency Project. December 28, 2002. https://www.presidency.ucsb.edu/documents/the-presidents-radio-address-719.

Bush, George W. 2002d. "The President's Radio Address." The American Presidency Project. September 14, 2002. https://www.presidency.ucsb.edu/documents/the-presidents-radio-address-704.

Bush, George W. 2003a. "Address Before a Joint Session of the Congress on the State of the Union." Public Papers of the Presidents.

Bush, George W. 2003b. "Remarks on Improving Counterterrorism Intelligence." Public Papers of the Presidents.

Bush, George W. 2003c. "The President's Radio Address | The American Presidency Project." The American Presidency Project. March 15, 2003. https://www.presidency.ucsb.edu/documents/the-presidents-radio-address-730.

Bush, George W. 2004. "Address Before a Joint Session of the Congress on the State of the Union." The American Presidency Project. January 20, 2004. https://www.presidency.ucsb.edu/documents/address-before-joint-session-the-congress-the-state-the-union-24.

"Cable, Gulf Public Diplomacy During Hostilities." n.d. FOIA 1998-0099-F, National Security Council, Nancy Bearg Dyke Files, Subject File, folder "Persian Gulf-Public Diplomacy [5]" OA/ID: CF01933. George H.W. Bush Presidential Library.

Caldwell, Leigh Ann, and Marianna Sotomayor. 2024. "The Evolution of Mike Johnson on Ukraine." *Washington Post*, April 21, 2024. https://www.washingtonpost.com/politics/2024/04/21/ukraine-aid-mike-johnson-house-speaker/.

Canes-Wrone, Brandice, William G. Howell, and David E. Lewis. 2008. "Toward a Broader Understanding of Presidential Power: A Reevaluation of the Two Presidencies Thesis." *Journal of Politics* 70 (1): 1–16.

Carson, Austin. 2016. "Facing Off and Saving Face: Covert Intervention and Escalation Management in the Korean War." *International Organization* 70 (1): 103–31.

Cavari, Amnon. 2012. "The Short-Term Effect of Going Public." *Political Research Quarterly* 66 (2): 336–51.

CBS News Poll, *The New York Times*. 1990. "Americans on the Gulf." Box 22, White House Press Office, Marlin Fitzwater Files, Alphabetical Subject Files, folder "Poll Data - [Gulf War]" OA/ID: 12923-007. George H.W. Bush Presidential Library.

Chapman, Terrance L. 2011. *Securing Approval: Domestic Politics and Multilateral Authorization for War*. University of Chicago Press.

Chaudoin, Stephen, Helen Milner, and Dustin Tingley. 2010. "The Center Still Holds: Liberal Internationalism Survives." *International Security* 35 (1): 75–94.

Chong, Dennis, and James Druckman. 2007. "Framing Public Opinion in Competitive Democracies." *American Political Science Review* 101 (4): 637–55.

Christopher, Warren. 2001. *Chances of a Lifetime*. Scribner.

Clinton, William J. 1993. "Remarks at the United States Military Academy Commencement Ceremony in West Point, New York." Public Papers of the Presidents.

Clinton, William J. 1994a. "The President's Radio Address." Public Papers of the Presidents.

Clinton, William J. 1994b. "The President's Radio Address and an Exchange With Reporters." Public Papers of the Presidents.

Clinton, William J. 1995a. "Address to the Nation on Implementation of the Peace Agreement in Bosnia-Herzegovina." Public Papers of the Presidents.

Clinton, William J. 1995b. "Remarks Announcing the Bosnia-Herzegovina Peace Agreement and an Exchange With Reporters." Public Papers of the Presidents.

Clinton, William J. 1995c. "Remarks on Arrival in Honolulu, Hawaii." The American Presidency Project. August 31, 1995. https://www.presidency.ucsb.edu/documents/remarks-arrival-honolulu-hawaii-0.

Clinton, William J. 1998. "Remarks on Departure for Silver Spring, Maryland, and an Exchange with Reporters." Public Papers of the Presidents.

Clymer, Adam. 1991. "Confrontation in the Gulf; Congress Acts to Authorize War in Gulf; Margins Are 5 Votes in Senate, 67 in House." *The New York Times*, January 13, 1991, sec. World. http://www.nytimes.com/1991/01/13/world/confrontation-gulf-congress-acts-authorize-war-gulf-margins-are-5-votes-senate.html.

CNBC. 2023. "CNBC All-America Economic Survey, Question 8, 31120679.00007, Hart Research Associates/Public Opinion Strategies." Survey Question. Cornell University, Ithaca, NY: Roper Center for Public Opinion Research, 2023. https://doi.org/10.25940/ROPER-31120679.

CNN/Time Magazine. 2003. "Time Magazine/CNN Poll # 2003-08: George W. Bush/2004 Presidential Election/Terrorism/Life After 9/11, Question 1, USHARRIS.Y090503.RD, Harris Interactive." Question 1, USHARRIS.Y090503.RD. Cornell University, Ithaca, NY: Roper Center for Public Opinion Research, 2003. DOI: 10.25940/ROPER-31092220.

"Collection of Documents, Polls/Persian Gulf." 1991. Box 81, White House Office of Public Affairs, Kristen Gear Files, folder "Polls of Persian Gulf" OA/ID: 03418-016. George H.W. Bush Presidential Library.

Connolly, Kate. 2001. "Schröder Warns Greens as Military Prepares to Enter the Fray." *The Guardian*, October 17, 2001, sec. World news. https://www.theguardian.com/world/2001/oct/17/afghanistan.terrorism9.

Conrad, Frederick G., Mick P. Couper, Roger Tourangeau, and Chan Zhang. 2017. "Reducing Speeding in Web Surveys by Providing Immediate Feedback." *Survey Research Methods* 11 (1): 45–61.

Convention. 2022. "Convention on Cluster Munitions." *The Convention on Cluster Munitions* (blog), 2022. https://www.clusterconvention.org/.

Coppock, Alexander. 2019. "Generalizing from Survey Experiments Conducted on Mechanical Turk: A Replication Approach." *Political Science Research and Methods* 7 (3): 1–16.

Crawford, Neta. 2002. *Argument and Change in World Politics: Ethics, Decolonization, and Humanitarian Intervention*. Cambridge University Press.

Crawford, Neta. 2013. *Accountability for Killing: Moral Responsibility for Collateral Damage in America's Post-9/11 Wars*. Oxford University Press.

Crawford, Neta. 2014. "Targeting Civilians and U.S. Strategic Bombing Norms." In *The American Way of Bombing: Changing Ethical and Legal Norms, From Flying Fortresses to Drones*, Matthew Evangelista and Henry Shue (eds). Cornell University Press.

Crowder, Richard T. 1990. "Memorandum, Richard T. Crowder to Ede Holiday." Box 81, White House Office of Chief of Staff, John Sununu Files, Issues File, folder "Persian Gulf War 1991 [6]" OA/ID: 29166-008. George H.W. Bush Presidential Library.

Davenport, Christian, and David A. Armstrong. 2004. "Democracy and the Violation of Human Rights: A Statistical Analysis from 1976 to 1996." *American Journal of Political Science* 68 (3): 538–54.

Demarest, David. 1990a. "Memorandum, David Demarest to Governor Sununu, Communications Plan—Operation Desert Shield." Box 82, White House Office of Chief of Staff, John Sununu Files, Issues Files, folder "Persian Gulf Working Group" OA/ID: 29167-005. George H.W. Bush Presidential Library.

Demarest, David. 1990b. "Memorandum, David Demarest to Governor Sununu, Presidential Participation with Outside Groups." Box 82, White House Office of Chief of Staff, John Sununu Files, Issues Files, folder "Persian Gulf Working Group" OA/ID CF00472. George H.W. Bush Presidential Library.

Demarest, David. 1990c. "Memorandum, David Demarest to Gulf Working Group, Ideas for Future Tactics." Box 81, White House Office of Public Affairs, Kristen Gear Files, folder "Tips/Fact Sheets Persian Gulf" OA/ID: 03417-004. George H.W. Bush Presidential Library.

Demarest, David. 1990d. "Memorandum, David Demarest to The President, Communications Plan for Operation Desert Shield." Box 82, White House Office of Chief of Staff, John Sununu Files, Issues Files, folder "Persian Gulf Working Group" OA/ID: 29167-005. George H.W. Bush Presidential Library.

Department of the Army. 2014. "Field Manual 3–24 Insurgencies and Countering Insurgencies." June 2, 2014. https://armypubs.army.mil/ProductMaps/PubForm/Details.aspx?PUB_ID=83748.

Desch, Michael C. 2003. "It Is Kind to Be Cruel: The Humanity of American Realism." *Review of International Studies* 29: 415–26.

DeYoung, Karen, Alex Horton, and Missy Ryan. 2023. "Biden Approves Cluster Munition Supply to Ukraine." *Washington Post*, July 9, 2023. https://www.washingtonpost.com/national-security/2023/07/06/biden-cluster-bombs-ukraine/.

Dole, Bob, and Joseph Lieberman. 1994. "Letter, Senators to the President." FOIA 2008-0994-F, Clinton Presidential Records National Security Council, European Affairs-Holl, Jane, folder "Bosnia-Hercegovina, February 1994 [1]" OA/ID: 348. William J. Clinton Presidential Library.

"Draft 1, Presidential Remarks: Address to Joint Session of Congress." 1990. Box 66, White House Office of Speechwriting, Speech File Draft Files, Chron Files, 1989–1993, folder "Address to Joint Session of Congress, 9/11/90 [4]" OA/ID 13539-011. George H.W. Bush Presidential Library.

"Draft Comments, McGroarty/Dooley, Presidential Remarks: Video Address to the Iraqi People." 1990. Box 66, White House Office of Speechwriting, Speech File Draft Files, Chron Files, 1989–1993, folder "Video Address to Iraqi People, 9/12/90" OA/ID: 13539-012. George H.W. Bush Presidential Library.

"Draft, Christmas Eve Message to the Troops." 1990. Box 91, White House Press Office, Marlin Fitzwater Files, Guidance Files, folder "Monday, December 24, 1990" OA/ID: 12992-008. George H.W. Bush Presidential Library.

Drezner, Daniel W. 2008. "The Realist Tradition in American Public Opinion." *Perspectives on Politics* 6 (1): 51–70.

Dropp, Kyle, Joshua D. Kertzer, and Thomas Zeitzoff. 2014. "The Less Americans Know about Ukraine's Location, the More They Want U.S. to Intervene." *Washington Post: The Monkey Cage*, April 7, 2014. https://www.washingtonpost.com/news/monkey-cage/wp/2014/04/07/the-less-americans-know-about-ukraines-location-the-more-they-want-u-s-to-intervene/.

Druckman, James, and Lawrence Jacobs. 2011. "Segmented Representation: The Reagan White House and Disproportionate Responsiveness." In *Who Gets Represented?* Peter K. Enns and Christopher Wlezien (eds.). Russell Sage Foundation.

Druckman, James, and Lawrence Jacobs. 2015. *Who Governs? Presidents, Public Opinion, and Manipulation.* The University of Chicago Press.

Druckman, James N., Cari Lynn Hennessy, Kristi St. Charles, and Jonathan Webber. 2010. "Competing Rhetoric Over Time: Frames Versus Cues." *The Journal of Politics* 72 (1): 136–48.

Druckman, James N., and Justin W. Holmes. 2004. "Does Presidential Rhetoric Matter? Priming and Presidential Approval." *Presidential Studies Quarterly* 34 (4): 755–78.

Dugan, Andrew. 2015. "Fewer in U.S. View Iraq, Afghanistan Wars as Mistakes." *Gallup.* June 12, 2015. https://news.gallup.com/poll/183575/fewer-view-iraq-afghanistan-wars-mistakes.aspx.

Dyke, Nancy Bearg. 1990a. "Notes, Persian Gulf [1]." George H.W. Bush Presidential Records, National Security Council, Nancy Bearg Dyke Files, Subject FIle, Persian Gulf [1]. George H.W. Bush Presidential Library.

Dyke, Nancy Bearg. 1990b. "Persian Gulf Public Diplomacy Plan - Diplomacy Phase." FOIA 1998-0099-F, National Security Council, Nancy Bearg Dyke Files, Subject File, folder "Persian Gulf-Public Diplomacy [2]." OA/ID: CF01933-009. George H.W. Bush Presidential Library.

Dyke, Nancy Bearg. 1990c. "Public Diplomacy Themes to Target on Iraqis." George H.W. Bush Presidential Records, National Security Council, Nancy Bearg Dyke Files, Subject File, Persian Gulf-Public Diplomacy [1]. George H.W. Bush Presidential Library.

Dyke, Nancy Bearg. 1991a. "Memorandum, Nancy Bearg Dyke to Brent Scowcroft through R. Rand Beers." FOIA 1998-0099-F, National Security Council, Nancy Bearg Dyke Files, Subject File, folder "Persian Gulf-Humanitarian [3]" OA/ID: CF01076-014. George H.W. Bush Presidential Library.

Dyke, Nancy Bearg. 1991b. "Memorandum, Nancy Bearg Dyke to Brent Scowcroft through R. Rand Beers, Gulf Humanitarian Assistance—Now and After the War." FOIA 1998-0099-F, National Security Council, Nancy Bearg Dyke Files, Subject File, folder "Persian Gulf-Humanitarian [3]" OA/ID: CF01076-014. George H.W. Bush Presidential Library.

Dyke, Nancy Bearg. 1991c. "Themes, Public Diplomacy Themes on War Length." FOIA 1998-0099-F, National Security Council, Nancy Bearg Dyke Files, Subject File, folder "Persian Gulf-Public Diplomacy [5]" OA/ID: CF01933. George H.W. Bush Presidential Library.

Eichenberg, Richard. 2005. "Victory Has Many Friends: US Public Opinion and the Use of Military Force." *International Security* 30 (1): 140–77.

Eurobarometer. 2024. "EU Humanitarian Aid." *Eurobarometer*, 2024. https://europa.eu/eurobarometer/surveys/detail/2976.

Evangelista, Matthew, and Henry Shue, eds. 2014. *The American Way of Bombing: Changing Ethical and Legal Norms, From Flying Fortresses to Drones.* Cornell University Press.

Evans, Gareth. 2004. "When Is It Right to Fight?" *Survival* 46 (3): 59–81.

Fabrizio, Tony. 1990. "Memorandum, From Tony Fabrizio to Ambassador Sam Zakhem, Summary of National Voter Survey: Voter Attitudes Towards U.S. Policy in the Middle East." Box 81, White House Office of Public Affairs, Kristen Gear Files, folder "Iraq-Pos-Comments" OA/ID: 03418-013. George H.W. Bush Presidential Library.

Feeley, John F. 1995. "Guidance, John F. Feeley to Brian P. Cullin, James L. Fetig, David T. Johnson, Steven J. Naplan, Jill A. Schuker, Natalie S. Woznick, Nov 17 Guidance/Bosnia." Box 6, NSC Emails, MSMail-Record (Sept 94–Sept 97) [Srebrencia and Ethnic Cleanse. . .], folder "08/18/1995-01/30/1997" OA/ID: 590000. William J. Clinton Presidential Library.

Finn, E. R. 2024. "Schroeder Ties Vote of Confidence To War Plan." *Washington Post*, February 26, 2024. https://www.washingtonpost.com/archive/politics/2001/11/14/schroeder-ties-vote-of-confidence-to-war-plan/4cec7fe9-1c3b-4aeb-a499-4909280fab37/.

Finnemore, Martha. 1996. "Constructing Norms of Humanitarian Intervention." In *The Culture of National Security*, edited by Peter Katzenstein. Columbia University Press.

Finnemore, Martha. 2003. *The Purpose of Intervention*. Cornell University Press.

Fitch, Greg. 1990. "Memorandum, Greg Fitch to Speechwriters and Researchers, Religious Reaction to Operation Desert Shield." Box 5, White House Office of Speechwriting, Tony Snow Files, Subject Files, 1988–1993, folder "Memoranda-Speeches 1991–1992" OA/ID: 13896–002. George H.W. Bush Presidential Library.

Fitch, Greg. 1991. "Note, Greg Fitch to Beverly, Letter to U.S. Catholic Conference, Archbishop Pilarczyk." FOIA 1998-0099-F, White House Office of Public Liaison, Leigh Ann Metzger Files, folder "Operation Desert Shield-Religious Leaders, Negative" OA/ID: 04380-030. George H.W. Bush Presidential Library.

Fitzwater, Marlin. 1990a. "Press Briefing by Marlin Fitzwater." George H.W. Bush Presidential Library.

Fitzwater, Marlin. 1990b. "Press Briefing by Marlin Fitzwater, August 30, 1990." Box 86, White House Press Office, Marlin Fitzwater Files, Guidance Files, folder "Friday, August 3, 1990" OA/ID: 12987-030. George H.W. Bush Presidential Library.

Fitzwater, Marlin. 1991a. "Memorandum, Marlin Fitzwater to Governor Sununu, General Scowcroft, 10-Day Gulf Media Plan." Box 25, Marlin Fitzwater Files, Alphabetical Subject Files, folder "Press Strategy," OA/ID 12926-002. George H.W. Bush Presidential Library.

Fitzwater, Marlin. 1991b. "Notes, Baker Calls Pres." Box 91, White House Press Office, Marlin Fitzwater Files, Guidance Files, folder "Wednesday, January 9, 1991" OA/ID: 12992-021. George H.W. Bush Presidential Library.

Fitzwater, Marlin. 1991c. "Notes, Bush Ph. Calls." Box 92, White House Press Office, Marlin Fitzwater Files, Guidance Files, folder "Friday, January 11, 1991" OA/ID: 12993-001. George H.W. Bush Presidential Library.

Fitzwater, Marlin. 1991d. "Notes, Marlin Fitzwater." Box 91, White House Press Office, Marlin Fitzwater Files, Guidance Files, folder "Wednesday, January 2, 1991" OA/ID: 12992-015. George H.W. Bush Presidential Library.

Fitzwater, Marlin. 1993. "Statement by Press Secretary Fitzwater on the Situation in Iraq." The American Presidency Project. January 8, 1993. https://www.presidency.ucsb.edu/documents/statement-press-secretary-fitzwater-the-situation-iraq.

"Folder, Poll Data - [Gulf War]." 1991. Box 22, White House Press Office, Marlin Fitzwater Files, Alphabetical Subject Files, folder "Poll Data - [Gulf War]" OA/ID: 12923-007. George H.W. Bush Presidential Library.

Friedman, Jeffrey A. 2023. *The Commander-in-Chief Test: Public Opinion and the Politics of Image-Making in US Foreign Policy.* Cornell University Press.

Frontline. 2014. "Assassination: The Long Road to War." *Frontline, PBS.* https://www.pbs.org/wgbh/pages/frontline/shows/longroad/etc/assassination.html.

Gadarian, Shana Kushner. 2010. "The Politics of Threat: How Terrorism News Shapes Foreign Policy Attitudes." *Journal of Politics* 72 (2): 469–83.

Gadarian, Shana Kushner. 2014. "Scary Pictures: How Terrorism Imagery Affects Voter Evaluations." *Political Communication* 31 (2): 282–302.

Gallup. 2001. "Americans Believe U.S. Participation in Gulf War a Decade Ago Worthwhile." *Gallup News Service.* February 26, 2001. https://news.gallup.com/poll/1963/Americans-Believe-US-Participation-Gulf-War-Decade-Ago-Worthwhile.aspx.

Gallup. 2009. "Presidential Approval Ratings—George W. Bush." Gallup.Com.http://www.gallup.com/poll/116500/Presidential-Approval-Ratings-George-Bush.aspx.

Gartner, Scott Sigmund. 2008. "The Multiple Effects of Casualties on Public Support for War: An Experimental Approach." *American Political Science Review* 102 (1): 95–106.

Gear, Kristin. n.d. "Guidance, Themes for Military Operations Against Iraq." FOIA 1998-0099-F, Kristin Gear Files, folder "Energy/Persian Gulf", OA/ID 03418-008. George H.W. Bush Presidential Library.

Gelpi, Christopher, and Joseph M. Grieco. 2015. "Competency Costs in Foreign Affairs: Presidential Performance in International Conflicts and Domestic Legislative Success, 1953–2001." *American Journal of Political Science* 59 (2): 440–56.

Gelpi, Christopher, Peter Feaver, and Jason Reifler. 2009. *Paying the Human Costs of War: American Public Opinion and Casualties in Military Conflicts.* Princeton University Press.

George, Alexander L., and Andrew Bennett. 2005. *Case Studies and Theory Development in the Social Sciences.* MIT Press.

German Marshall Fund. 2023. "2023 Transatlantic Trends: Public Opinion in a Shifting Global Order." https://www.gmfus.org/sites/default/files/2023-09/TT2023_digital-3.pdf.

Gershkoff, Amy, and Shana Kushner. 2005. "Shaping Public Opinion: The 9/11-Iraq Connection in the Bush Administration's Rhetoric." *Perspectives on Politics* 3 (03): 525–37. https://doi.org/10.1017/S1537592705050334.

Geys, Benny. 2010. "Wars, Presidents, and Popularity: The Political Cost(s) of War Re-Examined." *Public Opinion Quarterly* 74 (2): 357–74.

Goddard, Stacie E., and Ronald R. Krebs. 2015. "Rhetoric, Legitimation, and Grand Strategy." *Security Studies* 24 (1): 5–36.

Gray, C. Boyden. 1990. "Memorandum, C. Boyden Gray to the President, Potential Significance of a Declaration of War Against Iraq." Box 81, White House Office of Chief of Staff, John Sununu Files, Issues File, folder "Persian Gulf War 1991 [6]" OA/ID: 29166-008. George H.W. Bush Presidential Library.

Grieco, Joseph M., Christopher Gelpi, Jason Reifler, and Peter Feaver. 2011. "Let's Get a Second Opinion: International Institutions and American Public Support for War." *International Organization* 55 (2): 563–83.

"Guidance, Iraq and War Crimes." 1991. Box 93, White House Press Office, Marlin Fitzwater Files, Guidance Files, folder "Sunday, January 20, 1991" OA/ID 12994-001. George H.W. Bush Presidential Library.

"Guidance, Gulf Policy Themes." 1990. Box 17, Marlin Fitzwater Files, Alphabetical subject files, folder "Iraq (1991) [1]." George H.W. Bush Presidential Library.

"Guidance, Gulf Strategy January Themes and Messages." 1991. Box 17, Marlin Fitzwater Files, Alphabetical Subject Files, folder "Iraq 1991 [1]" OA/ID:12918. George H.W. Bush Presidential Library.

"Guidance, Presidential Letter to the College Students." 1991. Box 92, White House Press Office, Marlin Fitzwater Files, Guidance File, folder "Monday, January 14, 1991" OA/ID: 12993-004. George H.W. Bush Presidential Library.

Guisinger, Alexandra, and Elizabeth N. Saunders. 2017. "Mapping the Boundaries of Elite Cues: How Elites Shape Mass Opinion across International Issues." *International Studies Quarterly* 61 (2): 425–41.

Haidt, Jonathan, and Jesse Graham. 2007. "When Morality Opposes Justice: Conservatives Have Moral Intuitions That Liberals May Not Recognize." *Social Justice Research* 20 (1): 98–116.

Heaney, Michael T., and Fabio Rojas. 2011. "The Partisan Dynamics of Contention: Demobilization of the Antiwar Movement in the United States, 2007–2009." *Mobilization* 16 (1): 45–64.

Heaney, Michael T., and Fabio Rojas. 2015. *Party in the Street: The Antiwar Movement and the Democratic Party After 9/11.* Cambridge University Press.

Helman, Gerald B. 1991. "Memorandum, Gerald Helman to Robert M. Gates, Paul Wolfowitz, William P. Barr, Richard J. Kerr, and Admiral David E. Jeremiah, Public Opinion Assessment #13." FOIA 1998-0099-F, National Security Council, Nancy Bearg Dyke Files, Subject File, folder "Persian Gulf-Public Diplomacy [1]" OA/ID: CF01933-008. George H.W. Bush Presidential Library.

Herrmann, Richard, Philip Tetlock, and Penny Visser. 1999. "Mass Public Decisions to Go to War: A Cognitive-Interactionist Framework." *American Political Science Review* 93 (3): 553–73.

Hildebrandt, Timothy, Courtney Hillebrecht, Peter M. Holm, and Jon Pevehouse. 2013. "The Domestic Politics of Humanitarian Intervention: Public Opinion, Partisanship, and Ideology." *Foreign Policy Analysis* 9 (3): 243–66.

Holsti, Ole R. 1979. "The Three-Headed Eagle: The United States and System Change." *International Studies Quarterly* 23 (3): 339–59.

Holsti, Ole R. 1992. "Public Opinion and Foreign Policy: Challenges to the Almond-Lippmann Consensus." *International Studies Quarterly, Mershon Series: Research Programs and Debates,* 36 (4): 439–66.

Holsti, Ole R., and James N. Rosenau. 1990. "The Structure of Foreign Policy Attitudes among American Leaders." *The Journal of Politics* 52 (1): 94–125.

Holzgrefe, J. L., and Robert O. Keohane, eds. 2003. *Humanitarian Intervention: Ethical, Legal, and Political Dilemmas.* Cambridge University Press.

Howell, William G., and Jon Pevehouse. 2005. "Presidents, Congress, and the Use of Force." *International Organization* 59 (1): 209–32.

Human Rights Watch. 2023. "Ukraine: Civilian Deaths from Cluster Munitions." *Human Rights Watch* (blog). July 6, 2023. https://www.hrw.org/news/2023/07/06/ukraine-civilian-deaths-cluster-munitions.

Hurd, Ian. 1999. "Legitimacy and Authority in International Politics." *International Organization* 53 (2): 379–408.

Hurwitz, Jon, and Mark Peffley. 1987. "How Are Foreign Policy Attitudes Structured? A Hierarchical Model." *American Political Science Review* 81 (4): 1099–1120.

ICISS. 2001. "The Responsibility to Protect." Report of the International Commission on Intervention and State Sovereignty.

Ignatieff, Michael. 2007. "Getting Iraq Wrong." *The New York Times*, August 5, 2007, sec. Magazine. https://www.nytimes.com/2007/08/05/magazine/05iraq-t.html.

Ikenberry, G. John. 2009. "Liberal Internationalism 3.0: America and the Dilemmas of Liberal World Order." *Perspectives on Politics* 7 (1): 71–87.

Iyengar, Shanto, Yphtach Lelkes, Matthew S. Levendusky, Neil Malhotra, and Sean J. Westwood. 2019. "The Origins and Consequences of Affective Polarization in the United States." *Annual Review of Political Science* 22 (1): 129–46.

Iyer, Ravi, Spassena Koleva, Jesse Graham, Peter Ditto, and Jonathan Haidt. 2012. "Understanding Libertarian Morality: The Psychological Dispositions of Self-Identified Libertarians." *PLoS ONE* 7 (8): 1–23.

Jackson, Michael P. 1990. "Memorandum, Michael P. Jackson to Cabinet and Agency Contacts, Persian Gulf Policy—Communications Package #1." Box 82, White House Office of Chief of Staff, John Sununu Files, Issues Files, folder "Persian Gulf Working Group" OA/ID CF00472. George H.W. Bush Presidential Library.

Jackson, Michael P. 1991. "Draft Comments, Michael Jackson, Presidential Letter to College Students." Box 80, White House Office of Speechwriting, Speech File Draft File, Chron File, 1989-1993, folder "Letters to College Students, 1/7/1991" OA/ID: 13553-003. George H.W. Bush Presidential Library.

Jacobs, Lawrence, and Robert Shapiro. 2000. *Politicians Don't Pander: Political Manipulation and the Loss of Democratic Responsiveness.* University of Chicago Press.

Jentleson, Bruce. 1992. "The Pretty Prudent Public: Post Post-Vietnam American Opinion on the Use of Military Force." *International Studies Quarterly* 36 (1): 49–73.

Jentleson, Bruce, and Rebecca L. Britton. 1998. "Still Pretty Prudent: Post-Cold War American Public Opinion on the Use of Military Force." *Journal of Conflict Resolution* 42 (4): 395–17.

Johnson, Boris. 2022. "PM Statement on the Situation in Ukraine: 22 February 2022." *GOV.UK.*, February 22, 2022. https://www.gov.uk/government/speeches/pm-statement-on-the-situation-in-ukraine-22-february-2022.

Johnson, Lyndon B. 1965. "Statement by the President: 'Tragedy, Disappointment, and Progress' in Viet-Nam." The American Presidency Project. April 17, 1965. https://www.presidency.ucsb.edu/documents/statement-the-president-tragedy-disappointment-and-progress-viet-nam.

Johnson, Reed. 2002. "Revenge: A Family Affair." *Los Angeles Times*, December 11, 2002. https://www.latimes.com/archives/la-xpm-2002-dec-11-et-johnson11-story.html.

Keller, Bill. 2003. "The I-Can't-Believe-I'm-a-Hawk Club." *The New York Times*, February 8, 2003, sec. Opinion. https://www.nytimes.com/2003/02/08/opinion/the-i-cant-believe-i-m-a-hawk-club.html.

Kelly, Laura. 2022. "US Ambassador to UN Offers Condemnation of Russian Actions." *Text. The Hill* (blog). March 2, 2022. https://thehill.com/policy/international/596520-us-ambassador-to-un-offers-condemnation-of-russian-actions/.

Kennan, George F. 1984. *American Diplomacy*. University of Chicago Press.

Kennan, George F. 1985. "Morality and Foreign Policy." *Foreign Affairs* 64 (2): 205–18.

Kennan, George F. 1993. "Somalia, Through a Glass Darkly." *The New York Times*, September 30, 1993. http://www.nytimes.com/1993/09/30/opinion/somalia-through-a-glass-darkly.html?pagewanted=all.

Kernell, Samuel. 1997. *Going Public: New Strategies of Presidential Leadership*. 3rd ed. Washington, DC: Congressional Quarterly Inc.

Kertzer, Joshua D. 2013. "Making Sense of Isolationism: Foreign Policy Mood as a Multilevel Phenomenon." *Journal of Politics* 75 (1): 225–40.

Kertzer, Joshua D., Deborah Jordan Brooks, and Stephen G. Brooks. 2021. "Do Partisan Types Stop at the Water's Edge?" *The Journal of Politics* 83 (4): 1764–82.

Kertzer, Joshua D., Kathleen E. Powers, Brian C. Rathbun, and Ravi Iyer. 2014. "Moral Support: How Moral Values Shape Foreign Policy Attitudes." *Journal of Politics* 76 (3): 825–40.

Krebs, Ronald R. 2015. *Narrative and the Making of US National Security*. Cambridge University Press.

Krebs, Ronald R., and Jennifer K. Lobasz. 2007. "Fixing the Meaning of 9/11 Hegemony, Coercion, and the Road to War in Iraq." *Security Studies* 16 (3): 409–51.

Kreps, Sarah, Elizabeth N. Saunders, and Kenneth Schultz. 2018. "The Ratification Premium: Hawks, Doves, and Arms Control." *World Politics* 70 (4): 479–514.

Kreps, Sarah. 2010. "Elite Consensus as a Determinant of Alliance Cohesion: Why Public Opinion Hardly Matters for NATO-Led Operations in Afghanistan." *Foreign Policy Analysis* 6 (3): 191–215.

Kreps, Sarah. 2011. *Coalitions of Convenience: United States Military Interventions After the Cold War*. Oxford University Press.

Kreps, Sarah. 2018. *Taxing Wars: The American Way of War Finance and the Decline of Democracy*. Oxford University Press.

Kreps, Sarah, and Sarah Maxey. 2018. "Mechanisms of Morality: Sources of Support for Humanitarian Interventions." *Journal of Conflict Resolution* 62 (8): 1814–42.

Kriner, Douglas. 2010. *After the Rubicon: Congress, Presidents, and the Politics of Waging War*. University of Chicago Press.

Kriner, Douglas, and Francis Shen. 2014. "Responding to War on Capitol Hill: Battlefield Casualties, Congressional Response, and Public Support for the War in Iraq." *American Journal of Political Science* 58 (1): 157–74.

Kull, Steven, and I. M. Destler. 1999. *Misreading the Public: The Myth of a New Isolationism*. Brookings.

Kull, Steven, Clay Ramsay, and Evan Lewis. 2003. "Misperceptions, the Media, and the Iraq War." *Political Science Quarterly* 118 (4): 569–98.

Leahy, Patrick, and Jeff Merkley. 2023. "Here's Why Supplying Ukraine with Cluster Munitions Would Be a Terrible Mistake." *Washington Post*, July 7, 2023. https://www.washingtonpost.com/opinions/2023/07/07/leahy-merkley-ukraine-cluster-munitions/.

Lee, Carrie A. 2022. "Polarization, Casualty Sensitivity, and Military Operations: Evidence from a Survey Experiment." *International Politics* 59 (5): 981–1003.

Lee, Frances E. 2015. "How Party Polarization Affects Governance." *Annual Review of Political Science* 18 (1): 261–82.

Levendusky, Matthew S., and Michael C. Horowitz. 2012. "When Backing Down Is the Right Decision: Partisanship, New Information and Audience Costs." *Journal of Politics* 74 (2): 323–38.

Liberman, Peter. 2006. "An Eye for an Eye: Public Support for War against Evildoers." *International Organization* 60 (3): 687–722.

Lifton, Robert K., and Henry Siegman. 1993. "Letter, American Jewish Congress to the President." FOIA 2008-0994-F, Box 10, Clinton Presidential Records National Security Council, European Affairs-Holl, Jane, folder "Bosnia-Hercegovina, July-August 1993 [8]" OA/ID: 17. William J. Clinton Presidential Library.

Lippmann, Walter. 1922. *Public Opinion*. Macmillan.

Lorin, Matthew E. 1995. "Email, Matthew E. Lorin to Kathleen H. Cooper, War Crimes Statement FINAL." Box 6, NSC Emails, MSMail-Record (Sept 94-Sept 97) [Srebrenica and Ethnic Cleanse. . .], folder "07/12/1995-08/04/1995" OA/ID: 590000. William J. Clinton Presidential Library.

Lowe, Will. 2015. "Yoshikoder: Cross-Platform Multilingual Content Analysis." Java Software Version 0.6.5.

Lupton, Danielle L. 2017. "Out of the Service, Into the House: Military Experience and Congressional War Oversight." *Political Research Quarterly* 70 (2): 327–39.

Lupton, Danielle L. 2022. "Military Experience and Elite Decision-Making: Self-Selection, Socialization, and the Vietnam Draft Lottery." *International Studies Quarterly* 66: 1–14.

Lupton, Danielle L., and Clayton Webb. 2022. "Wither Elites? The Role of Elite Credibility and Knowledge in Public Perceptions of Foreign Policy." *International Studies Quarterly* 66 (3): 1–13. https://doi.org/10.1093/isq/sqac057.

Malhotra, Neil. 2008. "Completion Time and Response Order Effects in Web Surveys." *Public Opinion Quarterly* 72 (5): 914–34.

Malhotra, Neil, and Elizabeth Popp. 2012. "Bridging Partisan Divisions over Antiterrorism Policies: The Role of Threat Perceptions." *Political Research Quarterly* 65 (1): 34–47.

Malone, Noreen. 2021. "Why So Many Liberals Supported Invading Iraq." *Slate*, May 14, 2021. https://slate.com/news-and-politics/2021/05/iraq-war-liberal-media-support-humanitarian-intervention.html.

Mandelbaum, Michael. 1996. "Foreign Policy as Social Work." *Foreign Affairs* 75 (1): 16–32.

Mandelbaum, Michael, and William Schneider. 1979. "The New Internationalisms: Public Opinion and American Foreign Policy." In *Eagle Entangled: U.S. Foreign Policy in a*

Complex World, edited by Kenneth A. Oye, Donald Rothchild, and Robert J. Lieber. Longman, Inc.

Mason, Lilliana. 2018. *Uncivil Agreement: How Politics Became Our Identity*. University of Chicago Press.

Mattes, Michaela, and Jessica L. P. Weeks. 2019. "Hawks, Doves, and Peace: An Experimental Approach." *American Journal of Political Science* 63 (1): 53–66.

Mattes, Michaela, and Jessica L. P. Weeks. 2022. "Reacting to the Olive Branch: Hawks, Doves, and Public Support for Cooperation." *International Organization* 76: 957–76.

Maxey, Sarah. 2020. "The Power of Humanitarian Narratives: A Domestic Coalition Theory of Justifications for Military Action." *Political Research Quarterly* 73 (3): 680–95.

Maxey, Sarah. 2021a. "Finding the Water's Edge: When Negative Partisanship Influences Foreign Policy Attitudes." *International Politics* Online First: 1–25. https://doi.org/10. 1057/s41311-021-00354-9.

Maxey, Sarah. 2021b. "Limited Spin: When the Public Punishes Leaders Who Lie about Military Action." *Journal of Conflict Resolution* 65 (2–3): 283–312.

McClure, Frederick D. 1991. "Meeting with Bipartisan Group of House Members." Box 91, White House Press Office, Marlin Fitzwater Files, Guidance Files, folder "Wednesday, January 9, 1991" OA/ID: 12992-021. George H.W. Bush Presidential Library.

McFarland, Sam, and Melissa Mathews. 2005. "Do Americans Care About Human Rights?" *Journal of Human Rights* 4 (3): 305–19.

Mcgroarty, Dan. 1991. "Memorandum, Dan Mcgroarty to the President through David Demarest, Video Address to the Community of Nations United Against Iraqi Aggression." Box 80, White House Office of Speechwriting, Speech File Draft File, Chron File, 1989-1993, folder "Video Address on Iraqi Aggression, 1/8/9." OA/ID: 13553-004. George H.W. Bush Presidential Library.

McNally, and Simon. 1990. "Draft Two, McNally/Simon, Presidential Remarks: Officers and Troops at Hickam Airfield." Box 73, White House Office of Speechwriting, Speech File Draft Diles, Chron File, 1989-1993, folder "Officers and Troops at Hickam Airfield, 10/28/9." OA/ID: 13546-014. George H.W. Bush Presidential Library.

Mearsheimer, John J. 2011. *Why Leaders Lie: The Truth About Lying in International Politics*. Oxford University Press.

Meer, Jeff. 2023. "Cluster Munitions Are Too Risky for Use in Ukraine." *Washington Post*, March 6, 2023, sec. Opinion. https://www.washingtonpost.com/opinions/2023/ 03/06/cluster-munitions-ukraine-risk/.

"Meeting with Bipartisan Congressional Leadership." 1991. Box 91, White House Press Office, Marlin Fitzwater Files, Guidance Files, folder "Friday, January 4, 1991 [2]" OA/ID: 4541-016. George H.W. Bush Presidential Library.

"Memorandum, Summary of Iraq Public Diplomacy Meeting." 1991. FOIA 1998-0099-F, National Security Council, Nancy Bearg Dyke Files, Subject File, folder "Persian Gulf-Public Diplomacy [2]" OA/ID: CF01933-009. George H.W. Bush Presidential Library.

Metzger, Leigh Ann. 1990a. "Memorandum, Leigh Ann Metzger to David Demarest, Address Veterans of Foreign Wars Convention." Box 86, White House Press Office,

Marlin Fitzwater Files, Guidance Files, folder "Monday, August 20, 1990" OA/ID: 12988-012. George H.W. Bush Presidential Library.

Metzger, Leigh Ann. 1990b. "Memorandum, Leigh Ann Metzger to Governor Sununu through David Demarest, OPL 'Desert Shield' Activities." FOIA 1998-0099-F, White House Office of Public Liaison, Leigh Ann Metzger Files, folder "Kuwait" OA/ID: 06887-026. George H.W. Bush Presidential Library.

Metzger, Leigh Ann. 1990c. "Notes, Leigh Ann Metzger, Defense/National Security." FOIA 1998-0099-F, White House Office of Public Liaison, Leigh Ann Metzger Files, folder "Kuwait" OA/ID: 06887-026. George H.W. Bush Presidential Library.

Metzger, Leigh Ann. 1991. "Briefing with Leaders of Veterans Services Organizations, Leign Ann Metzger through David Demarest." Box 97, White House Press Office, Marlin Fitzwater Files, Guidance Files, folder "Monday, March 4, 1991" OA/ID: 12998-009. George H.W. Bush Presidential Library.

Milner, Helen, and Dustin Tingley. 2013. "The Choice for Multilateralism: Foreign Aid and American Foreign Policy." *Review of International Organizations* 8 (3): 313–41.

Milner, Helen, and Dustin Tingley. 2015. *Sailing the Water's Edge: The Domestic Politics of American Foreign Policy*. Princeton University Press.

Molinari, Susan. 1993. "Letter, Susan Molinari to the President." FOIA 2008-0994-F, Clinton Presidential Records National Security Council, European Affairs-Holl, Jane, Folder "Bosnia-Hercegovina, August 1993 [2]" OA/ID: 17. William J. Clinton Presidential Library.

Morgenthau, Hans J. 1951. *In Defense of the National Interest*. Alfred A. Knopf.

Morin, Richard. 1991. "Wash Post/ABC Poll, Gulf Poll: Most Americans Want Hill to Back Bush." Box 22, White House Press Office, Marlin Fitzwater Files, Alphabetical Subject Files, folder "Poll Data - [Gulf War]" OA/ID: 12923-007. George H.W. Bush Presidential Library.

Moyn, Samuel. 2021. *Humane: How the United States Abandoned Peace and Reinvented War*. Farrar, Straus, and Giroux.

Mueller, John. 1973. *War, Presidents, and Public Opinion*. Wiley.

Myrick, Rachel. 2022. "The Reputational Consequences of Polarization for American Foreign Policy: Evidence from the US-UK Bilateral Relationship." *International Politics* 59 (5): 1004–27.

National Archives. 2016. "Public Papers of the Presidents." National Archives. August 15, 2016. https://www.archives.gov/federal-register/publications/presidential-papers.html.

National Security Council. 1990a. "Memorandum, Iraq/Kuwait—The Military Option." Box 73, National Security Council, Richard N. Haass Files, Working Files, folder "Iraq-October 1990 [2]" OA/ID:CF01584-032. George H.W. Bush Presidential Library.

National Security Council. 1990b. "Memorandum, Next Steps in the Gulf." Box 73, National Security Council, Richard N. Haass Files, Working Files, folder "Iraq-October 1990 [2]" OA/ID:CF01584-032. George H.W. Bush Presidential Library.

Nelson, Thomas E., and Zoe M. Oxley. 1999. "Issue Framing Effects on Belief Importance and Opinion." *The Journal of Politics* 61 (4): 1040–67.

Nelson, Thomas E., Zoe M. Oxley, and Rosalee A. Clawson. 1997. "Toward a Psychology of Framing Effects." *Political Behavior* 19 (3): 221–46.

Newport, Frank. 2001. "Public Opinion of the War in Afghanistan." *Gallup News Service*, October 31, 2001. https://news.gallup.com/poll/9994/Public-Opinion-War-Afghanistan.aspx.

Nincic, Miroslav. 1997. "Domestic Costs, the U.S. Public, and the Isolationist Calculus." *International Studies Quarterly* 41 (4): 593–609.

O'Rourke, Lindsey A. 2018. *Covert Regime Change. Cornell Studies in Security Affairs.* Cornell University Press.

Oakes, Amy. 2012. *Diversionary War: Domestic Unrest and International Conflict.* Stanford University Press.

Obama, Barack. 2011. "Address to the Nation on the Situation in Libya." Public Papers of the Presidents.

Obama, Barack. 2013. "Remarks by the President in Address to the Nation on Syria." Office of the Press Secretary. September 10, 2013. https://www.whitehouse.gov/the-press-office/2013/09/10/remarks-president-address-nation-syria.

Obama, Barack. 2014. "Address to the Nation on United States Strategy to Combat the Islamic State of Iraq and the Levant Terrorist Organization (ISIL)." Public Papers of the Presidents.

Office of Communications. 1991. "Polling Data, Prepared by the Office of Communications." FOIA 1998-0099-F, White House Office of Public Affairs, Kristen Gear Files, folder "Polls of Persian Gulf" OA/ID: 03418-016. George H.W. Bush Presidential Library.

PA/Opinion Analysis. 1990. "First Poll on Release of Hostages Shows No Decline in Willingness to Use Force to Free Kuwait." FOIA 1998-0099-F, White House Office of Public Affairs, Kristen Gear Files, folder "Polls of Persian Gulf" OA/ID: 03418-016. George H.W. Bush Presidential Library.

PA/Opinion Analysis. 1991. "Majority of Americans Now Expect War to Last at Least 6 Months." FOIA 1998-0099-F, White House Office of Public Affairs, Kristen Gear Files, folder "Polls of Persian Gulf" OA/ID: 03418-016. George H.W. Bush Presidential Library.

Palmer, Glenn, Vito D'Orazio, Michael Kenwick, and Matthew Lane. 2015. "The MID4 Data Set: Procedures, Coding Rules, and Description." *Conflict Management and Peace Science* 32 (2): 222–42.

Panagopoulos, Costas. 2016. "All about That Base: Changing Campaign Strategies in U.S. Presidential Elections." *Party Politics* 22 (2): 179–90.

Pattison, James. 2010. *Humanitarian Intervention and the Responsibility to Protect: Who Should Intervene.* Oxford University Press.

Payne, Andrew. 2023. *War on the Ballot: How the Election Cycle Shapes Presidential Decision-Making In War.* Columbia University Press.

Perry, Kati, Hannah Dormido, Dylan Moriarty, Kevin Uhrmacher, and Adrián Blanco. 2024. "How Every House Member Voted on Aid to Ukraine, Israel and More." *Washington Post*, April 20, 2024. https://www.washingtonpost.com/politics/interactive/2024/04/20/ukraine-israel-border-funding-house-vote/.

Pettersson, Therése, and Peter Wallensteen. 2015. "Armed Conflicts, 1946-2014." *Journal of Peace Research* 52 (4): 536–50.

Pevehouse, Jon, and William G. Howell. 2007. *While Dangers Gather: Congressional Checks on Presidential War Powers*. Princeton University Press.

Pickering, Jeffrey, and Emizet Kisangani. 2009. "The International Military Intervention Dataset: An Updated Resource for Conflict Scholars." *Journal of Peace Research* 46 (4): 589–99.

Pinkerton, James P. 1990. "Note, James P. Pinkerton to Chriss Winston." Box 75, White House Office of Speechwriting, Speech File Draft Files, Chron File, 1989-1993, folder "GOP Senate Leadership, 11/13/90" OA/ID: 13548-010. George H.W. Bush Presidential Library.

Pinkerton, Jim. 1990. "Memorandum, Jim Pinkerton to Chriss Winston, VFW Address Speech Draft." Box No. 65, Stack G, OA/ID:13538-011, folder "VFW National Convention, 8/20/90 [2] OA/ID 05376." George H.W. Bush Presidential Library.

Pomeranz, William E. 2022. "Putin's Pretext?" The Wilson Center. February 20, 2022. https://www.wilsoncenter.org/article/putins-pretext.

Post, Abigail. 2023. "Words Matter: The Effect of Moral Language on International Bargaining." *International Security* 48 (1): 125–65.

Power, Samantha. 2002. *A Problem from Hell: America and the Age of Genocide*. Basic Books.

Psaki, Jen. 2022. "Press Briefing by Press Secretary Jen Psaki." The American Presidency Project. February 28, 2022. https://www.presidency.ucsb.edu/documents/press-briefing-press-secretary-jen-psaki-132.

Quealy, Kevin. 2017. "If Americans Can Find North Korea on a Map, They're More Likely to Prefer Diplomacy." *The New York Times*, July 5, 2017. https://www.nytimes.com/interactive/2017/05/14/upshot/if-americans-can-find-north-korea-on-a-map-theyre-more-likely-to-prefer-diplomacy.html.

Rainey, Carlisle. 2014. "Arguing for a Negligible Effect." *American Journal of Political Science* 58 (4): 1083–91.

Rathbun, Brian C. 2004. *Partisan Interventions: European Party Politics and Peace Enforcement in the Balkans*. Cornell University Press.

Rathbun, Brian C., Joshua D. Kertzer, Jason Reifler, Paul Goren, and Thomas Scotto. 2016. "Taking Foreign Policy Personally: Personal Values and Foreign Policy Attitudes." *International Studies Quarterly* 60: 124–37.

Rathbun, Brian C., and Rachel M. Stein. 2020. "Greater Goods: Morality and Attitudes Towards the Use of Nuclear Weapons." *Journal of Conflict Resolution* 64 (5): 787–816.

Reid, John. 2022. "Putin, Pretext, and the Dark Side of the 'Responsibility to Protect.'" War on the Rocks. May 27, 2022. https://warontherocks.com/2022/05/putin-pretext-and-the-dark-side-of-the-responsibility-to-protect/.

Reiter, Dan. 2012. "Democracy, Deception, and Entry into War." *Security Studies* 21 (4): 594–623.

Reiter, Dan, and Allan Stam. 2002. *Democracies at War*. Princeton University Press.

"Report, Iraq: Impact of the Sanctions." 1990. Box 6, White House Office of Speech-writing, Carol Aarhus Files, Alpha File, 1990-1992, folder "Persian Gulf [2]" OA/ID: 13864-007. George H.W. Bush Presidential Library.

Richman, Alvin. 1993. "Memorandum, Alving Richman to Ann Pincus, U.S. Public's Views on International Involvement and the Use of Force: Key Findings." Box 9, National Security Council, Legislative Affairs-Rosner, Jeremy, folder "Polling" OA/ID: 3. William J. Clinton Presidential Library.

Riker, William H. 1962. *The Theory of Political Coalitions.* Yale University Press.

Robinson, Piers. 1999. "The CNN Effect: Can the News Media Drive Foreign Policy?" *Review of International Studies* 25 (2): 301–09.

Robinson, Piers. 2011. "The CNN Effect Reconsidered: Mapping a Research Agenda for the Future." *Media, War, & Conflict* 4 (1): 3–11.

Rogers, E. d. 1990. "White House Staffing Memorandum, Ed Rogers to Chriss Winston, Presidential Remarks: Armed Forces Radio Network." Box 66, White House Office of Speechwriting, Speech File Draft Files, Chron Files, 1989-1993, folder "Armed Forces Radio Network, 8/29/90" OA/ID: 13539-001. George H.W. Bush Presidential Library.

Roosevelt, Franklin D. 1942. *"Fireside Chat."* Edited by Gerhard Peters and John T. Woolley. The American Presidency Project. http://www.presidency.ucsb.edu/ws/?pid=16252.

Rosenblast, L. 1991. "Fax, L. Rosenblast to Nancy Dyke." FOIA 1998-0099-F, National Security Council, Nancy Bearg Dyke Files, Subject File, folder "Refugees: Persian Gulf Pre-Kurds [2]" OA/ID: CF01458-022. George H.W. Bush Presidential Library.

Ross/Sonenshine. 1994. "Bosnia Public Affairs Strategy." FOIA 2008-0994-F, Box 22, Clinton Presidential Records National Security Council, European Affairs-Kerrick, Donald, folder "Bosnia-NATO [2]" OA/ID: 368. William J. Clinton Presidential Library.

Roy, J. Stapleton. 1990. "Memorandum, J. Stapleton Roy to Brent Scowcroft, Themes for the President's Speech to the UN General Assembly." Box 69, White House Office of Speechwriting, Speech File Draft Files, Chron File, 1989-1993, folder "United Nations General Assembly Address, 10/1/1990 [2]" OA/ID: 13542-011. George H.W. Bush Presidential Library.

Rugh, William. 1991a. "Memo, William A. Rugh to DOD Captain Larry Seaquist, Dr. Ed Hullender, Iraqi Disinformation-1/25." FOIA 1998-0099-F, National Security Council, Nancy Bearg Dyke Files, Subject File, folder "Persian Gulf-Public Diplomacy [1]" OA/ID: CF01933-008. George H.W. Bush Presidential Library.

Rugh, William. 1991b. "Memorandum, William A. Rugh to The Honorable John Kelly, January 25 Update of Public Reaction in NEA Countries." FOIA 1998-0099-F, National Security Council, Nancy Bearg Dyke Files, Subject File, folder "Persian Gulf-Public Diplomacy [2]" OA/ID: CF01933-009. George H.W. Bush Presidential Library.

Russett, Bruce. 1993. *Grasping the Democratic Peace: Principles for a Post-Cold War World.* Princeton University Press.

Sampson, Eve, Victoria Bisset, and Júlia Ledur. 2023. "What Are Cluster Munitions That Biden Is Sending to Ukraine?" *Washington Post*, July 12, 2023, sec. Europe. https://www.washingtonpost.com/world/2023/07/07/cluster-munitions-biden-ukraine/.

Saperstein, David. 1993. "Memo, Rabbi David Saperstein to Amy Zisook, 'Dallas Rally for Bosnia.'" 2008-0994-F, Clinton Presidential Records, National Security Council, European Affairs-Holl, Jane, folder "Bosnia-Hercegovina, July-August 1993 [1]" OA/ID: 17. William J. Clinton Presidential Library.

Saunders, Elizabeth N. 2011. *Leaders at War: How Presidents Shape Military Interventions.* Cornell University Press.

Saunders, Elizabeth N. 2015. "War and the Inner Circle: Democratic Elites and the Politics of Using Force." *Security Studies* 24 (1): 466–501.

Saunders, Elizabeth N. 2024. *The Insider's Game: How Elites Make War and Peace.* Princeton University Press.

Scholz, Olaf. 2022. "Federal Chancellor Scholz Strongly Condemns Russian Attack on Ukraine | Federal Government." Website of the Federal Government | Bundesregierung. February 24, 2022. https://www.bundesregierung.de/breg-en/news/federal-government-ukraine-war-russia-2007196.

Scholz, Olaf. 2024. "Federal Chancellor at Government Question Time in March 2024 | Federal Government." Website of the Federal Government | Bundesregierung. March 13, 2024. https://www.bundesregierung.de/breg-en/news/chancellor-government-question-time-march-2024-2265006.

Schröder, Gerhard. 2001. "Rede von Bundeskanzler Gerhard Schröder Zur Beteiligung Bewaffneter Deutscher Streitkräfte Am Einsatz Einer Internationalen Sicherheitsunterstützungstruppe in Afghanistan." In *A Corpus of German Political Speeches from the 21st Century,* edited by Adrien Barbaresi. https://politische-reden.eu/BR/t/356.html.

Schuessler, John M. 2015. *Deceit on the Road to War: Presidents, Politics, and American Democracy.* Cornell University Press.

Schultz, Kenneth. 2003. "Tying Hands and Washing Hands: The U.S. Congress and Multilateral Humanitarian Intervention." In *Locating the Proper Authorities: The Interaction of International and Domestic Institutions,* edited by Daniel W. Drezner. University of Michigan Press.

Schultz, Kenneth. 2017. "Perils of Polarization for U.S. Foreign Policy." *The Washington Quarterly* 40 (4): 7–28.

Sexton, Renard. 2016. "Aid as a Tool against Insurgency: Evidence from Contested and Controlled Territory in Afghanistan." *American Political Science Review* 110 (4): 731–49. https://doi.org/10.1017/S0003055416000356.

Shapiro, Robert, and Benjamin Page. 1988. "Foreign Policy and the Rational Public." *Journal of Conflict Resolution* 32 (2): 211–47.

Sittmann, William. 1990. "Memorandum, William Sittmann to Chriss Winston, Presidential Letter to College Students." Box 80, White House Office of Speechwriting, Speech File Draft File, Chron File, 1989-1993, folder "Letters to College Students, 1/7/1991" OA/ID: 13553-003. George H.W. Bush Presidential Library.

Smeltz, Dina, Ivo Daalder, and Craig Kafura. 2014. *"Foreign Policy in the Age of Retrenchment: Results of the 2014 Chicago Council Survey of American Public Opinion."* Chicago Council on Global Affairs.

Smeltz, Dina, Karl Friedhoff, Craig Kafura, and Lama El Baz. 2023. "2023 Survey of Public Opinion on US Foreign Policy." Research. The Chicago Council on Global

Affairs. October 4, 2023. https://globalaffairs.org/research/public-opinion-survey/2023-survey-public-opinion-us-foreign-policy.

Smith, Curt. 1990. "Memorandum, Curt Smith to the President through Chriss Winston, Remarks to VFW National Convention." Box 65, White House Office of Speechwriting, Speech File Draft Files, Chron Fil, 1989-1993, folder "VFW national Convention, 8/20/90 [1]" OA/ID: 13538-010. George H.W. Bush Presidential Library.

Smith, Curt. 1991. "Memorandum, Curt Smith to The President through Chriss Winston, Remarks at Religious Broadcasters Convention." Box 81, White House Office of Speechwriting, Speech File Draft Files, Chron File, 1989-1993, folder "Religious Broadcasters, 1/28/91" OA/ID: 13554-001. George H.W. Bush Presidential Library.

Snow, Tony. 1992a. "Speech Card, Defense, Clinton: No Experience, Will Gut Defense." George H.W. Bush Presidential Records, White House Office of Speechwriting, Tony Snow Files, Subject File, 1988-1993, Bush-Quayle '02 Communications Handbook [2]. George H.W. Bush Presidential Library.

Snow, Tony. 1992b. "Speech Card, Foreign Policy, Leader of the Free World." George H.W. Bush Presidential Records, White House Office of Speechwriting, Tony Snow Files, Subject File, 1988-1993, Bush-Quayle '02 Communications Handbook [2]. George H.W. Bush Presidential Library.

Snyder, Jack L. 1991. *Myths of Empire: Domestic Politics and International Ambition.* Cornell University Press.

Sonenshine, Tara D. 1994. "Memorandum, Tara D. Sonenshine, Bosnia." Box 25, National Security Council, European Affairs—Kerrick, Donald, folder "Bosnia-Talking Points [2]" OA/ID: 368. William J. Clinton Presidential Library.

Sonenshine, Tara D. n.d. "Memorandum, Tara D. Sonenshine, National Security Council, Bosnia-Press Strategy." Box 25, National Security Council, European Affairs—Kerrick, Donald, folder "Bosnia-Talking Points [2]" OA/ID: 368. William J. Clinton Presidential Library.

"Speech Cards, Republican Congressional Leadership." 1990. Box 88, White House Press Office, Marlin Fitzwater Files, Guidance Files, folder "Wednesday, September 26, 1990" OA/ID: 12989-010. George H.W. Bush Presidential Library.

Steeper, Fred. 1990a. "Report, Fred Steeper to Bob Teeter, U.S. National Survey." Box 68, Donated Historical Materials, Robert Teeter Collection, U.S. National Studies, folder "RNC National Survey-Summary-October 1990 [1]" OA/ID: 45798. George H.W. Bush Presidential Library.

Steeper, Fred. 1990b. "Report, Fred Steeper to Bob Teeter, U.S. National Survey: Iraq." Box 68, Donated Historical Materials, Robert Teeter Collection, U.S. National Studies, folder "RNC National Survey-Summary-October 1990 [1]" OA/ID: 45798. George H.W. Bush Presidential Library.

Steeper, Fred. 1991a. "Report, Fred Steeper to Ed Rogers, Highlights of RNC and Public Poll Results." Box 68, Donated Historical Materials, Robert Teeter Collection, U.S. National Studies, folder "U.S. National Tracking-Data & Summary-January 16-February 27, 1991 [Report on Public Opinion During the Persian Gulf War]. George H.W. Bush Presidential Library.

Steeper, Fred. 1991b. "Review of Persian Gulf Questionnaire and Results, Memo to Robert Teeter." Donated Historical Materials, Robert Teeter Collection, U.S. National Studies, U.S. National Tracking - Data & Summary - January 16-February 27, 1991 [Report on Public Opinion During the Persian Gulf War]. George H.W. Bush Presidential Library.

Steeper, Fred. 1992. "Research Findings and Strategy: Current Status and Recommendations." George H.W. Bush Presidential Records, White House Press Office, Marlin Fitzwater Files, Alphabetical Subject Files, Political Activity Advice. George H.W. Bush Presidential Library.

Stein, Jonathan, and Tim Dickinson. 2006. "Lie by Lie: A Timeline of How We Got Into Iraq." *Mother Jones* (blog). 2006. https://www.motherjones.com/politics/2011/12/leadup-iraq-war-timeline/.

Stein, Rachel M. 2015. "War and Revenge: Explaining Conflict Initiation by Democracies." *American Political Science Review* 109 (3): 556–73.

Sunak, Rishi. 2023. "Prime Minister: NATO Must Learn Lessons from Putin's Barbaric Tactics in Ukraine." *GOV.UK*, July 11, 2023. https://www.gov.uk/government/news/prime-minister-nato-must-learn-lessons-from-putins-barbaric-tactics-in-ukraine.

"Talking Points, Points to Be Made for Meeting with Republican Congressional Leadership." 1991. Box 93, White House Press Office, Marlin Fitzwater Files, Guidance Files, folder "Thursday, January 24, 1991" OA/ID: 12994-005. George H.W. Bush Presidential Library.

Tama, Jordan. 2024. *Bipartisanship and US Foreign Policy: Cooperation in a Polarized Age.* Oxford University Press.

Teeter, Robert. 1990a. "Iraq: Public Perceptions and Attitudes." Box 69, Donated Historical Materials, Robert Teeter Collection, U.S. National Studies, folder "U.S. National Survey-Summary Results-December 7-12, 1990" OA/ID 45799. George H.W. Bush Presidential Library.

Teeter, Robert. 1990b. "Report, Iraq: Public Perceptions and Attitudes, Use of Force: Reasons and Justifications." Box 69, Donated Historical Materials, Robert Teeter Collection, U.S. National Studies, folder "U.S. National Survey-Summary Results-December 7–12 1990" OA/ID: 45799. George H.W. Bush Presidential Library.

Teeter, Robert. 1990c. "U.S. National Survey." Donated Historical Materials, Robert Teeter Collection, U.S. National Studies, RNC National Survey-Summary-October, 1990[1]. George H.W. Bush Presidential Library.

Teeter, Robert. 1991. "Report on Public Opinion During the Persian Gulf War." Box 68, Donated Historical Materials, Robert Teeter Collection, U.S. National Studies, folder "U.S. National Tracking-Data & Summary-January 16-February 27, 1991 [Report on Public Opinion During the Persian Gulf War]. George H.W. Bush Presidential Library.

Thompson, Alexander. 2006. "Coercion through IOs: The Security Council and the Logic of Information Transmission." *International Organization* 60 (1): 1–34.

Tomz, Michael. 2007. "Domestic Audience Costs in International Relations: An Experimental Approach." *International Organization* 61 (4): 821–40.

Tomz, Michael, and Jessica Weeks. 2013. "Public Opinion and the Democratic Peace." *American Political Science Review* 107 (4): 849–65.

Tomz, Michael, and Jessica L. P. Weeks. 2019. "Human Rights and Public Support for War." *Journal of Politics* 82 (1): 182–94.

Tomz, Michael, Jessica L. P. Weeks, and Keren Yarhi-Milo. 2020. "Public Opinion and Decisions About Military Force in Democracies." *International Organization* 74 (1):19–43.

Trager, Robert F., and Lynn Vavreck. 2011. "The Political Costs of Crisis Bargaining: Presidential Rhetoric and the Role of Party." *American Journal of Political Science* 55 (3): 526–45.

Trump, Donald J. 2017a. "Donald J. Trump: Address Before a Joint Session of the Congress." The American Presidency Project. February 28, 2017. http://www.presidency.ucsb.edu/ws/index.php?pid=123408&st=&st1=.

Trump, Donald J. 2017b. "Donald J. Trump: Remarks Announcing Military Airstrikes on Syria in Palm Beach, Florida." The American Presidency Project. April 6, 2017. http://www.presidency.ucsb.edu/ws/index.php?pid=123706&st=&st1=.

Trump, Donald J. 2017c. "Remarks at MacDill Air Force Base, Florida." The American Presidency Project. February 6, 2017. https://www.presidency.ucsb.edu/documents/remarks-macdill-air-force-base-florida.

Trump, Donald J. 2018. "Address Before a Joint Session of the Congress on the State of the Union." The American Presidency Project. January 30, 2018. https://www.presidency.ucsb.edu/documents/address-before-joint-session-the-congress-the-state-the-union-25.

United Nations High Commissioner for Refugees. 1996. "High Commissioner for Refugees Announces End of Sarajevo Airlift." January 5, 1996. https://www.un.org/press/en/1996/19960105.ref1130.html.

United States Army. 2007. *The U.S. Army/Marine Corps Counterinsurgency Field Manual.* Vol. U.S. Army Field Manual No. 3-24, Marine Corps Warfighting Publication No. 3-33.5. University of Chicago Press. https://press.uchicago.edu/ucp/books/book/chicago/U/bo5748917.html.

UNSC. 1990a. "Resolution 660." United Nations. https://documents-dds-ny.un.org/doc/RESOLUTION/GEN/NR0/575/10/IMG/NR057510.pdf?OpenElement.

UNSC. 1990b. "Resolution 665." United Nations. https://documents-dds-ny.un.org/doc/RESOLUTION/GEN/NR0/575/15/IMG/NR057515.pdf?OpenElement.

UNSC. 1990c. "Resolution 678." United Nations. https://documents-dds-ny.un.org/doc/RESOLUTION/GEN/NR0/575/28/IMG/NR057528.pdf?OpenElement.

Urbatsch, R. 2010. "Isolationism and Domestic Politics." *Journal of Conflict Resolution* 54 (3): 471–92.

Valentino, Benjamin A., Paul Huth, and Sarah E. Croco. 2010. "Bear Any Burden? How Democracies Minimize the Costs of War." *Journal of Politics* 72 (2): 528–44.

Voeten, Erik. 2005. "The Political Origins of the UN Security Council's Ability to Legitimize the Use of Force." *International Organization* 59 (3): 527–57.

Wallace, Geoffrey P. R. 2013. "International Law and Public Attitudes Towards Torture: An Experimental Study." *International Organization* 67 (1): 105–40.

Weinberg, Jill, Jeremy Freese, and David McElhattan. 2014. "Comparing Data Characteristics and Results of an Online Factorial Survey between a Population-Based and a Crowdsource-Recruited Sample." *Sociological Science* August 2014 (1): 292–310.

Western, Jon. 2005. *Selling Intervention and War: The Presidency, the Media, and the American Public*. The Johns Hopkins University Press.

Western, Jon, and Joshua S. Goldstein. 2011. "Humanitarian Intervention Comes of Age: Lessons from Somalia to Libya." *Foreign Affairs* 90 (6): 48–59.

Weyrich, Paul M. 1990. "Letter, Paul M. Weyrich to President George Bush." FOIA 1998-0099-F, White House Office of Public Liaison, Leigh Ann Metzger Files, folder "Operation Desert Shield Religious Opinions/Criticism" OA/ID: 07164-040. George H.W. Bush Presidential Library.

Wheeler, Nicholas. 2000. *Saving Strangers: Humanitarian Intervention in International Society*. Oxford University Press.

"White House News Summary, 11:15 A.M. EST News Update, Gulf/Bishops (Los Angeles/AP)." 1990. FOIA 1998-0099-F, Presidential Records, White House Office of Public Liaison, Metzger, Leigh Ann, Files, folder "Operation Desert Shield Religious Opinions/Criticism" OA/ID 07164-040. George H.W. Bush Presidential Library.

White House Office of Public Affairs. 1990. "Communications Plan—Gulf Policy." Box 81, White House Office of Public Affairs, Kristen Gear Files, folder "Tips/Fact Sheets Persian Gulf" OA/ID:03417-004. George H.W. Bush Presidential Library.

Wilkenfeld, Jonathan, and Michale Brecher. 1984. "International Crises, 1945–1975: The UN Dimension." *International Studies Quarterly* 28 (1): 45–67.

Wittkopf, Eugene R. 1990. *Face of Internationalism: Public Opinion and American Foreign Policy*. Duke University Press.

Wolfowitz, Paul. 1991. "Note, Paul Wolfowitz to Bob Gates, Bob Kimmitt, Dick Kerr, Dave Jeremiah." FOIA 1998-0099-F, National Security Council, Nancy Bearg Dyke Files, Subject File, folder "Refugees: Persian Gulf Pre-Kurds [1]" OA/ID: CF01458-021. George H.W. Bush Presidential Library.

Wood, B. Dan, and Jeffrey Peake. 1998. "The Dynamics of Foreign Policy Agenda Setting." *American Political Science Review* 92 (1): 173–84.

Woodward, Bob. 2004. *Plan of Attack: The Definitive Account of the Decision to Invade Iraq*. Simon and Schuster Paperbacks.

Woolley, John T., and Gerhard Peters. n.d. "The American Presidency Project." Accessed January 21, 2023. https://www.presidency.ucsb.edu/.

Zacher, Mark W. 2001. "The Territorial Integrity Norm: International Boundaries and the Use of Force." *International Organization* 55 (2): 215–50.

Zvobgo, Kelebogile. 2019. "Human Rights versus National Interests: Shifting US Public Attitudes on the International Criminal Court." *International Studies Quarterly* 63: 1065–78.

Index